# Windows® 10 Computer
## *for* Seniors

Michael Miller

**QUE**®

800 East 96th Street,
Indianapolis, Indiana 46240

**AARP**®
Real Possibilities

# My Windows® 10 Computer for Seniors, Second Edition

**Copyright © 2018 by Pearson Education, Inc.**

ISBN-13: 9780789759788
ISBN-10: 0789759780

Library of Congress Control Number: 2017961717

Printed in the United States on America

1  18

## Trademarks

All terms mentioned in this book that are known to be trademarks or service marks have been appropriately capitalized. Que Publishing cannot attest to the accuracy of this information. Use of a term in this book should not be regarded as affecting the validity of any trademark or service mark.

Microsoft and/or its respective suppliers make no representations about the suitability of the information contained in the documents and related graphics published as part of the services for any purpose. All such documents and related graphics are provided "as is" without warranty of any kind. Microsoft and/or its respective suppliers hereby disclaim all warranties and conditions with regard to this information, including all warranties and conditions of merchantability, whether express, implied or statutory, fitness for a particular purpose, title and non-infringement. In no event shall Microsoft and/or its respective suppliers be liable for any special, indirect or consequential damages or any damages whatsoever resulting from loss of use, data or profits, whether in an action of contract, negligence or other tortious action, arising out of or in connection with the use or performance of information available from the services.

The documents and related graphics contained herein could include technical inaccuracies or typographical errors. Changes are periodically added to the information herein. Microsoft and/or its respective suppliers may make improvements and/or changes in the product(s) and/or the program(s) described herein at any time. Partial screenshots may be viewed in full within the software version specified.

Microsoft® and Windows® are registered trademarks of the Microsoft Corporation in the U.S.A. and other countries. Screenshots and icons reprinted with permission from the Microsoft Corporation. This book is not sponsored or endorsed by or affiliated with the Microsoft Corporation.

## Warning and Disclaimer

## Special Sales

For information about buying this title in bulk quantities, or for special sales opportunities (which may include electronic versions; custom cover designs; and content particular to your business, training goals, marketing focus, or branding interests), please contact our corporate sales department at corpsales@pearsoned.com or (800) 382-3419.

For government sales inquiries, please contact governmentsales@pearsoned.com.

For questions about sales outside the U.S., please contact international@pearsoned.com.

**Editor-in-Chief**
Greg Wiegand

**Senior Acquisitions Editor**
Laura Norman

**Director, AARP Books**
Jodi Lipson

**Development Editor**
Charlotte Kughen

**Managing Editor**
Sandra Schroeder

**Editorial Services**
The Wordsmithery LLC

**Indexer**
Cheryl Lenser

**Proofreader**
Katherin Ruiz

**Technical Editor**
Jeri Usbay

**Editorial Assistant**
Cindy J. Teeters

**Designer**
Chuti Prasertsith

**Compositor**
Bronkella Publishing

**Graphics**
TJ Graham Art

# Contents at a Glance

# Table of Contents

## 10   Finding and Installing Traditional Software     129

## 11   Connecting to the Internet—at Home or Away     137

## 12   Browsing and Searching the Web     145

# About the Author

**Michael Miller** is a prolific and popular writer of more than 200 nonfiction books who is known for his ability to explain complex topics to everyday readers. He writes about a variety of topics, including technology, business, and music. His best-selling books for Que and AARP include *My iPad for Seniors, My Social Media for Seniors, My Facebook for Seniors, My Smart Home for Seniors, My Samsung Galaxy S7 for Seniors, My Internet for Seniors,* and *My eBay for Seniors.* Worldwide, his books have sold more than 1.5 million copies.

Find out more at the author's website: www.millerwriter.com

Follow the author on Twitter: @molehillgroup

# Dedication

*To Sherry. As always.*

# Acknowledgments

Thanks to all the folks at Que who helped turn this manuscript into a book, including Laura Norman, Greg Wiegand, Charlotte Kughen, and technical editor Jeri Usbay. Thanks also to Jodi Lipson and the good folks at AARP for supporting and promoting this and other books.

# About AARP

AARP is a nonprofit, nonpartisan organization, with a membership of nearly 38 million, that helps people turn their goals and dreams into *real possibilities*™, strengthens communities, and fights for the issues that matter most to families such as healthcare, employment and income security, retirement planning, affordable utilities, and protection from financial abuse. Learn more at aarp.org.

# We Want to Hear from You!

As the reader of this book, *you* are our most important critic and commentator. We value your opinion and want to know what we're doing right, what we could do better, what areas you'd like to see us publish in, and any other words of wisdom you're willing to pass our way.

You can email or write to let us know what you did or didn't like about this book—as well as what we can do to make our books better.

*Please note that we cannot help you with technical problems related to the topic of this book.*

When you write, please be sure to include this book's title and author as well as your name, email address, and phone number. We will carefully review your comments and share them with the author and editors who worked on the book.

**Email:**  feedback@quepublishing.com

**Mail:**  Que Publishing

ATTN: Reader Feedback

800 East 96th Street

Indianapolis, IN 46240 USA

# Reader Services

Register your copy of *My Windows 10 Computer for Seniors* on the InformIT site for convenient access to updates and corrections as they become available. To start the registration process, go to informit.com/register and log in or create an account. Enter the product ISBN (9780789759788) and click Submit. If you would like to be notified of exclusive offers on new editions and updates, please check the box to receive email from us.

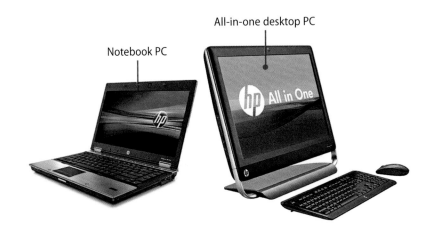

Notebook PC

All-in-one desktop PC

In this chapter, you find out what components are in a typical computer system—what they are and how they work.

# Understanding Computer Basics

What should you look for if you need a new computer? What are all those pieces and parts? And how do you connect everything together?

These are common questions for anyone just getting started out with computers. Read on to learn more about the key components of a typical computer system—and how they all work together.

## Examining Key Components

All computers do pretty much the same things, in pretty much the same ways. There are differences, however, in the capacities and capabilities of key components, which can affect how fast your computer operates. And when you're shopping for a new PC, you need to keep these options in mind.

# Hard Disk Drive

All computers feature some form of long-term storage for your documents, photos, music, and videos. On most desktop PCs and many smaller notebook (portable) computers, this storage is in the form of an *internal hard disk drive*. This is a device that stores data magnetically, on multiple metallic platters—kind of like a high-tech electronic juke box.

## Lettered Drives

All storage drives are assigned specific letters by Windows. On most systems, the main hard drive is called the c: drive. If you have a second hard drive, it will be the d: drive. Any external drives attached to your PC will pick up the lettering from there.

Most computers today come with very large hard drives, capable of storing just about anything you can imagine. While 1 terabyte (TB) is probably the most common size, you can find computers with hard drives from 500 gigabytes (GB) to 4 TB. The more hard disk storage the better, especially if you have lots of digital photos or videos to store.

## Kilobytes, Megabytes, Gigabytes, and Terabytes

The most basic unit of digital storage is called a byte; a byte typically equals one character of text. One thousand bytes equal one *kilobyte* (KB). One thousand kilobytes, or one million bytes, equal one *megabyte* (MB). One thousand megabytes, or one billion bytes, equal one *gigabyte* (GB). One thousand gigabytes, or one trillion bytes, equal one *terabyte* (TB).

Many newer notebook PCs use solid-state memory instead of hard disk drives for long-term storage. Unlike traditional hard disks, solid-state storage devices have no moving parts, instead storing data electronically on silicon microchips. That makes solid-state storage smaller, lighter, and faster than hard disk storage. On the downside, PCs with solid-state storage provide less storage space (typically in the 128GB to 256GB range) than those with traditional hard drives. It's a tradeoff, but one that many people are making in the notebook market.

# Memory

Hard disks and solid-state memory devices provide long-term storage for your data. Your computer also needs short-term storage to temporarily store documents as you're working on them or photos you're viewing.

This short-term storage is provided by your PC's *random access memory*, or RAM. Most PCs today offer anywhere from 4 to 32 gigabytes (GB) of RAM. The more memory in your computer, the faster it operates.

# Processor

The other major factor that affects the speed of your PC is its *central processing unit* (CPU) or *processor*. The more powerful your computer's CPU, measured in terms of gigahertz (GHz), the faster your system runs.

Today's CPUs often contain more than one processing unit. A dual-core CPU contains the equivalent of two processors in one unit and should be roughly twice as fast as a comparable single-core CPU; a quad-core CPU should be four times as fast as a single-core CPU.

## System Unit

On a traditional desktop computer, the hard disk, memory, and CPU are contained within a separate system unit that also sports various connectors and ports for monitors and other devices. On an all-in-one desktop, the system unit is built in to the monitor display. On a notebook PC, the hard disk and other components are all part of the notebook itself.

# Display

All computers today come with liquid crystal display (LCD) screens. The screen can be in an external monitor in desktop systems, combined with the system unit for all-in-one systems, or built in to a notebook PC. Screens come in a variety of sizes, from 10" diagonal in small notebook PCs to 24" diagonal or more in larger desktop systems. Naturally, you should choose a screen size that's easy for you to read.

**LCD monitor**

Some LCD monitors offer touchscreen operation, so that you can perform some operations with the swipe of a fingertip. Since touchscreen displays cost more than traditional displays, they're typically not found on lower-end models.

### Touchpads for Touchscreens

Some touchpads on newer notebook PCs let you emulate a touchscreen display. That is, you can perform similar touch gestures on one of these touchpads as you can on a touchscreen. (Learn more about touchpad input later in this chapter.)

## Keyboard

When it comes to typing letters, emails, and other documents, as well as posting updates to websites such as Facebook, you need an alphanumeric keyboard. On a desktop PC, the keyboard is an external component (called a *peripheral*); the keyboard is built in to all laptop PCs, also called *notebook PCs*.

**Function keys**    **External keyboard**

**Numeric keypad**

**Windows key**    **Arrow (direction) keys**

Computer keyboards include typical typewriter keys, as well as a set of so-called *function keys* (designated F1 through F12) aligned on the top row of the keyboard; these function keys provide one-touch access to many computer functions. For example, pressing the F1 key in many programs brings up the program's help system.

Also, several keys that aren't letters or numbers are used to perform general functions. For example, the Escape (Esc) key typically undoes the current action, the Backspace key deletes the previous character, and the Delete (Del) key deletes the current character. And, as you'll learn later in this book, there are also Windows and Menu keys that have specific functionality within the Windows operating system.

In addition, most external (and some notebook) keyboards have a separate numeric keypad, which makes it easier to enter numbers. There are also number keys beneath the function keys on all computer keyboards.

### External Input on a Notebook PC

Even though notebook PCs come with built-in keyboards and touchpads, you can still connect external keyboards and mice (pointing devices) if you like, via the PC's USB ports. (Read more about USB ports later in this chapter in the "Connectors" section.) Some users prefer the feel of a full-size keyboard and mouse to the smaller versions included in their notebooks.

## Pointing Device

You use a pointing device of some sort to move the cursor from place to place on the computer screen. On a desktop PC, the pointing device of choice is called a *mouse*; it's about the size of a bar of soap, and you make it work by rolling it across a hard surface, such as a desktop.

Scroll wheel

Left button

Right button

External mouse

Most notebook PCs have a built-in pointing device called a *touchpad*. You move your fingers across the touchpad to move the cursor across the computer screen.

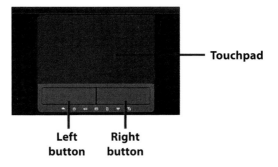

Touchpad

Left
button

Right
button

Both mice and touchpads have accompanying buttons that you click to perform various operations. Most devices include both left and right buttons; clicking the left button activates most common functions, whereas clicking the right button provides additional functionality in select situations.

## Virtual Buttons

Some touchpads don't have discrete buttons. Instead, the lower part of the touch-pad is designated as the button area; you tap on the lower-left quadrant to left-click, and tap on the lower-right quadrant to right-click.

# Connectors

Every computer comes with a variety of connectors (called *ports*) to which you can connect external components (called *peripherals*), such as keyboards, print-ers, and the like. A number of different connectors are available, and not all com-puters offer the same assortment.

On today's computers, the most common type of connector is called the *univer-sal serial bus*, or USB. Most external devices connect to your computer via USB.

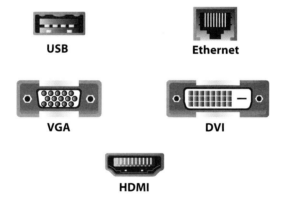

Your computer (even notebook models) also has one or more connectors for an external monitor. This can be a traditional *video graphics array* (VGA) connector, a newer *digital visual interface* (DVI) connector, or a *high definition multimedia inter-face* (HDMI) connector, like the ones you have on your living room TV. HDMI and DVI provide the best picture, so you should use whichever of these your external monitor supports.

### HDMI

Because HDMI transmits both video and audio, you can use this port to connect your computer to your living room TV. (HDMI is also used to connect DVD players, Blu-ray players, cable boxes, and other devices to television sets.)

Most computers today also have an Ethernet port to connect to wired home and office networks. Notebook computers (and some desktops) also offer wireless network connectivity, via a technology called *Wi-Fi*. If your computer has Wi-Fi, you don't have to connect via a cable.

# Exploring Different Types of PCs

If you're in the market for a new PC, you'll find two general types available—desktops and notebooks. All types of computers do pretty much the same thing, and they do it in similar ways; the differences between desktop and notebook computers are more about how they're configured than how they perform.

## Desktop PCs

The first general type of PC is the desktop system. A desktop computer is designed to be used in one place; it's a stationary computer, not a portable one.

All desktop PCs have a separate keyboard and mouse, used for typing and navigating the screen. You also have a monitor, or computer screen, and a system unit that houses all the internal electronics for the entire system.

In a traditional desktop PC system, the monitor and system unit are two separate components; you can store the system unit under your desk or in some other out-of-the-way place. So-called all-in-one systems combine the monitor and system unit (as well as speakers) into one piece of equipment, which reduces the number of connections you have to make. Some all-in-ones offer touchscreen monitors.

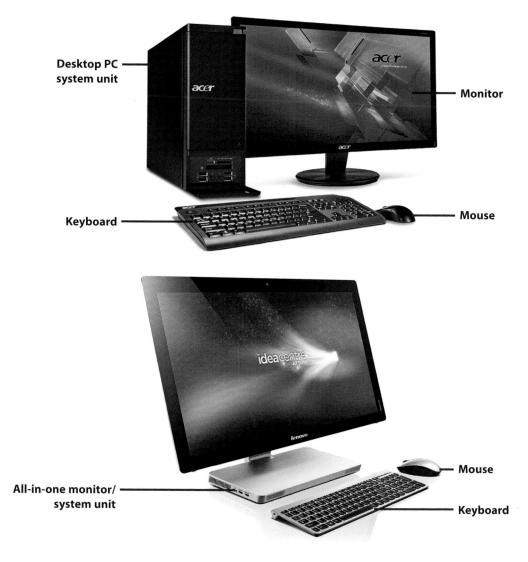

Desktop PC system unit

Monitor

Keyboard

Mouse

All-in-one monitor/ system unit

Mouse

Keyboard

For many users, the major advantage of a traditional desktop or all-in-one PC is the larger monitor screen, full-size keyboard, and separate mouse. It's easier to read many documents on a larger desktop monitor, and most full-size keyboards also offer numeric keypads, which are easier for entering numbers when you're doing online banking or budgeting. Many users also find the separate mouse easier to use than the small touchpad found on most notebook PCs.

### Monitor Screens

Most desktop computer monitors have screens that measure 19" to 24" diagonally. Most notebook PC screens measure 10" to 16" diagonally, so they are considerably smaller than their desktop counterparts.

On the downside, a desktop PC isn't portable; you have to leave it in one place in your home. In addition, a desktop system—even an all-in-one—is a little more complicated to set up, with all its external components. What's more, you'll likely pay a little more for a desktop system than you will for a similarly configured notebook PC.

## Notebook PCs

A notebook PC, sometimes called a laptop computer, combines all the components of a desktop system into a single unit with built-in screen, keyboard, and touchpad. Notebook PCs are not only small and lightweight, but also portable because they're capable of operating from a built-in battery that can last anywhere from 2 to 6 hours on a charge. (Naturally, a notebook PC can also be plugged in to a wall to use standard AC power.)

Screen

Keyboard

Notebook PC

Touchpad

In addition, you can take a notebook PC just about anywhere. You can move your notebook to your living room or bedroom as you desire, and even take it with you when you're traveling or use it in public places such as coffeehouses.

On the downside, the typical notebook PC has a smaller screen than a desktop system, which could be problematic if you experience deteriorating vision. In addition, the compact keyboard of a notebook model might be more difficult to type on. Most notebook PCs also use a small touchpad to navigate onscreen, as opposed to the larger mouse of a desktop system, which some people might find difficult to use. (You can always connect an external mouse to your notebook, as discussed later in this chapter.)

### 2-in-1 Notebooks

When you get to the higher end of the notebook PC market, you find units that combine the features of a notebook PC with those of a tablet. (*Tablets* are portable touchscreen devices, such as the Amazon Fire or Apple iPad devices.) These *2-in-1 PCs*, as they're called, typically let you swivel the display against the keyboard to emulate touchscreen tablet operation, or swivel the display the other way to let you use the device with the traditional keyboard. These 2-in-1 units are great if you need the functionality of a notebook PC and the portability of a tablet—even if they do cost a bit more than a normal notebook.

# Which Type of PC Should You Buy?

Which type of PC you purchase depends on how and where you plan to use your new computer. Here are some recommendations:

- If you need a larger screen, prefer a full-sized keyboard and mouse, and don't need your computer to be portable, go with a desktop PC. Consider an all-in-one system for easier setup.

- If you don't want to bother with connecting cables and external devices, go with an all-in-one or notebook PC.

- If you want to be able to use your computer in different rooms of your home, go with a notebook PC.

- If you want to be able to easily take your computer with you when you travel, go with a notebook PC.

Naturally, every person has his or her unique needs and preferences. Always try out a system in the store to see if it is comfortable for you before making a purchase.

# Setting Up Your New Computer System

After you purchase a new PC, you need to set up and connect all of the system's hardware. As you might suspect, this is easier to do with a notebook PC than it is with a desktop system.

## Hardware and Software

All the physical parts of your computer—the screen, the system unit, the keyboard, and so forth—are referred to as *hardware*. The programs, apps, and games you run on your computer are called *software*.

## Set Up a Notebook PC

If you have a notebook PC, there isn't much you need to connect; everything's inside the case. Just connect your printer (and any other external peripherals, such as a mouse if you prefer to use one instead of a touchpad) via USB, plug your notebook into a power outlet, and you're ready to go.

( 1 ) Connect one end of your printer's USB cable to a USB port on your notebook; connect the other end of the cable to your printer. (If you have a printer that connects wirelessly via Wi-Fi, skip this step.)

( 2 ) Connect one end of your computer's power cable to the power connector on the side or back of your notebook.

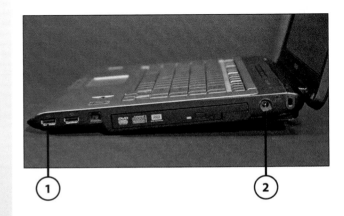

( 3 ) Connect the other end of the
computer's power cable to a
power source and then connect
your printer and other powered
external peripherals to the same
power source.

## Use a Surge Suppressor

For extra protection, connect the power
cable on your notebook or desktop system
unit to a power strip that incorporates a
surge suppressor rather than plugging
it directly into an electrical outlet. This
protects your PC from power-line surges
that can damage its delicate internal parts.
If you have a desktop system, be sure to
connect your monitor to the same surge
suppressor.

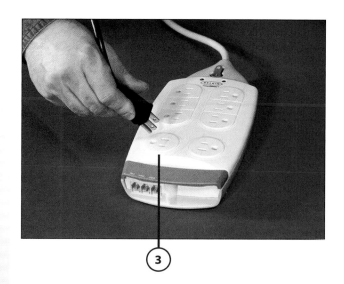

## Set Up a Traditional Desktop PC

If you have a traditional desktop
computer system, you need to connect
all the pieces and parts to your computer's system unit before powering it
on. When all your peripherals are connected, you can connect your system
unit to a power source.

( 1 ) Connect the mouse cable to a
USB port on the back of your
system unit.

( 2 ) Connect the keyboard cable to
a USB port on the back of your
system unit.

## Mice and Keyboards

Most newer mice and keyboards connect via USB. Some older models, however, connect to dedicated mouse and keyboard ports on your system unit. You should use whatever connection is appropriate.

**( 3 )** Connect a VGA, DVI, or HDMI monitor cable to the corresponding port on the back of your system unit. Make sure the other end is connected to your video monitor.

## Digital Connections

Most newer computer monitors include DVI or HDMI connections instead of or in addition to the older VGA-type connection. If you have a choice, a DVI or HDMI connection delivers a crisper picture than the older VGA (analog) connection.

**( 4 )** Connect the green phono cable from your main external speaker to the audio-out or sound-out connector on your system unit; connect the other end of the cable to the speaker. (Some external speakers connect via USB, which is even simpler; just connect the speaker cable to an open USB port on your system unit.)

**( 5 )** Connect one end of your printer's USB cable to a USB port on the back of your system unit; connect the other end of the cable to your printer. (If your printer connects wirelessly via Wi-Fi, skip this step.)

( **6** )  Connect one end of your computer's power cable to the power
connector on the back of your
system unit.

( **7** )  Connect the other end of the
power cable to a power source
and then connect your printer
and other powered external
peripherals to the same power
source.

( **6** )

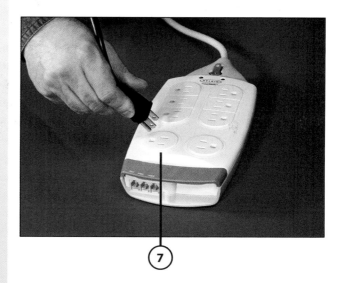

( **7** )

# Set Up an All-in-One Desktop PC

In an all-in-one desktop PC, the speakers and system unit are built in to the monitor, so there are fewer things to connect—just the mouse, keyboard, and any external peripherals, such as a printer. This makes for a much quicker and easier setup.

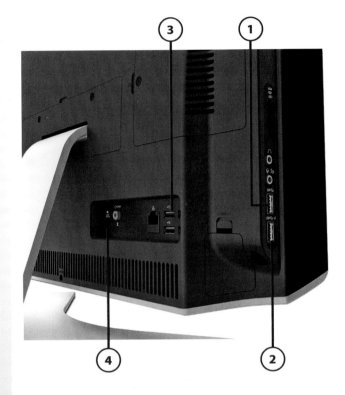

1. Connect the mouse cable to a USB port on the monitor.

2. Connect the keyboard cable to a USB port on the monitor.

3. Connect one end of your printer's USB cable to a USB port on the monitor; connect the other end of the cable to your printer. (If your printer connects wirelessly via Wi-Fi, skip this step.)

4. Connect one end of your computer's power cable to the power connector on the monitor.

5. Connect the other end of the power cable to a power source and then connect your printer and other powered external peripherals to the same power source.

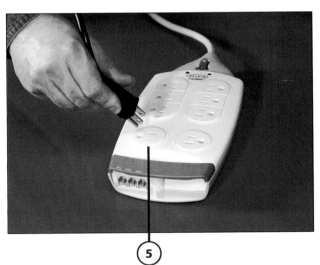

Keyboard

Mouse

In this chapter, you learn how to operate
Windows with your mouse or keyboard.

→ Using Windows with a Mouse or Touchpad
→ Using Windows with a Keyboard

2

# Performing Basic Operations

Whether you're completely new to computers or just new to Windows
10, you need to master some basic mouse and keyboard operations.

## Using Windows with a Mouse or Touchpad

To use Windows efficiently on a desktop or notebook PC, you need to
master a few simple operations with your mouse or touchpad, such as
pointing and clicking, dragging and dropping, and right-clicking.

# Mouse and Touchpad Operations

Of the various mouse and touchpad operations, the most common is pointing and clicking—that is, you point at something with the onscreen cursor and then click or tap the appropriate mouse or touchpad button. Normal clicking or tapping uses the left button; however, some operations require that you click or tap the right button instead.

( 1 ) To single-click (select) an item, position the cursor over the onscreen item and click or tap the left mouse or touchpad button.

( 2 ) To double-click (select or open) an item, position the cursor over the onscreen item and click or tap the left mouse or touchpad button twice in rapid succession.

( 3 ) To right-click an item (to display a context-sensitive options menu), position the cursor over the onscreen item and then click or tap the *right* mouse or touchpad button.

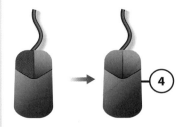

( 4 ) To drag and drop an item from one location to another, position the cursor over the item, click or tap and hold the left mouse or touchpad button, drag the item to a new position, and then release the button.

**5** To scroll through a window, mouse over the window to display the scroll bar; then move the mouse over the up or down arrow on the scroll bar and click or tap the left mouse or touchpad button.

**6** To move to a specific place in a long window or document, click the scroll box (between the up and down arrows) and drag it to a new position.

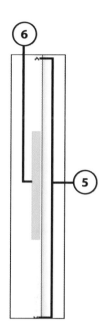

## Scroll Wheel

If your mouse has a scroll wheel, you can use it to scroll through a long document. Just roll the wheel back or forward to scroll down or up through a window. Likewise, some notebook touchpads let you drag your finger up or down to scroll through a window.

**7** To display the Windows Start menu, mouse over the lower-left corner of the screen and click the Start button. (The Start button is always present on the Windows desktop, at the far left side of the *taskbar*, the bar that runs horizontally across the bottom of the screen by default.)

---

### Mouse Over

Another common mouse operation is called the *mouse over*, or *hovering*, where you hold the cursor over an onscreen item without pressing either of the mouse or touchpad buttons. For example, when you mouse over an icon or menu item, Windows displays a *ToolTip* that tells you a little about the selected item.

---

# Using Windows with a Keyboard

You don't have to use your mouse or touchpad to perform many operations in Windows. Many users prefer to use their keyboards because it lets them keep their hands in one place when they're entering text and other information.

## Keyboard Operations

Many Windows operations can also be achieved from your computer keyboard, without touching your mouse or touchpad. Several of these operations use special keys that are unique to Windows PC keyboards, such as the Windows and Application keys.

 To scroll down any page or screen, press the PageDown key.

 To scroll up any page or screen, press the PageUp key.

   To launch a program or open a file, use the keyboard's arrow keys to move to the appropriate item and then press the Enter key.

 To display a context-sensitive pop-up menu (the equivalent of right-clicking an item), use the keyboard's arrow keys to move to that item and then press the Application key.

 To cancel or "back out" of the current operation, press the Escape key.

 To rename a file, use the keyboard's arrow keys to move to that file and then press the F2 key.

To access an application's Help system, press the F1 key.

 To display the Start menu, press the Windows key.

Desktop

Open application
window

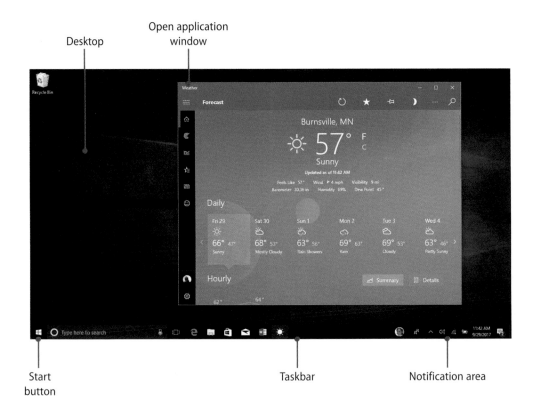

Start
button

Taskbar

Notification area

In this chapter, you find out how to turn on
and start using a new Windows 10 computer.

→ Powering Up and Powering Down
→ Finding Your Way Around Windows

# Using Your Windows 10 PC—If You've Never Used a Computer Before

Many people have used computers before and have probably owned at least one PC over the years—but not everyone is an experienced computer user. If you've just purchased your first PC, there's a lot to learn—especially when it comes to using the Windows operating system.

This chapter, then, is for those of you just starting out with your first PC. If you're a more experienced user, feel free to skip ahead to Chapter 4, "Using Your Windows 10 PC—If You've Used Windows Before"; otherwise, read on to learn how to get started with your new computer and Windows 10.

# Powering Up and Powering Down

If you've already read Chapter 1, "Understanding Computer Basics," you've learned how to connect all the components of your new computer system. Now that you have everything connected, it's time to turn everything on.

### Booting Up

Technical types call the procedure of starting up a computer *booting* or *booting up* the system. Restarting a system (turning it off and then back on) is called rebooting.

## Turn On and Configure Your New PC—For the First Time

The first time you power up your new PC, you're led through an initial setup and configuration process so that you can get Windows ready to use.

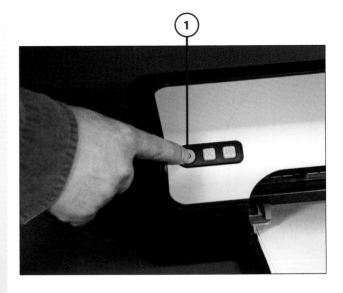

1. Turn on your printer, monitor (for a traditional desktop PC), and other powered external peripherals.

### Go in Order

Your computer is the *last* thing you turn on in your system, after all other connected devices. That's because when it powers on, it has to sense all the other components—which it can do only if the other components are plugged in and turned on.

( 2 ) If you're using a notebook PC, open the notebook's case so that you can see the screen and access the keyboard.

( 3 ) Press the power or "on" button on your computer. Windows starts up and begins displaying a series of Setup windows and screens.

( 4 ) You see a welcome screen, powered by Cortana, the personal digital assistant in Windows. You can continue by using your keyboard to make selections or by speaking to Cortana on your computer.

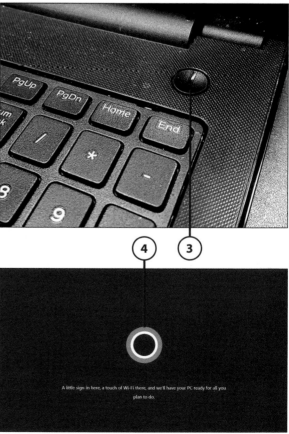

A little sign-in here, a touch of Wi-Fi there, and we'll have your PC ready for all you plan to do.

**5** When prompted, select the region where you live and click Yes. (Windows should have already suggested the correct region, but you can change this if it's not correct.)

**6** On the next screen, make sure Windows has selected the right country for your keyboard layout—and if not, click the correct country. (If you're in the U.S., that should be selected.) Click Yes to proceed.

**7** If you're asked to add a second keyboard layout, click Skip. (You don't need this unless you use your computer in two different languages—in which case, click Add Layout and follow the onscreen instructions.)

## Wireless Networking

If any wireless networks are nearby, the installation process prompts you to select your network from the list. Learn more about connecting your computer to a wireless network in Chapter 11, "Connecting to the Internet—at Home or Away."

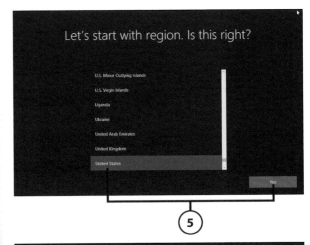

**5**

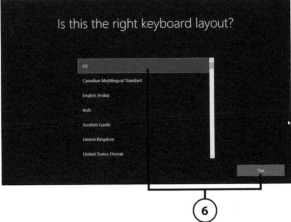

**6**

**7**

8  If you connected to a wired or wireless network, Windows goes online and checks for any necessary updates. If any are found, they're downloaded and installed at this point.

9  When prompted if you're setting up for an organization or for your own personal use, click Set Up for Personal Use and then click Next.

10  You're prompted to enter the email address for your Microsoft account. If you don't have a Microsoft account, click Create Account and follow the onscreen instructions.

11  If you already have a Microsoft account (for Outlook.com, OneDrive, Skype, or another Microsoft service), enter your email address and click Next. When prompted for your password, enter it.

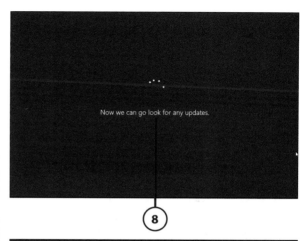

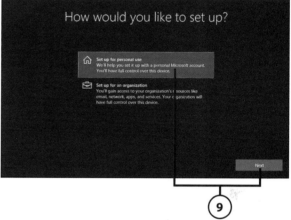

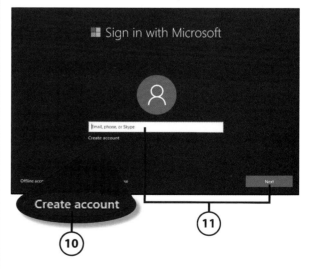

**12** You're asked if you want to set up a PIN instead of a password. Click Do This Later—unless you really want to do this now, in which case click Set a PIN and follow the onscreen instructions.

**13** In the Fall Creators Update, Microsoft lets you link your Windows 10 computer to your cell phone. If you want to do this now, enter your phone number and click Send. When you're done, click Next.

**14** You're prompted to make Cortana your personal assistant. You want to do this, so click Yes and follow the onscreen instructions to do so.

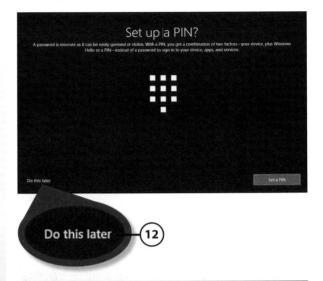

**15** Next up are Windows 10's privacy settings. You can enable or disable any of the following: Location (turn on to take advantage of location-based experiences in certain apps); Diagnostics (Basic or Full, which sends system information to Microsoft for troubleshooting purposes); Relevant Ads (turn on if you want the ads you're served to match your personal usage and interests); Speech Recognition (turn on to speak to Cortana and other apps that support voice recognition); and Tailored Experience with Diagnostic Data (turn on to send your usage data to Microsoft to tailor tips and recommendations within Windows). Click "on" those items you want to enable and then click Accept.

**16** Windows now continues the installation process and displays the Windows desktop when everything is set up and ready to use.

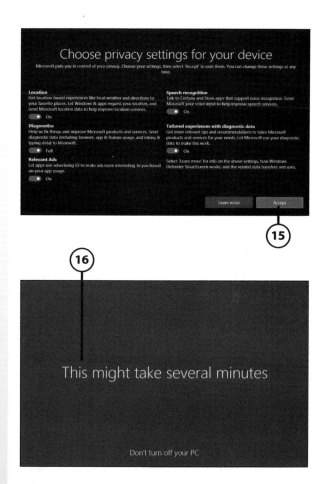

## >>>Go Further

## WINDOWS ACCOUNTS

As you've seen, part of the initial setup process for a new Windows 10 computer involves setting a *user account* for this computer. If you have an existing account with any Microsoft service, you simply link to that account during the setup process. If you don't have an existing Microsoft account, you can create a new one using any existing email address.

If you don't have an existing email address (or don't want to use it, for some reason or another), Microsoft lets you create a new email account at the same time you're activating Windows. Just follow the onscreen instructions, and Microsoft will use this new email account/address for your computer user account.

Learn more about user accounts, passwords, and the like in Chapter 6, "Personalizing Windows."

## Turn On Your System— Normally

Each subsequent time you turn on your computer, you go through pretty much the same routine—but without the initial configuration steps.

( 1 ) Turn on your printer, monitor (for a traditional desktop PC), and other powered external peripherals.

( 2 ) If you're using a notebook PC, open the notebook's case so that you can see the screen and access the keyboard.

**(3)** Press the power or "on" button on your computer. Windows launches automatically and displays the lock screen.

## Lock Screen Information

The Windows lock screen displays a photographic background along with some useful information—including the date and time, power status, and Wi-Fi (connectivity) status.

**(4)** Press any key or move your mouse to display the sign-in screen.

**(5)** Enter your password (if necessary), and then press the Enter key on your keyboard or click the next arrow key onscreen. Windows displays the desktop, ready for use.

**(4)**

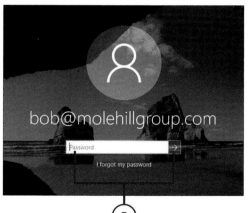

bob@molehillgroup.com

Password

I forgot my password

**(5)**

## Turn Off Your Computer

How you turn off your PC depends on what type of computer you have. If you have a notebook or tablet model, you can press the unit's power (on/off) button—although that typically will put your PC into Sleep mode, not turn it all the way off. The better approach is to shut down your system through Windows.

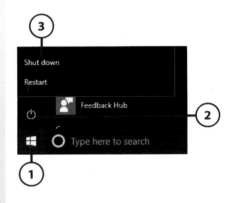

(1) Click the Start button at the far left side of the taskbar (or press the Windows key on your computer keyboard) to display the Start menu.

(2) Click Power to display the submenu of options.

(3) Click Shut Down.

---

### Sleep Mode

If you're using a notebook PC, Windows includes a special Sleep mode that keeps your computer running in a low-power state, ready to start up quickly when you open the lid or turn it on again. You can enter Sleep mode from the Power Options menu—or, with many notebook PCs, by pressing the unit's power button.

---

# Finding Your Way Around Windows

When it comes to finding your way around Windows 10, it's all about learning the different parts of the desktop.

## Use the Start Menu

All the software programs and utilities on your computer are accessed via the Windows Start menu. Your most frequently used programs and basic Windows tools are listed on the left side of the Start menu; your favorite programs are "pinned" as tiles to the right side. To open a specific program, just click the icon or tile.

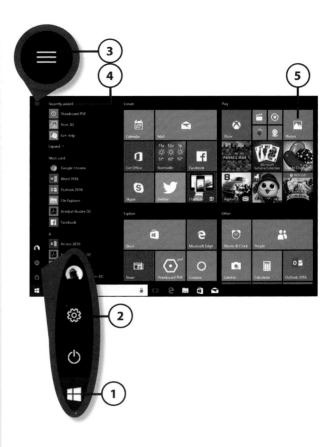

( 1 )  Click the Start button (or press the Windows key on your keyboard) to open the Start menu.

( 2 )  Icons for basic operations (Power, Settings, and your account) are listed on the far left of the Start menu.

( 3 )  To expand the left section to display icon labels, click the Expand button at the top of the Start menu.

( 4 )  All applications are listed in the middle portion of the Start menu. You see Most Used and Recently Added apps first, then a complete list of all installed apps, in alphabetical order. Scroll down to view additional apps; click an app to open it. (Some apps are organized in folders by publisher or type of application; click a folder to view its contents.)

( 5 )  Favorite programs are "pinned" to the right of the main Start menu in resizable tiles. To launch an application, click an item with your mouse, or move to that item using the arrow keys and press Enter on your keyboard.

## Different Looks

Your Start screen probably looks a little different from the ones shown in this chapter—in particular the tiles you see. That's because every person's system is different, depending on the particular programs and apps you have installed on your PC.

## Quick Access Menu

Right-click the Start button to display the Quick Access menu. This is a menu of advanced options, including direct links to File Explorer, Mobility Center, and Task Manager.

# Use the Taskbar

The taskbar is that area at the bottom of the Windows desktop. Icons on the taskbar can represent frequently used programs, open programs, or open documents.

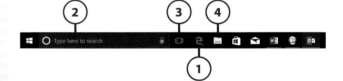

1. To open an application from the taskbar, click the application's icon.

2. To search your computer for files and apps, or the Web for additional information, click within the Cortana search box ("Type here to search") and type your query.

3. To view all open applications in thumbnail form, click the Task View button.

4. To open File Explorer, click the File Explorer icon.

**5** The far right side of the taskbar is called the notification area, and it displays icons for essential Windows operations—sound, networking, power, time and date, and so forth. To view more details about any item displayed in this area, click that item's icon.

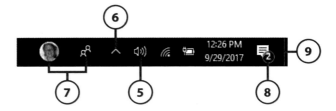

**6** Click the up arrow to view icons for more items, normally hidden.

**7** The taskbar might also include icons for your favorite contacts. Click a person's icon to contact that person, or click the People icon to add other contacts to the taskbar.

**8** To open the Windows Action Center, which includes system notifications and key actions, click the Notifications icon.

**9** To minimize all open applications, click the slim Peek button at the far right of the taskbar.

## Taskbar Icons

A taskbar icon with a plain background represents an unopened application. A taskbar icon with a line underneath represents a running application. A taskbar icon with a shaded background represents the highlighted or topmost window on your desktop. An application with multiple documents open is represented by "stacked" lines underneath the icon.

Start menu

Start button                                                     Tiles

4

# Using Your Windows 10 PC—If You've Used Windows Before

Windows 10 is the latest version of Windows, the operating system from Microsoft that's been driving personal computers since the late 1980s. Windows 10, released in 2015, is a considerable improvement over the previous version (Windows 8) and a worthwhile upgrade if you're using any older version of Windows.

## Windows 10 for Windows 8/8.1 Users

The Windows operating system has been around for more than 30 years now. Version 1.0 of Windows was released in November of 1985 and has gone through numerous small and more significant revisions since then.

Prior to Windows 10 there was Windows 8, released in 2012. (Microsoft skipped the Windows 9 title.) With Windows 8, Microsoft attempted a complete overhaul of the operating system's interface and operation, in order to better compete in the burgeoning touchscreen tablet computer market. These changes included deprecating the traditional desktop, removing the Start button and Start menu, and forcing users to use touch gestures instead of the mouse and keyboard.

Unfortunately, these changes ill served the billions of people using traditional desktop and notebook computers, and was met by widespread resistance—and anemic sales. Microsoft tried to reverse some of the damage with the rapid release of Windows 8.1 in 2013, which brought back the Start button (but not the Start menu), but the other changes weren't significant enough to make much of a difference.

Fortunately, Microsoft learned from its mistakes and changed things dramatically (for the better) with Windows 10. This latest operating system is a worthy successor to the much-beloved Windows 7—and to Windows 8, of course.

If you're a Windows 8/8.1 user, what will you find new in Windows 10? Lots! Here's a short list of the most important changes:

- The Start button is back, as is the Start menu. Click the Start button and you see a new and (really) improved version of the Start menu, with all your installed programs listed.

- Programs pinned to the Start menu now appear as resizable tiles, some of which display live information without having to be opened.

- Windows boots directly to the desktop.

- The much-despised Start screen from Windows 8 is no more. If you're using Windows 10 on a tablet or other smaller device, you instead see a full-screen version of the new Start menu, complete with a slightly different version of the taskbar.

- Also gone is the Windows 8 Charms bar, used to configure many system settings. These system settings (and more) are now accessible from a new Settings window, which also replaces much of the functionality of the traditional Control Panel. (Although the Control Panel remains—well-hidden—in Windows 10, you'll probably use the Settings tool instead.)

- Although you can operate Windows 10 with touch gestures, you don't have to. Everything you need to do you can do with your mouse and keyboard.

- The full-screen Modern apps from Windows 8 have been rewritten to appear in resizable windows on the traditional desktop.

- There's a new Action Center, accessible from the taskbar, that displays important system messages and key system operations.

- Traditional system search has been replaced by the Cortana virtual assistant, which functions similarly to Siri on an Apple iPhone. You can operate Cortana with the keyboard or with voice commands.

- There's a new web browser, called Microsoft Edge, that's faster and more streamlined than the old Internet Explorer—and that adds several new features, as well.

There are even more new features, including some nice changes to the interface design, but that gives you a feel of what's new and different. If you're still running Windows 8 or Windows 8.1, you want to upgrade to Windows 10—which should be a relatively easy and painless process. See the Microsoft website for details.

# Windows 10 for Windows 7 Users

Prior to the release of Windows 10, it's fair to say that the last great version of Windows was Windows 7. It was so beloved that most Windows 7 users didn't upgrade to Windows 8 or 8.1; they kept running 7 on their old machines, and avoided buying new PCs so they wouldn't have to run the dreaded Windows 8.

But Windows 7 is starting to get a little long in the tooth, and many of those older Windows 7 PCs are really starting to show their age. Fortunately, it's easy to upgrade from Windows 7 directly to Windows 10—and if your computer is still running Windows 7, it's something you probably should do.

If you're a Windows 7 user, you'll find Windows 10 familiar. I view Windows 10 as the natural upgrade to Windows 7 that Windows 8 should have been but wasn't. Windows 10 sticks with everything that people liked about Windows 7 and makes some natural and quite useful enhancements.

What will Windows 7 users find new in Windows 10? Here's a short list:

- The interface looks a little different, using a more contemporary flat design with minimal windows "chrome" (which means almost borderless windows).

- There aren't any desktop "gadgets" in Windows 10. Sorry about that.

- The Start menu has been substantially revamped. Pinned apps now appear as live resizable tiles on the Start menu, and the Start menu itself is resizable.

- You now sign in to Windows with a Microsoft account. You can sign in to multiple PCs (all running Windows 10) with the same account and have your personal options appear on the other PCs.

- The newer, faster Microsoft Edge web browser replaces the older, slower Internet Explorer.

- Windows Explorer is renamed to File Explorer, with a new ribbon interface.

- The Task Manager tool is completely overhauled to make it more functional.

- You use Windows 10's Settings tool, instead of the old Control Panel, to configure most of the operating system's settings.

- The Windows Defender antivirus/antispyware tool is now included, free of charge.

- Windows added options to both refresh and reset the operating system in case of severe system problems.

In terms of compatibility, Windows 10 should run just fine on a Windows 7 PC. You may find some compatibility issues with some older software, so check with Microsoft or your software publisher to make sure everything works well together.

You should be able to upgrade from Windows 7 to Windows 10 without losing any of your files, programs, or settings. See the Microsoft website for more information.

# Windows 10 for Windows XP Users

Techie types might find it hard to believe, but there are tens of millions of people and companies still using Windows XP, more than 15 years after its initial release—and several years since Microsoft quit officially supporting it. That loss of support is reason enough to upgrade from XP to Windows 10, and you'll gain a lot of functionality by moving to a more modern operating system.

**Windows XP for Work**

Why are so many companies still using a 15-year-old operating system? In a lot of cases, it's because those companies use purpose-built software that was designed specifically for the Windows XP platform. If this is the main software your company uses, there has been little need to upgrade operating systems—especially if the old software won't run on newer versions of Windows.

The challenge with upgrading a computer directly from Windows XP to Windows 10 is that you're moving from a 15-year-old operating system to a brand-new state-of-the-art one. If you're using a computer that's as old as the operating system, it may not be able to run Windows 10 at all; certainly, you're likely to run into some compatibility issues with older peripherals and software programs.

In addition, the upgrade itself won't be easy. You can't just upgrade the operating system; you have to wipe your computer's hard disk completely clean and then install Windows 10 fresh on top of that. (This is called a *clean install*.) You'll lose all your files and programs and settings, so you'll want to back up your files first and then restore them after you install Windows 10. You'll need to reinstall all your software programs from scratch, as well.

For these reasons, it's difficult to recommend upgrading from Windows XP to Windows 10, even with all the benefits that might come from such a move. A better approach is to ditch your older computer (or give it to one of your children or grandchildren) and buy a new computer with Windows 10 already installed. New computers are a lot less expensive than they were a decade ago, and getting a new PC up and running will take a lot less time and effort than trying to upgrade a Windows XP machine to Windows 10.

# The 10 Most Important New Features of Windows 10

Now that you know what's new and different in this latest version of Windows, let's take a more in-depth look at the most important new features in Windows 10.

## 1: Back to the Desktop (Goodbye, Start Screen)

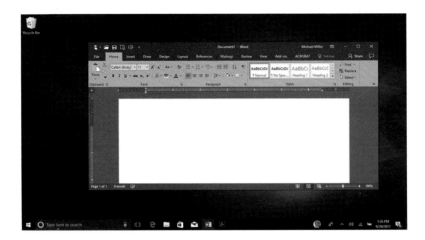

The biggest mistake that Microsoft made with Windows 8 was trying to apply a single interface paradigm to all possible devices—and then picking the wrong interface. Microsoft assumed that tablets would obliterate desktop and notebook PCs, developed a touch-based, full-screen interface that worked fine on those touchscreen devices, but then forced that interface on all traditional PC users. Bad decision.

The biggest change in Windows 10 is the abandonment of the entire touch-based approach. When you boot Windows 10 with a traditional PC, you're booted directly to the desktop. There's no Start screen (which is how you had to open apps in Windows 8), no Charms bar you have to swipe in from the right (which is where many system settings were located in Windows 8), and no "Modern" or "Metro" apps that take up the entire screen to display a minimal amount of information. You start your PC, you see the same old desktop you've grown to love and expect, and you're off to the races.

If you're familiar with Windows 7, the Windows 10 desktop looks pretty much like the one you're used to. You'll find a taskbar at the bottom of the screen, application shortcuts on the desktop itself, and even a Start button in the lower-left corner. (More on that in a moment.) You don't need to touch it to make it work (although you can, on a touchscreen PC); it's designed for use with your mouse and keyboard, just as you're used to. In short, it's the Windows desktop you want, with no unnecessary interference.

## Tablet Mode

If you're running Windows 10 on a touchscreen tablet, things look a little different. Windows senses that you're using a device without a keyboard and automatically switches to what it calls Tablet mode, with a full-screen Start menu and full-screen apps. Learn more about this version of Windows 10 in Chapter 8, "Using Windows 10 on a Touchscreen Device."

# 2: The Start Menu Returns—Better Than Ever

Perhaps the most significant change in Windows 10 is that little piece of real estate in the lower-left corner. That's right, the Start button and the Start menu are back!

The dumbest thing Microsoft did in Windows 8 might have been removing the Start menu, which is how we've all been launching programs since the advent of Windows 95 two decades ago. In Windows 8, you had to navigate to the Start screen, which took up the entire screen (of course), find your app among the dozens or hundreds displayed there, and then do the tap or click thing. There was no compelling reason for this change, nobody was demanding it, and users quite frankly despised it.

Well, Microsoft heard your complaints, and the Start menu is back in Windows 10. Click the Start button and you see the Start menu—although it looks a little different from what you were used to in Windows 7.

The Start menu now has three sections, left to right. The left section contains icons for common operations (such as Power and Settings), and the middle displays a list of all the applications installed on your system. These look different but function much like similar sections on the Windows 7 Start menu.

It's the right side of the Start menu that's radically different. Here is where you see any apps you've pinned to the Start menu, but not in the traditional list. Instead, you see a "tile" for each item. Depending on the app, a tile can be "live"— that is, it can display current information when available. If you pin the Weather app, for example, the Weather tile displays current temperature and weather conditions. The News tile displays current news headlines, and so forth.

These tiles are resizable, and the Start menu itself can be resized vertically and horizontally. The tiles create a new level of usability for the Start menu, resulting in a nice addition of Windows 8 functionality into the traditional Windows desktop paradigm.

## 3: Things Look a Little Different

Microsoft always tweaks the interface a little with each new version of Windows, and Windows 10 is no different. The new color schemes result in a darker taskbar, and all the system icons have been redesigned. More important, it's a flat interface; windows have a slight drop shadow and look as if they're floating on the desktop. Microsoft also removed most of the unnecessary "chrome" in the interface, so there's little to no frame around most windows.

And, in the Fall Creators Update, you get the option of displaying a Dark Theme, which makes most app backgrounds black with white text. There's also the introduction of a new design aesthetic called Fluent Design, which makes window backgrounds look like translucent acrylic; the background also slightly changes color when you move your mouse around. These are subtle changes, but they make for a more enjoyable computing experience.

## 4: Take Control with the Action Center

At the far-right corner of the notification area of the taskbar is a new Notifications icon. Click this to display the Action Center, which serves multiple purposes.

First, it displays important system messages. Second, if you're using Microsoft Outlook or a similarly compatible email client, it displays new messages in your email inbox. And third, the Action Center displays Quick Actions—tiles that link into key system operations, such as turning Wi-Fi on or off, switching to Tablet mode, and the like. It's kind of like a quick access pane to some pretty important stuff.

# 5: Manage System Settings with the Settings Tool

In all older versions of Windows, all system settings were accessible from the Control Panel. In Windows 8, that changed with some (but not all) settings accessible from a Charms bar that swiped in from the right side of the screen.

In Windows 10, the Charms bar is no more and the Control Panel has been effectively hidden. Instead, there's a new Settings tool, accessible from either the Start menu or the Action Center, that contains just about all of your system settings. It's the place to go to when you want to configure something about your system.

## 6: Windows Apps on the Desktop

In Windows 8, Microsoft introduced a new class of applications, originally dubbed Metro (then Modern, then Windows Store, then Universal Windows Platform) apps. These apps ran full screen and were designed to be used on touch interfaces—not on the traditional Windows desktop.

In Windows 10, Microsoft has redesigned these apps —now called simply Windows apps—to appear in traditional windows on the desktop. You can resize the windows as you like and display multiple app windows at a time. You get all the functionality of these newer apps but in a desktop-friendly package—just as it should be.

# 7: Smart Searching—and More—with Cortana

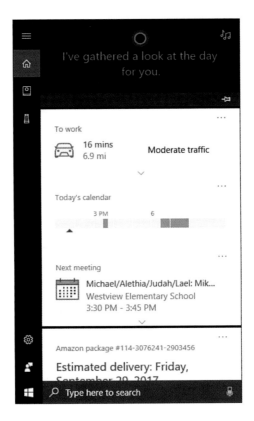

Whereas most Windows 10 changes are evolutionary improvements, there's one completely new technology. Cortana is a virtual assistant, much like Apple's Siri, that serves multiple functions. You use Cortana to search for content on your PC or on the Web, and it does a good job of that, learning your behavior as it goes along. You can also use Cortana to set reminders, schedule tasks, view the latest news and weather, and such. Again, with use, Cortana learns what you like and dislike, and thus gets smarter about the options it offers you.

You can search with Cortana from your computer keyboard or speak voice commands into your PC's microphone. Just click the search box on the taskbar or say "Hey, Cortana" into your computer's microphone.

## 8: A New Way to Browse the Web

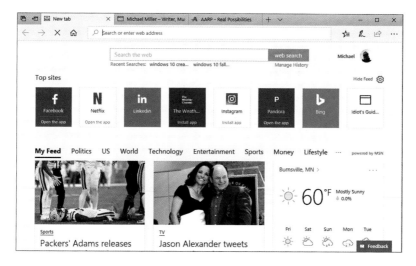

Windows 10 features a new web browser, named Microsoft Edge. This new browser looks and feels more like the more modern Chrome and Firefox browsers and, like those browsers, supports tabbed browsing. Edge also includes a new Reading View which removes annoying ads from many web pages, and lets you mark up the pages you view with Web Notes. In addition, Edge is considerably faster than the older Internet Explorer browser, and more compatible with today's state-of-the-art websites. It's a great replacement for an older browser that was showing its age.

## 9: Improved Task Switching

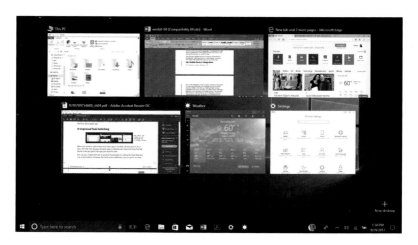

When you want to switch from one open app to another, all you have to do is press Alt+Tab. This displays all open apps as thumbnails; keep pressing that Tab button until you get to the app you want to view.

You can also display this list of window thumbnails by clicking the Task View button on the taskbar. However, this button has additional uses, as you'll see next.

## 10: Mobile Device Integration

New in the Windows 10 Fall Creators Update is the ability to sync your Windows 10 computer with your mobile phone or tablet. This lets you read and reply to text messages from your computer, as well as share data files between your computer and mobile device. You can now start work on a document on your computer, continue working on it with your Android or iOS smartphone or tablet, and finish things up back at your PC. This feature recognizes how we use our devices today, and puts your documents and files front and center—no matter which device you're using.

## And More...

Windows 10 offers even more changes, big and small, under the hood and hiding in plain sight. This makes Windows 10 (now with the latest Fall Creators Update) a must-have upgrade for both beleaguered Windows 8 users and expectant Windows 7 devotees. It's the upgrade to Windows 7 that Windows 8 should have been—and it's now available on your personal computer.

# Windows 10 Updates for Windows 10 Users

If you've been running Windows 10 for a while, you know that Microsoft has made some important updates to its core operating system since its initial release. The latest version of Windows 10, dubbed the Fall Creators Update, was released in October of 2017 and, along with previous updates, has improved upon the original release in significant ways.

It's important to know that Microsoft thinks of Windows 10 as an operating system as a service, which means it's not a static piece of software you install once and forget about. Microsoft is constantly revising the operating system and periodically releases important updates to the user base. Some of these revisions are in the form of monthly updates (managed in the Windows Update section of the Settings tool) designed to fix bugs and improve performance. Other updates are more major and include new features and interface changes.

Since the original release of Windows 10 in 2015, there have been three major updates—the Anniversary Update, Creators Update, and Fall Creators Update. Microsoft intends to release subsequent major updates every six months or so.

So what's new in these Windows 10 updates? There are a slew of features and changes, both major and minor. If you've been using Windows 10 all along, look for these new features.

## Anniversary Update

Microsoft released its first major Windows 10 update on the operating system's first anniversary, in August, 2016. This update included a lot of bug fixes and performance enhancements, including the following new features:

- Dark Theme, to display apps with a black background instead of the traditional white
- New Skype app for video, audio, and text messaging
- Windows Ink for drawing in select apps.

## Creators Update

The Creators Update was released eight months after the Anniversary Update, in April, 2017. This release saw even more new features and changes to how a few things looked and worked. These changes included the following:

- Changes to how Windows updates are delivered, so that you can opt not to automatically receive some minor updates
- Game Mode to enhance game playback
- New interface for the Windows Defender anti-malware app
- Paint 3D app for drawing three-dimensional shapes
- Virtual reality functionality

## Fall Creators Update

The latest update to Windows 10 was released in October, 2017. This update added even more new functionality to the operating system, along with some important interface changes. These changes included

- The ability to pin individual websites to the taskbar
- Controlled folder access in Windows Defender to guard against ransomware attacks
- Fluent Design elements to improve the look of the operating system and apps

- Integration with Android, iOS, and Windows phones and tablets, to share data and messages between multiple devices

- My People app to manage your favorite contacts directly from the Windows taskbar

- OneDrive Files on Demand for working with files stored online

- Story Remix in the Photos app, to create "highlight reels" of your pictures and videos

- Support for "mixed reality" headsets and apps

All three of the major updates have also included enhanced functionality for the Cortana virtual digital assistant, Microsoft Edge browser, Action Center, and Settings tool. These changes are designed to make Windows more functional and easier to use.

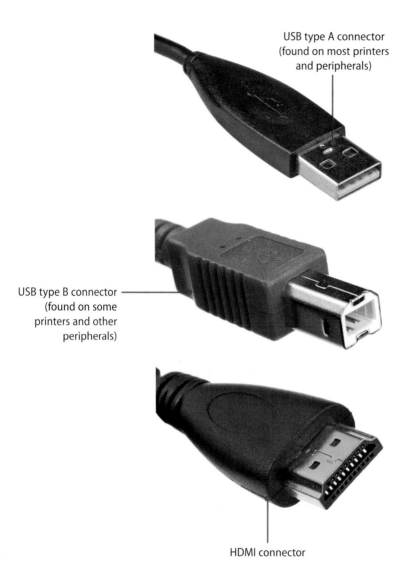

USB type A connector
(found on most printers
and peripherals)

USB type B connector
(found on some
printers and other
peripherals)

HDMI connector

In this chapter, you find out how to connect your new computer to printers and other USB devices.

→ Connecting Devices via USB
→ Connecting Your PC to Your TV

5

# Connecting Printers and Other Peripherals

Your Windows 10 computer doesn't operate in a vacuum. To get the most out of your machine, you might want to connect it to other devices—such as a printer, or even your living room TV.

## Connecting Devices via USB

Most external devices—including printers and scanners—connect to your PC via USB. This is a type of connection common on computers and other electronic devices; it carries data and provides power for some connected devices. USB is popular because it's so easy to use. All you have to do is connect a device via USB and your computer should automatically recognize it.

## USB

USB stands for *universal serial bus*, and is an industry standard developed in the mid-1990s. There have been three different versions of USB to date—1.0, 2.0, and 3.0. Chances are your computer includes a mixture of USB 2.0 and 3.0 ports. All USB cables use similar connectors, but each successive version transmits data faster than the previous versions.

## Connect a Printer

Most printers today connect to your computer via an easy-to-use USB cable. Once you've connected the printer, you can then configure it from within Windows.

### Wireless Printers

Some newer printers offer the option of connecting to your computer wirelessly, via Wi-Fi. This offers the convenience of placing your printer anywhere in your house without having to physically tether it to your PC. I've found USB connections more reliable than wireless ones, but if you opt to go the wireless route make sure you follow the printer manufacturer's instructions for getting everything set up and properly configured.

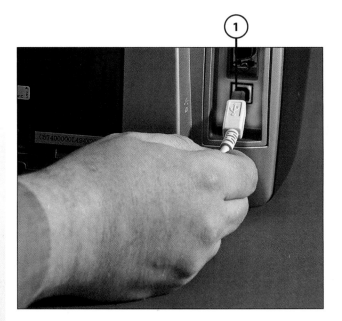

1. Connect one end of a USB cable to the USB port on your printer.

2. Connect the other end of the USB cable to a USB port on your computer.

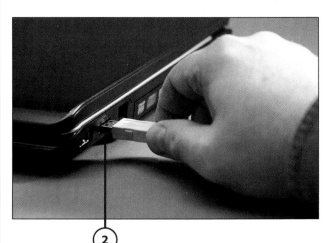

(3) Connect the printer's power cable to a power outlet.

(4) You must now install the printer within Windows. Click the Notifications icon in the taskbar to display the Action panel.

(5) Click All Settings to display the Settings window.

(6) Click Devices.

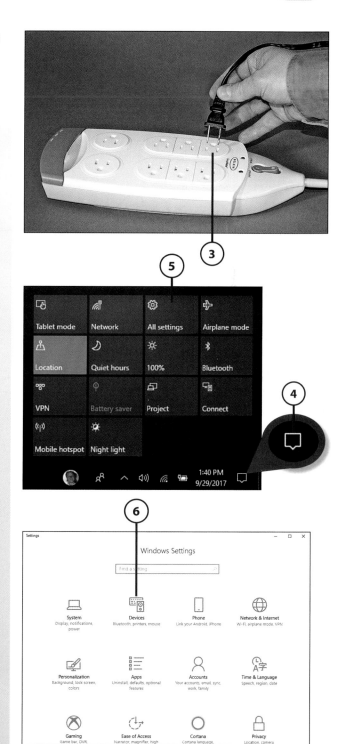

( 7 ) In the left-hand column, click to select Printers & Scanners.

( 8 ) In the right column, click Add a Printer or Scanner and let Windows search for it. When your printer is found, follow the onscreen instructions to complete the installation.

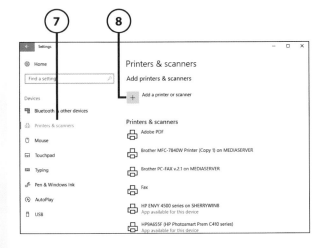

## Connect Other Peripherals

You can connect a variety of peripherals to your computer via USB. These include mice, keyboards, digital cameras, external hard drives, scanners, and more.

( 1 ) Connect one end of a USB cable to your new device.

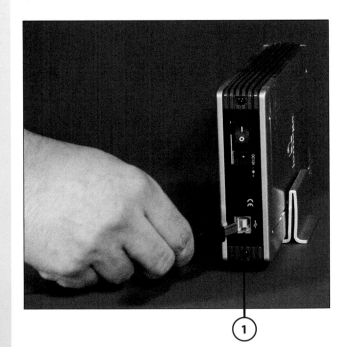

( 2 ) Connect the other end of the cable to a free USB port on your PC.

( 3 ) In most cases, Windows recognizes the new devices and automatically installs the proper system drivers and files. If Windows can perform multiple actions for a given device (such as viewing or downloading photos from a digital camera), you might be prompted to select which action you wish to take. Click the prompt to make a selection.

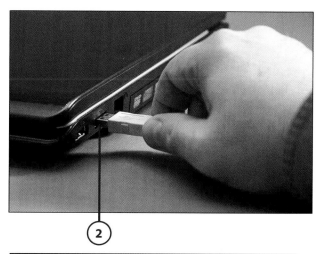

### USB Hubs

If you connect too many USB devices, you can run out of USB connectors on your PC. If that happens, buy an add-on USB hub, which lets you plug multiple USB peripherals into a single USB port.

# Connecting Your PC to Your TV

If you want to watch Internet streaming video (from Netflix and other services) on your TV, you can simply connect your TV to your PC via an HDMI cable. Connected this way, anything you watch on your PC will display on your TV screen.

## Connect via HDMI

HDMI is the easiest way to connect your PC to your TV. HDMI stands for high definition multimedia interface, and has become the connection standard for high definition TVs. All newer TV sets have two or more HDMI inputs, typically used to connect cable boxes, Blu-ray players, and the like. HDMI transmits both audio and video signals.

Most new computers, both desktops and laptops, have either a full-sized or mini HDMI port. (Laptops are more likely to have a mini HDMI port.) All you have to do is connect the appropriate HDMI cable between your two devices.

( 1 ) Connect one end of an HDMI or mini HDMI cable to the HDMI port on your computer.

( 2 ) Connect the other end of the HDMI cable to an open HDMI connector on your TV.

**(3)** Switch your TV to the HDMI input you connected to. Your computer screen should now appear on your TV display.

**(4)** To view programming in full screen, click the full-screen button in the app or window you're viewing.

## Mini HDMI Connectors

Not all PCs have full-sized HDMI ports. Some (particularly laptops) have mini HDMI connectors, which require the use of a special HDMI cable with a mini connector on one end and a standard-sized connector on the other.

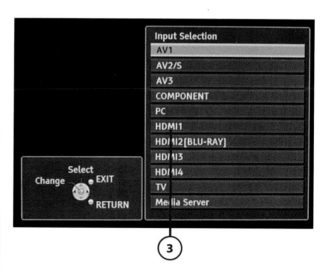

**(3)**

**(4)**

Settings tool (light theme)

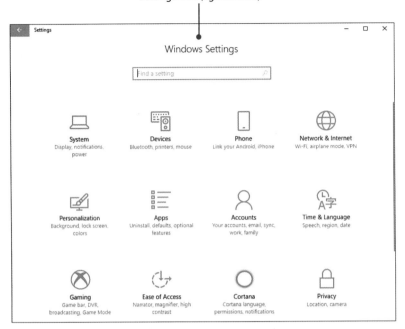

Settings tool
(dark theme)

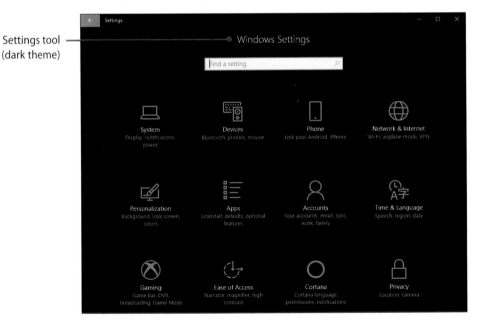

In this chapter, you find out how to customize the look and feel of Windows to your own personal satisfaction.

6

# Personalizing Windows

When you first turn on your new computer system, you see the Windows lock screen, and then the Windows desktop, complete with the Start menu. You can accept the default look for each of these items, or you can customize them to your own personal tastes. It's one way to make Windows look like *your* version of Windows, different from anybody else's.

## Personalizing the Windows Desktop

You can personalize several elements on the Windows desktop itself. You can change the color scheme, the desktop background, and even "pin" your favorite programs to the taskbar or the Start menu.

# Personalize the Start Menu

The Windows 10 Start menu can be customized to display tiles for your favorite programs. These tiles can be moved or resized, as you like.

**(1)** Click the Start button to open the Start menu.

**(2)** To resize the Start menu, mouse over the top or right edge; then click and drag the window to the desired size.

**(3)** To "pin" a program to the right side of the Start menu, right-click the name of the app and then select Pin to Start. (You can also use your mouse to click and drag the app to where you want it on the right side of the Start menu.)

---

## Pinning

"Pinning" an app creates a permanent shortcut to that app. You can pin programs to either the Start menu or the taskbar.

---

**(4)** To rearrange tiles on the Start menu, click and hold a tile and then drag it to a new position.

**(5)** To resize a tile, right-click the tile, select Resize, and then select the desired size. Tiles come in four possible sizes: Small, Medium, Wide, and Large.

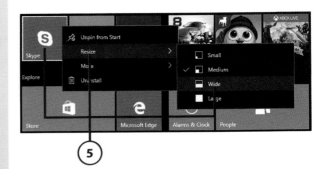

( 6 ) To remove a tile from the Start menu, right-click the tile and select Unpin from Start.

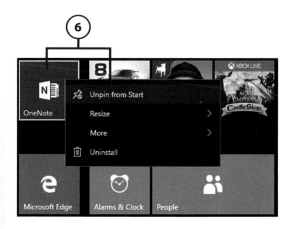

## Live Tiles

Tiles for some apps display "live" information—that is, current data in real time. For example, the Weather tile displays current weather conditions; the News tile displays current news headlines.

# Change the Desktop Background

The Windows desktop displays across your entire computer screen. One of the most popular ways to personalize the desktop is to use a favorite picture or color as the desktop background.

( 1 ) Right-click in any open area of the desktop and select Personalize from the pop-up menu. The Personalization window displays.

( 2 ) Click to select the Background tab.

( 3 ) To use a picture as your desktop background, click the Background control and select Picture.

( 4 ) Click to select one of the thumbnail images displayed. *Or...*

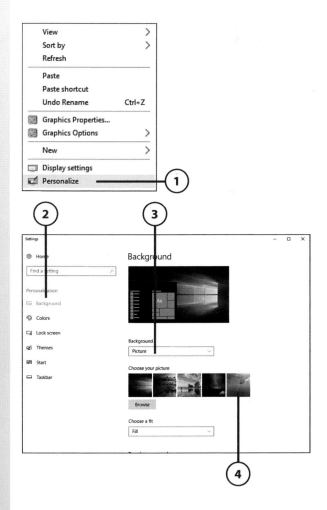

**5** Click Browse to select another picture stored on your computer.

**6** If the selected image is a different size from your Windows desktop, click the Choose a Fit list and select a display option—Fill (zooms into the picture to fill the screen), Fit (fits the image to fill the screen horizontally, but might leave black bars above and below the image), Stretch (distorts the picture to fill the screen), Tile (displays multiple instances of a smaller image), Center (displays a smaller image in the center of the screen, with black space around it), or Span (spans a single image across multiple monitors, if you have multiple monitors on your system).

**7** To set a color for your desktop background, click the Background list and select Solid Color.

**8** Click to select the color you want. (Or click Custom Color to choose from a broader palette.)

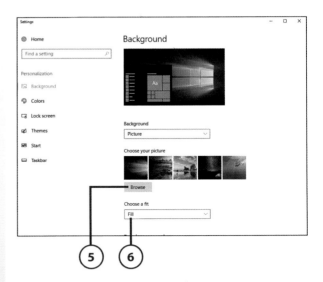

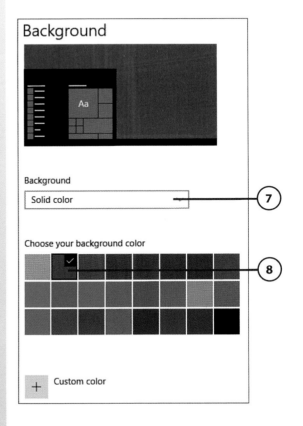

**9** To have your desktop background rotate through a variety of pictures, click the Background list and select Slideshow.

**10** By default, the slideshow chooses pictures from your Pictures folder. To select a different folder, click Browse.

**11** To change how long each photo is displayed, click the Change Picture Every list and make a new selection.

**12** To display pictures randomly, click "on" the Shuffle switch.

**13** Click the Choose a Fit list and select a display option.

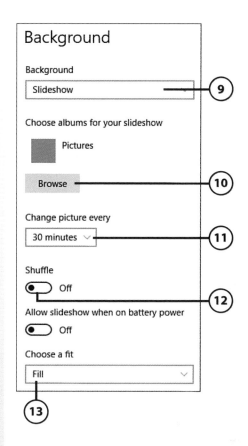

## Change the Accent Color

You can select any color for the title bar and frame that surrounds open windows on the desktop. You can also set the color for the Windows taskbar, Start menu, and Action Center.

**1** Right-click in any open area of the desktop and select Personalize from the pop-up menu. The Personalization window displays.

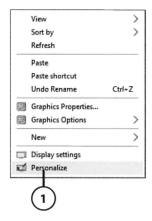

**2** Click to select the Colors tab.

**3** To have Windows automatically choose the accent color based on the color of the desktop image, click to check the Automatically Pick an Accent Color from My Background option.

**4** To select a different accent color, uncheck the Automatically Pick an Accent Color from My Background option, and then click to select the color you want.

**5** To make the Windows desktop elements transparent, scroll down the window and click "on" the Transparency Effects switch.

**6** To show the accent color on the Start menu, taskbar, and Action Center, click to select the Start, Taskbar, and Action Center option. Uncheck this option to display a black Start menu, taskbar, and Action Center.

**7** To show the accent color on windows title bars, click to select the Title Bars option.

**8** To switch to Windows 10's "Dark" mode (displays a black background in many windows), go to the Choose Your Default App Mode section and select the Dark option.

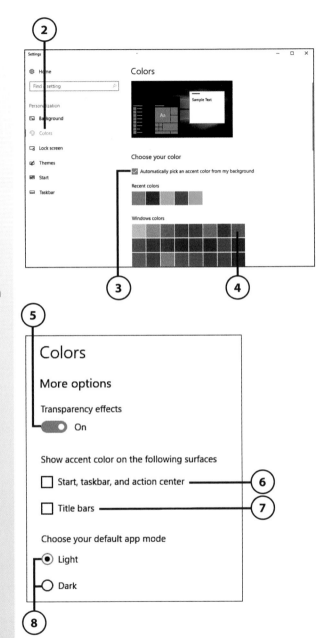

# Change the Desktop Theme

Although you can configure each element of the Windows desktop separately, it's often easier to choose a predesigned *theme* that changes all the elements in a visually pleasing configuration. A theme combines background images, color schemes, system sounds, and mouse cursor appearance to present a unified look and feel. Some themes even change the color scheme to match the current background picture.

(**1**) Right-click any open area of the desktop to display the options menu and then click Personalize to display the Personalization window.

(**2**) Click to select the Themes tab.

(**3**) To save the currently selected background, color, sound, and mouse scheme as a new theme, click Save Theme. When prompted, give this new theme a name.

(**4**) Scroll down to the Apply a Theme section to view all themes installed on your PC. Click any theme to change to that theme.

(**5**) Additional themes, most free of charge, are available from the Microsoft Store online. Click Get More Themes in the Store to view what's available.

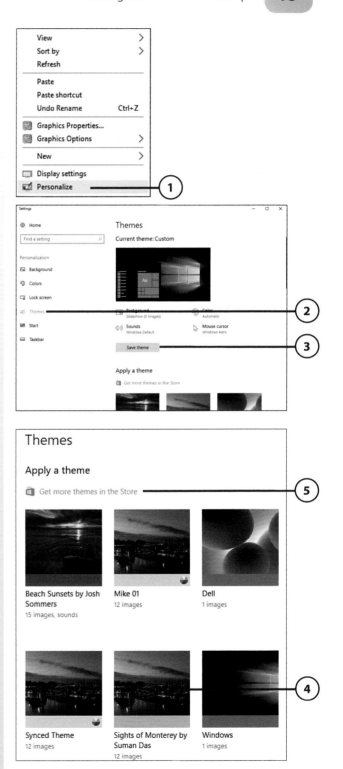

# Personalizing the Lock Screen

You can also personalize the lock screen, which you see when you first start or begin to log in to Windows. You can change the background picture of the lock screen, turn the lock screen into a photo slideshow, and add informational apps to the screen.

## Change the Lock Screen Background

You can choose from several stock images for the background of your lock screen, or you can upload your own photo to use as the background.

### Lock Screen

The lock screen appears when you first power on your PC and any time you log off from your personal account or switch users. It also appears when you awaken your computer from Sleep mode.

1. Right-click in any open area of the desktop and select Personalize from the pop-up menu. The Personalization window displays.

2. Click to select the Lock Screen tab.

3. Click the Background list and select Picture. (Or stick with the default Windows Spotlight to have Windows choose new background pictures for you every few days.)

4. Click the thumbnail for the picture you want to use.

5. Alternatively, click the Browse button to use your own picture as the background.

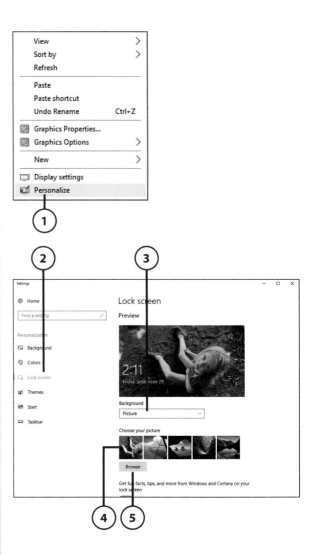

# Display a Slideshow on the Lock Screen

Windows lets you turn your computer into a kind of digital picture frame, by displaying a slideshow of your photos on the lock screen while your PC isn't being used.

## >>>Go Further

### DISPLAY THE LOCK SCREEN

You can display the lock screen (and your photo slideshow) at any time by opening the Start menu, clicking your profile picture, and selecting Lock.

**1** Right-click in any open area of the desktop and select Personalize from the pop-up menu. The Personalization window displays.

**2** Click to select the Lock Screen tab.

**3** Click the Background list and select Slideshow.

**4** By default, Windows displays pictures from your Pictures folder. Click Add a Folder to select a different picture folder you want to display in your slideshow.

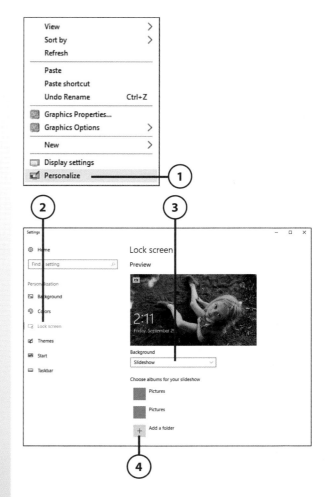

## >>>Go Further
## ADVANCED SETTINGS

Click Advanced Slideshow Settings to configure the slideshow to include Camera Roll folders from this PC and your OneDrive account, use only pictures that best fit your screen, not play a slideshow when on battery power, and show the lock screen instead of turning off the screen when your PC is inactive. You can even choose to turn off your computer's screen after the slideshow has played for a specified period of time.

## Add Apps to the Lock Screen

The lock screen can display a number of apps that run in the background and display useful or interesting information, even while your computer is locked. By default, you see the date/time, power status, and connection status, but it's easy to add other apps and information (such as weather conditions and unread email messages) to the lock screen.

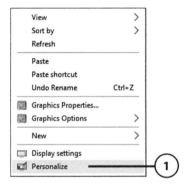

① Right-click in any open area of the desktop and select Personalize from the pop-up menu. The Personalization window displays.

② Click to select the Lock Screen tab.

③ Go to the Choose Apps to Show Quick Status section and click one of the + buttons to display the Choose an App panel.

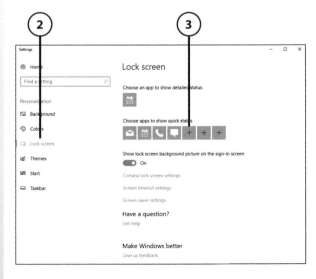

**4** Click the app you want to add.

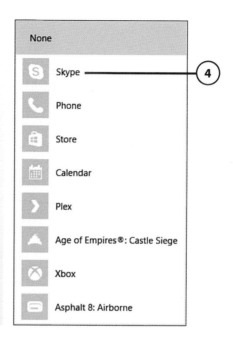

None

S   Skype ———————————— **4**

📞   Phone

🏪   Store

📅   Calendar

›   Plex

▲   Age of Empires®: Castle Siege

⊗   Xbox

▭   Asphalt 8: Airborne

# >>>Go Further

## LIVE INFORMATION

You can also opt for one of the apps on the lock screen to display detailed live information. For example, you might want the lock screen to display current weather conditions from the Weather app or upcoming appointments from the Calendar app.

To select which app displays detailed information, click the app button in the Choose an App to Show Detailed Status section to display a list of apps on your system that can provide live information.

# Change Your Account Picture

Windows displays a small thumbnail image next to your account name when you log in to Windows from the lock screen; this same image displays next to your name on the Windows Start menu. When you first configured Windows, you were prompted to select a default image to use as this profile picture. You can, at any time, change this picture to something more to your liking.

1. Click the Start button to display the Start menu.

2. Click your name or picture on the left side of the Start menu to display the options menu.

3. Click Change Account Settings to display the Settings tool with the Your Info tab selected.

4. If you've previously selected a profile picture, click one of the images displayed at the top of the page.

5. To use another picture stored on your computer (or online at OneDrive), scroll to the Create Your Picture section, click Browse for One, and then select the picture you want.

6. Alternatively, you can take a picture with your computer's webcam to use for your account picture. Click Camera then follow the onscreen directions from there.

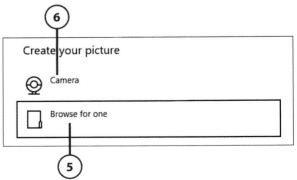

# Configuring Other Windows Settings

You can configure many other Windows system settings. In most cases, the default settings work fine and you don't need to change a thing. However, you *can* change these settings, if you want to or need to.

## Configure Settings from the Settings Tool

You configure most Windows settings from the Settings tool, which consists of a series of tabs, accessible from the left side of the window, that present different types of settings.

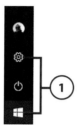

1. Click the Start button to display the Start menu, then click Settings.

2. Alternatively, click the Notifications icon on the taskbar then click All Settings.

3. Windows now opens the Settings tool. To search for a specific setting, type your query into the Find a Setting box and click the Search (magnifying glass) icon. *Or...*

4. Click a category icon to display settings of that type.

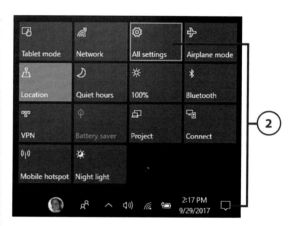

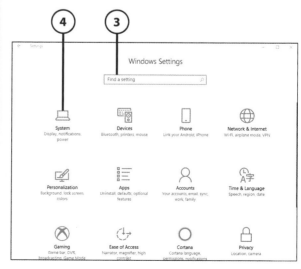

**5** Click the tab on the left to select the type of settings you want to configure.

**6** Configure the necessary options from the right side of the window.

**7** Click Home to return to the Settings tool's Home screen.

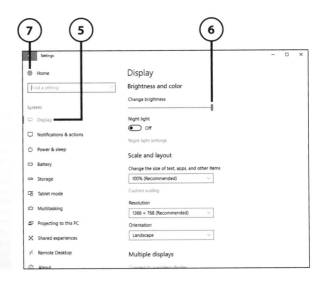

>>>Go Further

## CONTROL PANEL

In previous versions of Windows, most system settings were found in what was called the Control Panel. Since the initial release of Windows 10, Microsoft has been moving these settings from the Control Panel to the newer Settings app, so that the Control Panel is no longer necessary. You can still access the Control Panel if you want, however; just open the Start menu, click Windows System, and click Control Panel.

# Working with User Accounts

Chances are you're not the only person using your computer; it's likely that you'll be sharing your PC with your spouse or partner and maybe even your children and grandchildren. Fortunately, you can configure Windows so that different people using your computer sign on with their own custom settings—and access to their own personal files.

The best way for multiple people to use a single computer is to assign each person his or her own password-protected *user account*. For a given person to use the PC and access her own programs and files, she has to sign in to the computer with her personal password. If a person doesn't have an account or the proper password, she can't use the computer.

Windows lets you create two different types of user accounts—online and local. The default is the online account, which comes with some unique benefits.

## >>>Go Further

## SIGN-IN OPTIONS

When you set up a new user account, you can choose from several different ways to sign in to your PC. You can sign in to your account with a traditional password, with a personal identification number (PIN), or with something new, called a *picture password* that requires you to sketch a portion of a picture onscreen.

Some computers also let you sign in with a new technology called Windows Hello. With Windows Hello you can sign in with your fingerprint (on your notebook's touchpad) or facial recognition, via your PC's webcam. This technology is available only on select (typically higher-end) models, however.

Most of us will choose the traditional password option because it's easiest to set up and less confusing to use. Just enter your password when prompted on the lock screen and you're good to go!

An online account is linked to a new or existing Microsoft account. When you use a Microsoft account on your computer, Windows displays information from other Microsoft sites you use. For example, Windows displays the latest weather conditions in the Weather app, the latest news headlines in the News app, and the latest stock quotes in the Stock app—all based on settings you make when you configure your Microsoft account. Local accounts cannot access this personalized data.

For these reasons, I recommend you create (or use an existing) Microsoft Account for any new user you add to your computer.

## >>>Go Further

## DIFFERENT ACCOUNTS FOR DIFFERENT USERS

When you get your PC set up just the way you like, you may be hesitant to let anybody else use it. This goes doubly so for your children and grandchildren; you love 'em, but don't want them to mess up your computer with their games and tweeting and whatnot.

This is where creating separate user accounts has value. Create a user account for each user of your PC—for you, your spouse, and each of your kids and grandkids—and then make everybody sign in under their own personal accounts. The other family members can personalize their accounts however they want and there's nothing they can break, and nothing they can change. The next time you sign in to your user account, everything should look just the way you left it—no matter who used your computer in the meantime.

## Create a New User Account

You create one user account when you first launch Windows on your new PC. At any time, you can create additional user accounts for other people using your computer.

By default, Windows will use an existing Microsoft account to create your new Windows user account. So if you have an Outlook.com, OneDrive, Skype, Xbox Live, or other Microsoft account, you can use that account to sign in to Windows on your computer.

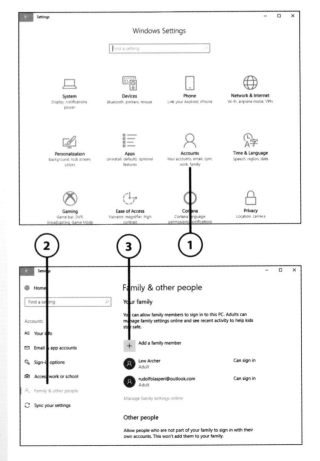

1. Open the Settings tool and click Accounts to display the Accounts page.

2. Click to select the Family & Other People tab.

3. Click Add a Family Member to display the Microsoft Account window.

**4** Select either Add a Child or Add an Adult.

**5** If the person already has an email address, enter it and click Next.

**6** If this person doesn't have an email address, click The Person I Want to Add Doesn't Have an Email Address.

**7** If you're creating a new email address, enter the desired email username into the New Email box. (You might have to try several names to get one that isn't already taken.)

**8** Enter the desired password into the Password box.

**9** Enter this person's birthdate.

**10** Click Next and follow the remaining instructions to create the new account.

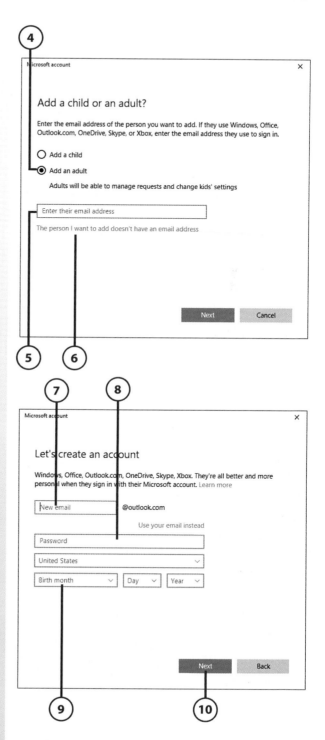

## >>>Go Further
### CHILD ACCOUNTS

If you're setting up an account on your computer for one of your younger family members, you might want to make that account a special *child account*. You see this option when you click Add a Family Member.

The big difference between a child account and a regular account is that Windows enables Family Safety Monitoring for the child account. With Family Safety Monitoring, you can turn on web filtering (to block access to undesirable websites), limit when younger children or grandchildren can use the PC and what websites they can visit, set limits on games and Windows Store app purchases, and monitor the kids' PC activity.

To do this, open the Security tool, select Update & Security, select the Windows Defender tab, and click Open Windows Defender Security Center. From here, click the Family Options icon and, on the next screen, click View Family Settings. This takes you to your Microsoft Account online, from where you can turn on and off Family Safety and activity reporting, as well as configure web filtering, time limits, Microsoft Store and game restrictions, and app restrictions for any account.

It's all about making Windows—and your Windows computer—safer for younger users. The younger members of your family will be the better for it.

## Switch Users

If other people are using your computer, they'll want to sign in with their own accounts. Fortunately, it's relatively easy to sign in and out of different accounts, and to switch users.

You can change users on your PC without restarting it.

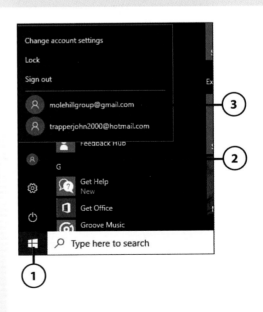

1. Click the Start button to display the Start menu.

2. Click your name or picture at the left side of the Start menu to display a list of other users.

3. Click the desired user's name.

**(4)** When prompted, enter the new user's password, and then press Enter.

**(4)**

## Sign In with Multiple Users

If you have more than one user assigned to Windows, the sign-in process is slightly different when you start up your computer.

**(1)** Power up your computer.

**(2)** When the Windows lock screen appears, press any key on your keyboard or click the mouse to display the sign-in screen. All users of this computer are listed here.

**(1)** **(2)**

( 3 ) Click your username to display your personal sign-in screen.

( 4 ) Enter your password as normal; then press the Enter key to display your personal desktop.

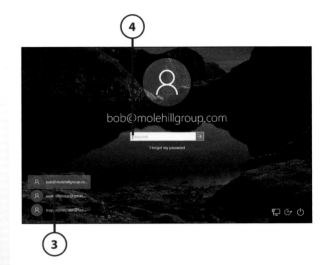

bob@molehillgroup.com

I forgot my password

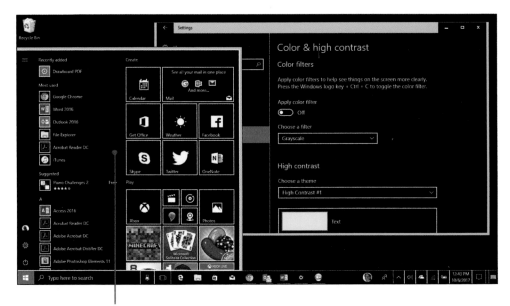

Windows desktop and Start
menu in high-contrast colors

In this chapter, you discover how to use the accessibility functions built in to Windows and other ways to make Windows easier to use if you have vision or mobility issues.

→ Employing Ease of Access Functions
→ Using Alternative Input Devices

# Making Windows Easier to Use

If you have 20/20 vision, perfect hearing, and the Samson-like grip of a circus strongman, good for you. For the rest of us, however, the default display settings of most computers, particularly notebook models with smaller screens and cramped keyboards, can affect our ability to use our PCs.

Fortunately, Microsoft offers some Ease of Access features that can make Windows—and your new PC—a little easier to use. Let's take a look.

## Employing Ease of Access Functions

Windows 10's Ease of Access features are designed to improve accessibility—that is, to make your computer easier and more comfortable to use, especially if you have vision, hearing, or dexterity issues. Microsoft offers several useful Ease of Access functions, including the capability to enlarge text on the screen, change the contrast to make text more readable, and to read the screen to aid those with vision problems.

# Access Ease of Access Features

The easiest way to get to Windows 10's Ease of Access settings is through the Settings window.

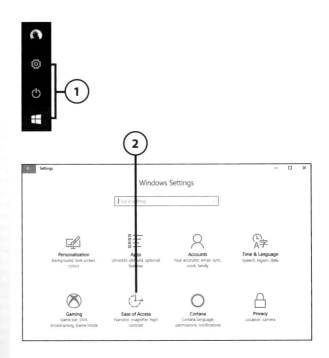

1. Click the Start button to display the Start menu; then click Settings to open the Settings window. (Alternatively, click the Notifications icon on the taskbar and then click All Settings.)

2. Click Ease of Access to display the Ease of Access screen.

# Enlarge the Screen

If you're having trouble reading what's onscreen because the text is too small, you can turn on the Magnifier tool. The Magnifier does just what the name implies—it magnifies an area of the screen to make it larger, for easier reading.

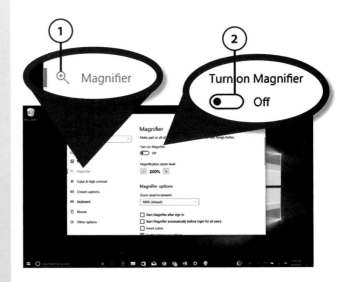

1. From the Ease of Access screen, click to select the Magnifier tab.

2. Click "on" the Magnifier control (that is, move the Magnifier slider to the On position).

## Invert Colors

To display the magnified screen with inverted colors (white text against a black background), select the Invert Colors option on the Magnifier tab.

**3** The screen enlarges to 200% of its original size. Navigate around the screen by moving your mouse to the edge of it. (For example, to move the screen to the right, move your mouse to the right edge of the screen.)

**4** To adjust Magnifier settings, click the onscreen magnifying glass icon to display the Magnifier dialog box.

**5** Click the + (plus) button to enlarge the screen further. (Alternatively, press Windows + the plus key on your keyboard.)

**6** Click the – (minus) button to reduce the size of the screen. (Alternatively, press Windows + the minus key on your keyboard.)

**7** Click the X to turn off the Magnifier. (Alternatively, press Windows + Esc on your keyboard.)

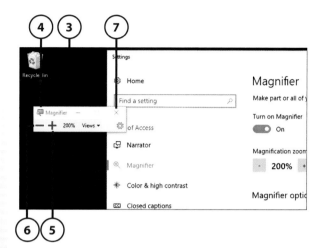

>>>Go Further

## MAKING WEB PAGES EASIER TO READ

If you're like me, you spend a lot of time on the Internet, reading articles and other content on the Web. Unfortunately, many web pages are difficult to read, cluttered with unnecessary ads and images and with text that's just a little too small.

There are a few things you can do to make web pages easier to read. The first is to increase the size of the onscreen text. In the Microsoft Edge browser, you do this by clicking the More Actions button, and then clicking the + zoom control. (In the Google Chrome browser, click Customize and Control in the top-right corner to access the zoom control.)

There's an even better approach in Microsoft Edge—a new feature called Reading view. In Reading view, Edge removes all the unnecessary ads and graphic elements; it displays only the text and accompanying pictures for the current web page. Reading view also increases the text size, so all around you get a much better reading experience. For those with vision problems, Reading view is a godsend. Check it out by going to your favorite web page and then clicking the Reading View button in the browser's Address bar. It really works!

Learn more about Reading view, and web browsing in general, in Chapter 12, "Browsing and Searching the Web."

## Improve Onscreen Contrast

Some people find it easier to view onscreen text if there's more of a contrast between the text and the background. To that end, Windows 10 lets you apply color filters that help you see different colors in grayscale, or a high contrast mode that displays lighter text on a dark background, instead of the normal black-on-white theme.

( 1 ) From the Ease of Access screen, click to select the Color & High Contrast tab.

( 2 ) To apply a color filter, click "on" the Apply Color Filter switch and then select a filter from the Choose a Filter list. (Color filters are particularly useful if you experience color blindness; it's easier to see grayscale elements than those in similar colors.)

( 3 ) To apply a high contrast theme, select a theme from the Choose a Theme list. Click the Apply button when done.

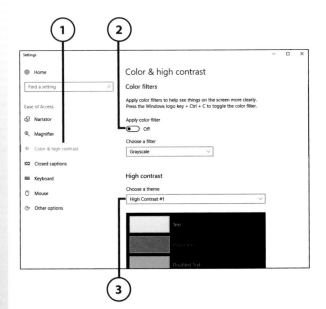

## Make the Cursor Easier to See

Another issue that many users have is seeing the cursor onscreen. The default cursor in Windows can be a little small and difficult to locate on a busy desktop; you can change the size and color of the cursor to make it easier to see. You can choose from Regular, Large, and Extra Large size settings, as well as from White, Black, and Inverting color settings.

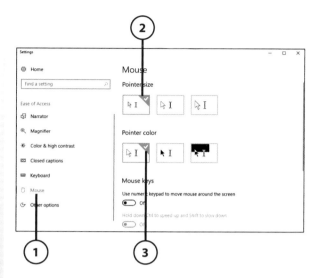

**( 1 )** From the Ease of Access screen, click to select the Mouse tab.

**( 2 )** In the Pointer Size section, select a larger pointer size.

**( 3 )** In the Pointer Color section, select a different pointer color—ideally, one that's easier to see onscreen.

## >>>Go Further

## CONNECTING A LARGER SCREEN

The easiest solution if you're having trouble seeing what's onscreen is to make the screen bigger—literally. This means connecting a larger computer monitor to your computer. Many people find that monitors sized 22" and larger are a lot easier to see than the standard 15" screens that are common today.

With most new computer monitors, both desktop and notebook models, you have the option of connecting via the traditional Video Graphics Array (VGA) connector, the newer Digital Visual Interface (DVI) connector, or even newer HDMI connector. A DVI or HDMI cable costs more than a VGA cable, but it provides a sharper digital picture.

# Read Text Aloud with Narrator

If your eyesight is really bad, even making the onscreen text and cursor super large won't help. To that end, Windows offers the Narrator utility, which speaks to you through your PC's speakers. When you press a key, Narrator tells you the name of that key. When you mouse over an item onscreen, Narrator tells you what it is. Narrator helps you operate your PC without having to see what's onscreen.

(1) From the Ease of Access screen, click to select the Narrator tab.

(2) Click "on" the Narrator control. If you want to use Narrator full time, click "on" the Start Narrator Automatically control as well.

### Keyboard Shortcut
You can also enable Narrator by pressing Windows+Ctrl+Enter on your keyboard.

(3) Pull down the Choose a Voice list and select from either David, Zira, or Mark.

(4) Use the Speed and Pitch controls to adjust how the voice sounds to you.

(5) Scroll down to the Sounds You Hear section and click "on" those items you want narrated.

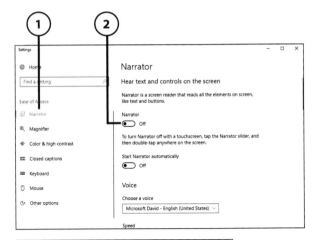

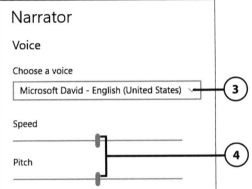

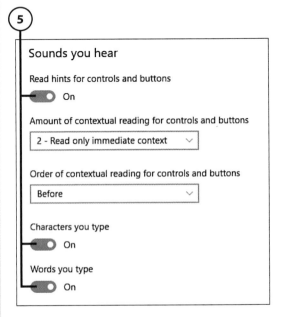

(**6**) Go to the Cursor and Keys section and click "on" those settings you prefer.

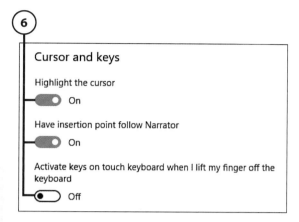

(**6**)

Cursor and keys

Highlight the cursor

On

Have insertion point follow Narrator

On

Activate keys on touch keyboard when I lift my finger off the keyboard

Off

# Use the On-Screen Keyboard

If you find that pressing the keys on your computer keyboard with your fingers is becoming too difficult, especially on a notebook PC with smaller keys, you might want to use the Windows On-Screen Keyboard. This is a virtual keyboard, displayed on your computer screen, that you can operate with your mouse instead of your fingers (or with your fingers, if you have a tablet PC without a traditional keyboard).

(**1**) From the Ease of Access screen in the Settings window, click Keyboard in the navigation sidebar.

(**2**) Click "on" the On-Screen Keyboard control. The On-Screen Keyboard displays.

(**3**) To "press" a key, click it with your mouse—or, on a touchscreen display, tap it with your finger.

(**4**) To close the On-Screen Keyboard, click the X in the top-right corner.

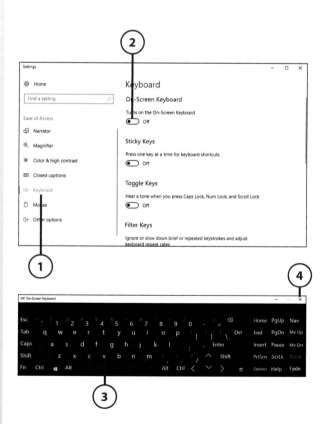

>>>*Go Further*

## MORE ACCESSIBILITY OPTIONS

I've covered the major Ease of Access functions here, but there are more where these came from. If you're having difficulty seeing items onscreen or operating Windows, you should explore all the options present on the Ease of Access settings screen. You can, for example, enable visual notifications for Windows sounds, opt to use the numeric keypad to move the mouse around the screen, and choose to activate a window by hovering over it with your mouse.

# Using Alternative Input Devices

Some of us might lose fine mobility in our hands and fingers, whether due to arthritis or some other condition. This might make it difficult to use the small touchpad found on most notebook PCs or to type on normal-sized keyboard keys.

The solution for this problem is to attach different input devices. You can easily connect an external mouse to a notebook PC that then replaces the built-in touchpad, or attach a keyboard with larger keys for easier use.

## Replace the Touchpad

Touchpads are convenient pointing devices for notebook PC users, but they can be difficult to use, especially if you have difficulty moving or holding your hand and fingers steady. The solution is to attach an external pointing device to a USB port on your notebook PC; when you do this, you use the (hopefully easier-to-use) external device instead of the built-in touchpad. There are two primary types of devices to choose from.

The first one is a simple external mouse that connects wirelessly to your computer via either USB cable or wirelessly via Bluetooth. Many people find that using a mouse is easier than trying to tap precise movements on a notebook's touchpad. If you're using a wireless mouse, connect the mouse's USB receiver into any open USB port on your computer, turn on the external mouse, and start using it. In most instances no additional setup is required.

In lieu of a touchpad or mouse, some users prefer an even larger trackball controller. This type of controller is typically used by youngsters who play computer games, but is also a terrific option for those with mobility issues. Use the large roller ball on top to move the cursor around the screen.

## Attach a Different Keyboard

Some notebook PC keyboards are a little smaller than the keyboard on a typical desktop PC, and use "chiclet" keys that don't respond much to your touch. You can remedy this situation by attaching a full-size external keyboard, either via USB cable or wirelessly via Bluetooth. Most external keyboards are easier to use and more ergonomic than the smaller keyboards found on most notebook computers.

Even the keys on a standard-sized keyboard might not be big enough if you have mobility issues. Several companies make keyboards with enlarged keys that are both easier to see and easier to use. Look for these online.

Tile for pinned application

Taskbar    Full-screen Start menu

In this chapter, you learn how to operate Windows 10 on a touchscreen device.

→ Using Windows in Tablet Mode
→ Using Windows with Touch Gestures

# Using Windows 10 on a Touchscreen Device

Many new PCs—both all-in-one desktop and notebook models—come with touchscreen displays. In addition, if you have a smaller device, such as a tablet, you can use Windows 10's Tablet mode, which displays the Start menu and application windows in full-screen mode.

Windows 10 was designed with touchscreens in mind, so you can perform many common operations with touch gestures. You just have to know how.

## Using Windows in Tablet Mode

If you have a notebook or desktop PC, Windows is displayed in the traditional desktop mode. If you have a device with a touchscreen, however, Windows can display in Tablet mode, specially designed for devices you operate via touch instead of a keyboard or mouse. Tablet mode is optimized for smaller-screen devices, displaying the Start menu and all applications full screen.

# Switch to Tablet Mode

If you have a tablet or 2-in-1 device, Windows 10's Continuum feature automatically senses your device (and how you're using it) and displays in the correct mode. For example, if you have a 2-in-1 tablet/notebook combo, when you remove the keyboard or flip the screen over to tablet operation, Windows asks you if you want to switch to Tablet mode. When you reattach the keyboard or flip the screen back for normal use, you're asked if you want to switch to Desktop mode.

Otherwise, you can manually switch to Tablet mode by following these steps.

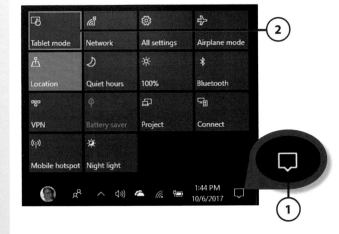

1. On the Windows taskbar, click or tap the Notification icon to display the Action Center.

2. Click or tap "on" the Tablet Mode tile. (It switches from gray to blue when activated.)

## Return to Normal Mode

To return to normal mode from Tablet mode, display the Action Center and click "off" the Tablet Mode tile.

# Use Windows 10's Tablet Mode

Tablet mode is designed for use with tablets, 2-in-1 notebooks, and other small-screen devices. In Tablet mode, the Start menu is displayed full screen, as are all open application windows. The taskbar remains visible so that you can easily open the Start menu, as well as pinned and open apps. And many apps—especially Windows apps—subtly adapt their interfaces for full-screen touch operation.

① Tap the Start button on the task-bar to display the Start menu full screen.

② Tap the All Apps button to display the All Apps list.

③ Tap any tile to launch the associated program in full-screen mode.

④ To display the Action Center, swipe in from the right side of the screen or tap the Notifications icon on the taskbar.

⑤ To switch to other open apps, swipe in from the left side of the screen and then tap the app you want.

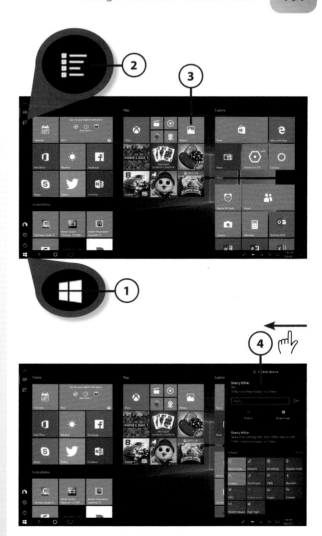

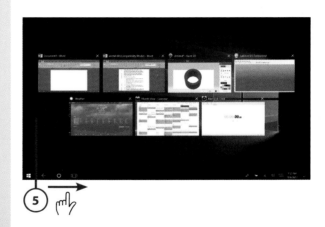

# Using Windows with Touch Gestures

If you're using Windows 10 on a computer or tablet with a touchscreen display, you can use your fingers instead of a mouse to do what you need to do. To that end, it's important to learn some essential touchscreen operations.

## Touchscreen Operations

Many operations in Windows 10 can be performed without a mouse or keyboard, using simple touch gestures instead.

 To "click" or select an item on a touchscreen display, tap the item with the tip of your finger and release.

 To "right-click" an item on a touchscreen display (typically displays a context-sensitive options menu), press, hold, and then release the item with the tip of your finger.

 To scroll up or down a page, swipe the screen in the desired direction.

 To zoom in on a given screen (that is, to make a selection larger), use two fingers to touch two points on the item, and then move your fingers apart.

 To zoom out of a given screen (that is, to make a selection smaller and see more of the surrounding page), use two fingers (or your thumb and first finger) to touch two points on the item, and then pinch your fingers in toward each other.

>>>Go Further

TOUCHPAD OPERATIONS

Many touchpads, found on notebook PCs, let you use touchscreen gestures, such as tapping and swiping. Consult your computer's operating manual to find out if your device has this functionality.

Windows
app

Minimize
button

Maximize
button

Close
button

Vertical
scroll bar

9

# Using Windows 10 Apps

You can run two types of programs in Windows 10. First are those
traditional software programs that run on the Windows desktop, which
is covered in Chapter 10, "Finding and Installing Traditional Software."
(These are programs that work as well in Windows 7 as they do in
Windows 10.)

Then there are those programs, called Windows apps, designed to work
specifically in the Windows 10 environment. These apps are subtly different from traditional software programs and offer a more uniform interface and operation.

## Launching Your Favorite Programs

Whether you're looking for a traditional software program or more modern Windows app, all of the applications you have installed on your PC
are displayed on the Start menu. Just click the Start button, scroll down
the app list, and click the one you want to run. You can also "pin" shortcuts to any program on the right side of the Start menu, the desktop
taskbar, or to the desktop itself.

# Pin a Tile to the Start Menu

Programs you pin to the Start menu appear as resizable tiles on the right side of the menu, which makes for easier access. To launch a pinned program, just open the Start menu and click the appropriate tile.

1. Click the Start button to display the Start menu.

2. From the apps list, scroll to and then right-click the application you want to pin.

3. Click Pin to Start.

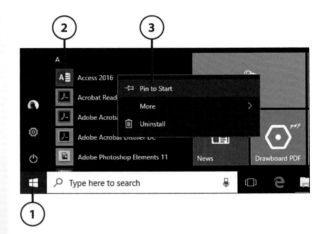

# Pin a Program to the Taskbar

You can also pin a shortcut to any program to the Windows taskbar—that strip of icons that appears at the bottom of the desktop.

1. Click the Start button to display the Start menu.

2. From the apps list, scroll to and then right-click the application you want to pin.

3. Click More.

4. Click Pin to Taskbar.

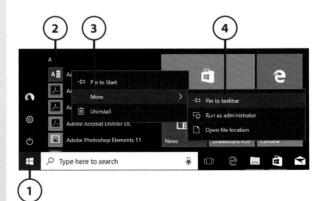

## Create a Shortcut on the Desktop

If you frequently use a particular program or file, you can create a shortcut to that item on the Windows desktop itself.

1. Click the Start button to display the Start menu.

2. Click and drag the icon for the application to the desktop. A new desktop shortcut is created for that app.

## Open a Program

How you open a desktop program depends on where the shortcut to that program is.

1. From the Windows Start menu, click the icon or tile for the program.

2. Alternatively, from the taskbar, click the icon for the program.

3. As yet another alternative, from the Windows Desktop, *double-click* the shortcut for the program.

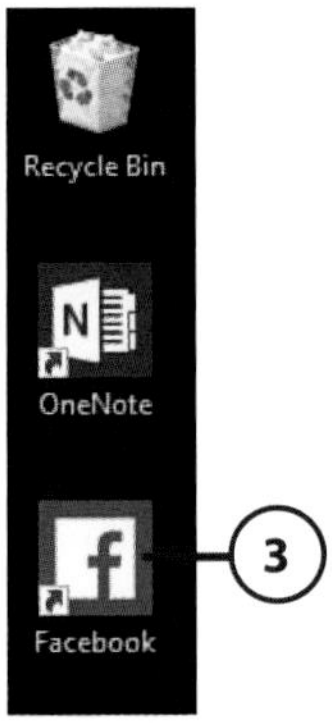


# Working with Apps on the Desktop

Every app opens in its own individual window on the Windows desktop. You can easily resize and rearrange all the open windows on the desktop.

## Maximize, Minimize, and Close a Window

After you've opened a window, you can maximize it to display full screen. You can also minimize it so that it disappears from the desktop and resides as a button on the Windows taskbar, and you can close it completely.

1. To maximize the window, click the Maximize button in the top-right corner. When the window is maximized, the Maximize button turns into a Restore Down button; click this button to return the window to its original size.

2. To minimize the window, click the Minimize button in the top-right corner. The window shrinks to an icon on the taskbar; to restore the window to its original size, click the window's icon on the taskbar.

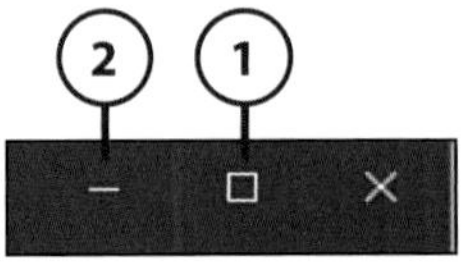

**(3)** To close the window completely (and shut down the program or document inside), click Close (the X) at the top-right corner.

## Resize a Window

You can resize any individual window to fill the entire screen or just a part of the screen.

**(1)** Use your mouse to click any side or corner of the window; the cursor should turn into a double-sided arrow.

**(2)** Keep the mouse button pressed and then drag the edge of the window to a new position.

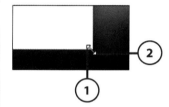

## Switch Between Open Windows

After you've launched a few programs, you can easily switch between one open program and another.

**(1)** Press Alt+Tab to display thumbnails of all open windows. Keep pressing Tab to cycle through the open apps. Release the keys to switch to the selected window.

**(2)** Alternatively, click the Task View button on the taskbar. This displays thumbnails of all open windows. Click the window you wish to switch to.

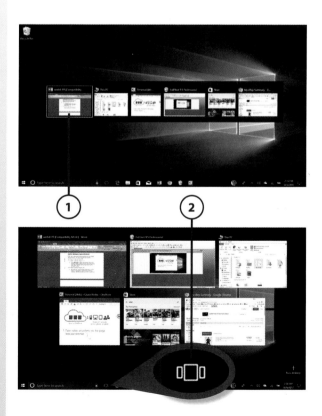

**3** When a program or document is open, an icon for that item (with a line underneath) appears in the Windows taskbar. Mouse over that icon to view a thumbnail preview of all open documents for that application.

**4** To switch to an open document from the taskbar, mouse over the icon for that item and then click the thumbnail for that document.

## Multiple Documents

If multiple documents or pages for an application are open, multiple thumbnails will appear when you hover over that application's icon in the taskbar.

## Snap a Window

Any open window can be "snapped" to the left or right side of the desktop, filling half the screen. This enables you to easily display two windows side-by-side.

**1** To snap a window to the left side of the desktop, click and drag the window to the left edge. (Alternatively, you can press Windows+Left Arrow on your keyboard.)

**2** Windows displays thumbnails of all your other open apps. Click a thumbnail to open that app on the right side of the desktop.

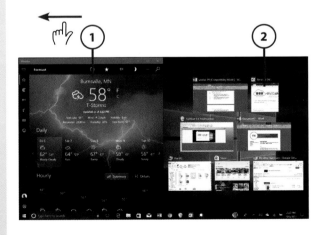

**3** To snap a window to the right side of the desktop, click and drag the window to the right edge. (Alternatively, you can press Windows+Right Arrow on your keyboard.)

**4** Windows displays thumbnails of all your other open apps. Click a thumbnail to open that app on the left side of the desktop.

**5** To display a window full screen, click and drag the window to the top of the desktop. (Alternatively, you can press Windows+Up Arrow on your keyboard.)

## Move a Window

To move a window to another position on the desktop, click and drag the window's title area.

# Scroll Through a Window

Many programs, documents, and web pages are longer than the containing window is high. To read the full page or document, you need to scroll through the window.

**1** Mouse over the open window to display the vertical scroll bar.

**2** Click the up arrow on the window's scroll bar to scroll up one line at a time.

**3** Click the down arrow on the window's scroll bar to scroll down one line at a time.

**4** Click and drag the scroll box (slider) to scroll up or down in a smooth motion.

---

### Other Ways to Scroll

You can also scroll up or down a window by pressing the PageUp and PageDn keys on your keyboard. In addition, if your mouse has a scroll wheel, you can use it to scroll through a window.

---

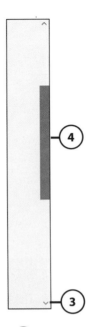

## Configure App Settings

Apps designed specifically for Windows 10 (and available from the Microsoft Store) offer a similar interface and operation. In particular, you can configure the settings for these apps with a simple click of the mouse.

**1** To configure the basic settings of a Windows app, click the Options (three-bar) button.

**2** Select app features or options.

**3** Click Settings to view and configure additional app settings.

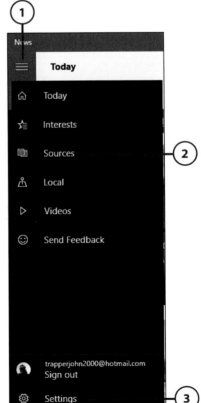

### Windows versus UWP versus Universal versus Metro versus Modern

The term "Windows app" is just the latest name for what Microsoft has variously called Universal Windows Platform (UWP), Universal, Metro, Modern, and Windows Store apps. So if you see any of these alternative monikers, know that they're referring to what in this book we call Windows apps.

# Using Windows 10's Built-in Apps

Windows 10 comes with numerous Windows apps preinstalled, including News, Weather, Sports, Money, and Calendar apps. You launch these apps from the Windows Start menu.

## News

When you want to read the latest headlines, use the News app, with news curated from various sources.

( **1** ) Click a headline or picture to read the complete story. Scroll down to view additional stories.

( **2** ) Click a tab to view specific types of stories—All, Top Stories, US, World, Crime, Technology, and so forth.

( **3** ) To customize the news you see, click the Interests icon and then click those items you're interested in.

# Weather

The Weather app is one of the better-looking and most useful apps available. The background image represents current conditions; for example, a sunny spring day is represented by a beautiful image of fresh leaves in the sunlight. Current conditions are on top—temperature, wind, humidity, and the like. The rest of the screen is devoted to a five-day forecast.

(**1**) Scroll down to view the daily and hourly forecasts and more detailed information.

(**2**) Click Maps to view the current radar weather map.

(**3**) Click Favorites to switch to different locations.

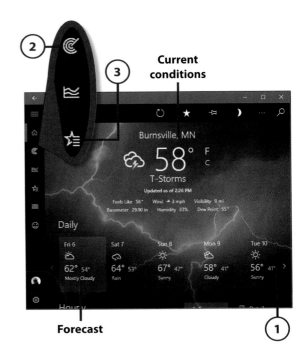

# Sports

You can use the Sports app to read the latest headlines from the world of sports, as well as follow your favorite sports and teams. When you launch the app, you see the top story of the day; click to read the complete story.

(**1**) Scroll down to view more stories, headlines, and videos.

(**2**) Click Scoreboard to view the latest scores for your favorite teams.

(**3**) Click a sport or league (NFL, NBA, MLB, and the like) in the left sidebar to view news and scores for that sport.

# Money

Windows 10's Money app is the perfect way to stay up to date on the latest financial news, as well as keep track of your personal investments.

( 1 ) The main screen displays current financial news and information. Click Watchlist to view your stock watchlist.

( 2 ) Click a stock to view more information about that stock.

( 3 ) Click the + to add a stock to your watch list; when the Add to Watchlist panel appears, enter the name or symbol of the stock and then click the one you want to add.

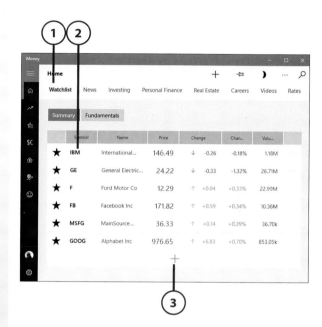

# Maps

The Maps app lets you create street maps and driving directions. It's based on Bing Maps, which is Microsoft's web-based mapping service.

You can click and drag your mouse to move the map in any direction—or, if you have a touchscreen device, just drag or swipe your finger to move the map. You can zoom in and out of the map by using the +/– zoom controls at the lower right. On a touchscreen device, you can zoom out by pinching the screen with your fingers, or you can zoom in by expanding your fingers on the screen.

( 1 ) By default, Maps displays a map of your current location. Click the + icon to zoom into this location, or the – to zoom out.

( 2 ) To search for nearby businesses, enter the name or type of business into the Search box.

( 3 ) To switch to another location, enter the street address, city, state, or ZIP Code into the Search box.

( 4 ) To display current traffic conditions or change to satellite (aerial) view, click Map Views and make a selection.

( 5 ) To generate driving directions, click Directions to display the Directions pane.

( 6 ) Enter the starting location into the A box, or accept your current location ("My Location").

( 7 ) Enter your destination into the B box.

( 8 ) Click Get Directions to generate step-by-step driving directions and a map of your route.

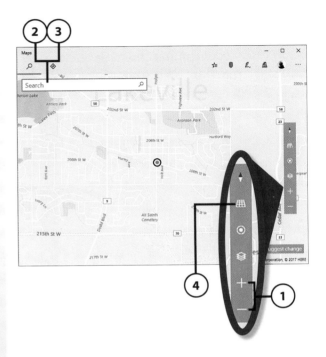

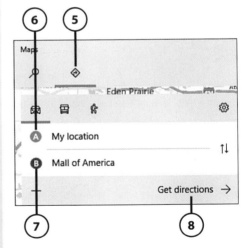

# Calendar

The Calendar app lets you keep track of appointments and to-do lists. By default, Calendar displays items synced from your Microsoft account and any other account connected to your computer.

When you launch the Calendar app, you see a monthly calendar, with all your scheduled appointments listed. To scroll back or forward through the months, use your keyboard's up and down arrow keys, or swipe the screen (on a touchscreen device).

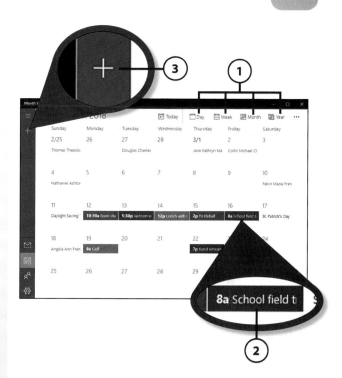

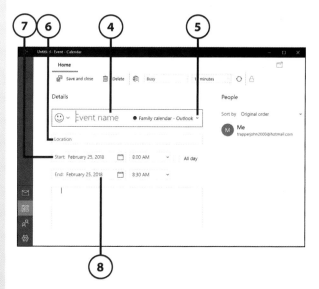

**(1)** Click Day, Week, Month, or Year to switch to another view.

**(2)** Click an item on the calendar to view more details about that appointment.

**(3)** Click + New Event in the left side-bar to create a new appointment.

**(4)** Enter the name of the appoint-ment into the Event Name box.

**(5)** If you're tracking multiple cal-endars, click the down arrow in the Event Name box and select a calendar for this event.

**(6)** Enter the location of the event into the Location box.

**(7)** Enter the start date and time of the event with the Start controls.

**(8)** Enter the end date and time with the End controls.

**9** If the event lasts all day (like a birthday or holiday), check the All Day box.

**10** Enter details about the appointment into the Event Description box.

**11** Click Save and Close to save the new appointment.

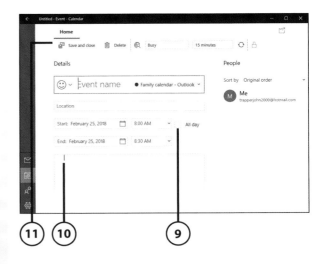

## Alarms & Clock

The Alarms & Clock app turns your computer into a digital alarm clock, and it also includes timer and stopwatch functions.

**1** Click or tap Alarm to enter the alarm function.

**2** Click the On/Off switch for an existing alarm to turn it on or off.

**3** Click or tap the + button to set a new alarm.

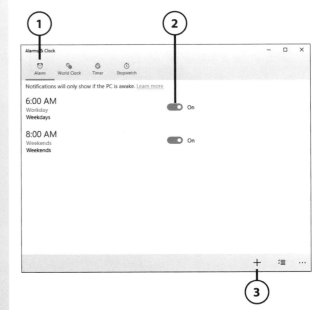

(**4**) Use the time controls to set the time for this alarm.

(**5**) Click Alarm Name then enter a name for the alarm.

(**6**) To repeat this alarm, click Repeats and make a selection.

(**7**) Click Sound to set the sound for this alarm.

(**8**) Click Snooze Time to set a snooze time for this alarm.

(**9**) Click Save to save this alarm.

(**10**) Click Timer to enter the timer function.

(**11**) Click the Start button to start any existing timer.

(**12**) Click the + button to create a new timer.

(**13**) Use the time controls to set the duration for this timer.

(**14**) Click Timer Name to enter a name for this timer.

(**15**) Click Save to return to the Timer screen.

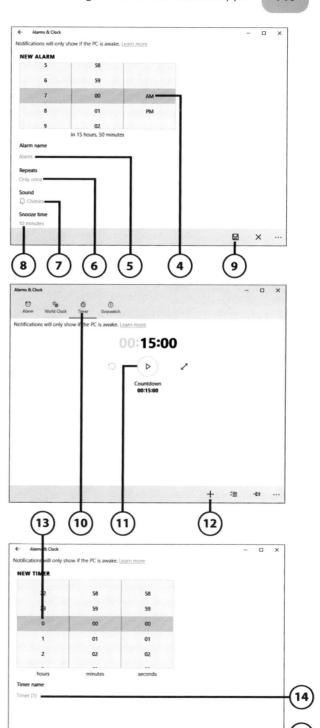

**16** Click or tap Stopwatch to enter the stopwatch function.

**17** Click or tap the Reset button to reset the stopwatch to zero.

**18** Click or tap the Play (arrow) button to start the stopwatch. The Play button changes to a Pause button.

**19** The stopwatch now displays the elapsed time.

**20** Click or tap the Pause button to stop the stopwatch.

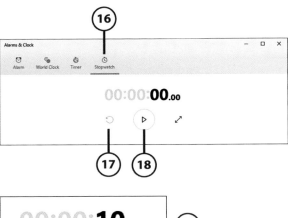

# Calculator

The Calculator app functions as a standard, scientific, or programmer calculator. It also lets you convert various measurements from one format to another (such as liters to teaspoons).

**1** Click the buttons with your mouse, tap them with your finger, or use your computer keyboard to enter numbers and operators.

**2** The answer to your calculation is displayed above the keypad.

**3** To switch between the Standard, Scientific, Programmer, or Date Calculation calculators, click the Menu (three-bar) button and make a selection.

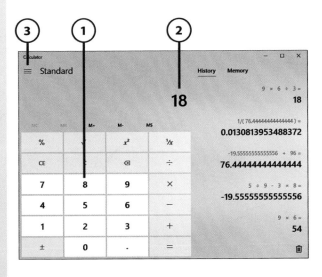

**4** To use the conversion function, click the Menu button, go to the Converter section, and then select what you want to convert—volume, length, weight and mass, and so forth.

**5** On the next screen, click the first down arrow to select the original unit of measurement.

**6** Click the second down arrow to select the converted unit of measurement.

**7** Use the onscreen keypad or your computer's numeric keypad to enter the original unit you want converted.

**8** The conversion appears in the bottom box.

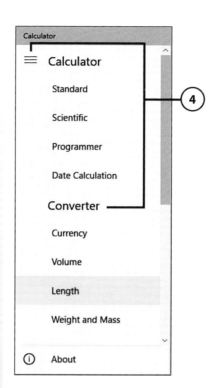

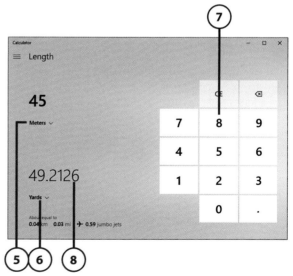

# Paint 3D

New to Windows 10's Fall Creators Update is program called Paint 3D. This is a significant update to the old Paint program that's been around since the beginning of Windows; Paint 3D lets you create three-dimensional constructs in addition to the simple drawings you could create in previous versions.

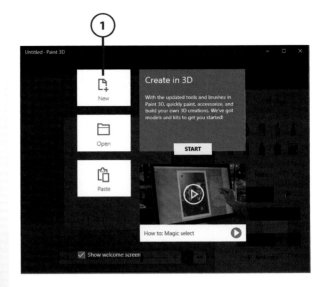

1. When Paint 3D first launches, click New to create a new drawing. (Or click Open to open something you've previously worked on.)

2. To draw in your project, click the Toolbar icon and select Art Tools.

3. Select the type of drawing tool you want to use—marker, oil brush, pixel pen, and so forth.

4. Select a color for your drawing tool.

5. Use your mouse to draw on the blank canvas.

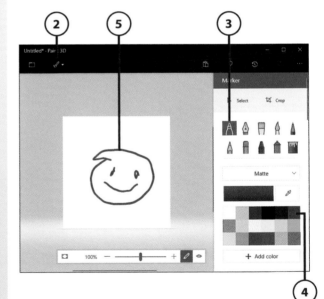

**6** To add a 3D object to your project, click the Toolbar icon and select 3D.

**7** Select the type of 3D model you want to add.

**8** Select a color for this 3D model.

**9** Use your mouse to add this model to your canvas.

**10** Use the rotation controls to rotate the 3D model.

**11** Click the Toolbar icon to add other types of graphics to your project—stickers, text, effects, and the like.

**12** To save your work, click the Expand Menu icon.

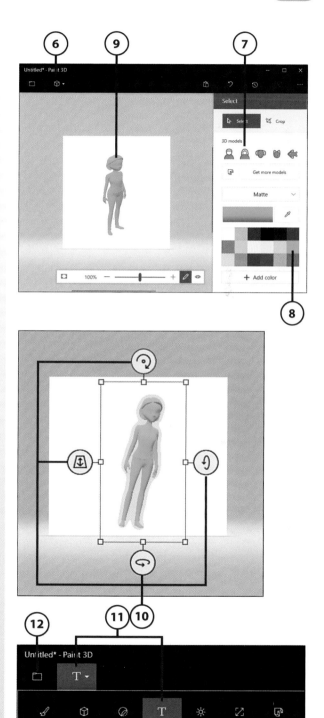

13. The first time you save your work, click Save As and give your file a name.

14. As you continue working on your project, click Save to save your work.

15. Click Print to print your work.

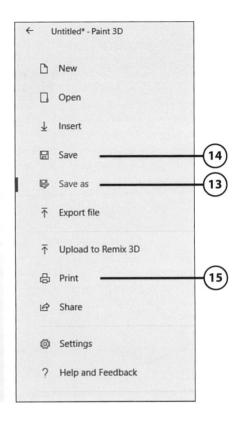

# Shopping the Microsoft Store

There are many more Windows apps than those included with Windows 10. You can shop for available Windows apps in the Microsoft Store (previously called the Windows Store). All of the apps in the Microsoft Store are the newer-style Windows apps, and many are free.

## Browse for Apps

The Microsoft Store is accessible as if it were another app, from the Start menu or its shortcut icon on the Windows taskbar. Click the Store icon to start the app.

### Pricing

Whereas a traditional computer software program can cost hundreds of dollars, most apps in the Windows Store cost $20 or less—and many are available for free. (Note that some of the free apps require in-app purchases to activate additional functionality.)

1. The Microsoft Store launches with featured apps at the top of the home page. Scroll down to view Picks for You, Most Popular, Top Free Apps, and the like.

2. To view different types of items in the Store, click the Menu (three-bar) button at the top of the window.

3. Click Apps to view only apps.

4. Click Games to view only games.

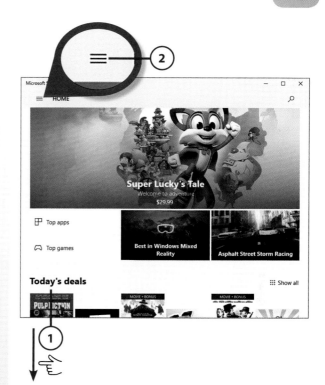

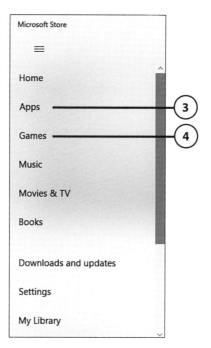

**5** Scroll to the bottom of the Apps or Games page to view all available categories; click a category to view all apps in that category.

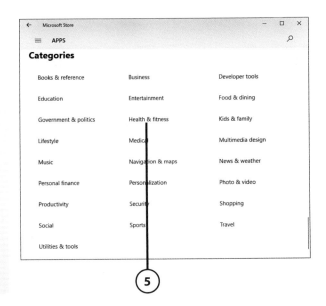

# >>>Go Further

## SEARCH THE STORE

Browsing is a good way to see everything that's available in the Microsoft Store. But if you have a specific app you're interested in, browsing might be inefficient.

In this instance, you can easily search for any given app. Just open the Store app and click the Search icon at the top of the screen to display the Search box. Enter the full or partial name of the app into the Search box and then press Enter. All matching apps are displayed.

# Download and Install a New App

After you've browsed to a given category, it's easy to find apps you might like.

( 1 ) Click the app in which you're interested to display the app's information page.

( 2 ) Click the Buy button to purchase the app; when prompted to confirm your purchase, click the Confirm button.

( 3 ) If the app is free, click the Get button to download it to your computer.

## First Time Purchase

The first time you purchase an app from the Microsoft Store, you're prompted to set up a payment method. Do so, and Microsoft remembers this information for future purchases.

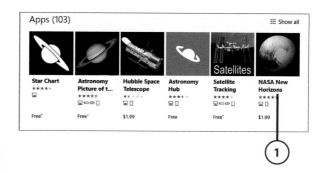

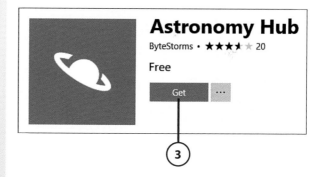

Minimize button

Maximize button

Close button

Title bar

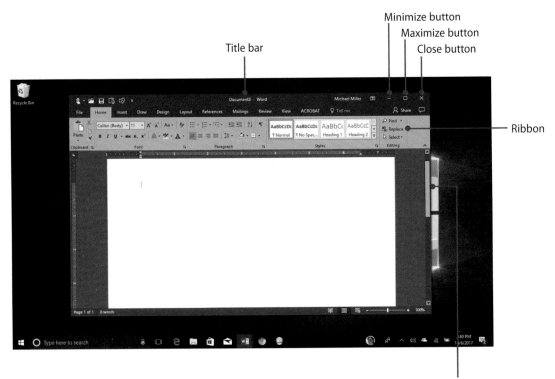

Ribbon

Vertical scroll bar

In this chapter, you learn how to find and install software programs for your PC.

→ Working with Traditional Software Programs
→ Finding and Installing Traditional Software Programs

10

# Finding and Installing Traditional Software

In the previous chapter we looked at the newer Windows apps that come preinstalled with Windows 10 and are available in the Microsoft Store. But you still might want to use some of the older style software programs that have been available for previous versions of Windows. These traditional programs look and work a little differently than the newer Windows apps.

## Working with Traditional Software Programs

Most traditional software programs have similar onscreen elements—menus, toolbars, ribbons, and such. Once you learn how to use one program, the others should be quite familiar.

## Use Pull-Down Menus

Many software programs use a set of pull-down *menus* to store all the commands and operations you can perform. The menus are aligned across the top of the window, just below the title bar, in what is called a *menu bar*.

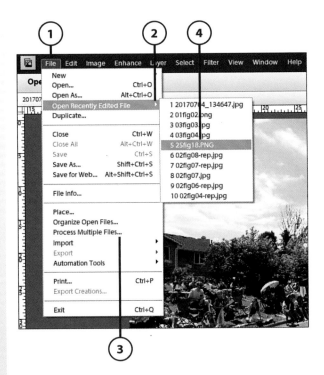

**①** Click the menu's name to pull down the menu.

**②** A little black arrow to the right of a menu item indicates that additional choices are available on a *submenu*. Click the menu item or the arrow to display the submenu.

**③** Three little dots (called an *ellipsis*) to the right of a menu item indicate that additional choices are available. Click the menu item to display a dialog box and to make a choice.

**④** Click the menu item to select it.

## Use Toolbars

Some older software programs put the most frequently used operations on one or more *toolbars*, which are usually located just below the menu bar. A toolbar looks like a row of buttons, each with a small picture (called an *icon*) and maybe a bit of text. You activate the associated command or operation by clicking the button with your mouse.

**Click a toolbar button to active the command.**

Click a button on the toolbar to select that operation.

### Long Toolbars

If the toolbar is too long to display fully on your screen, you see a right arrow at the far-right side of the toolbar. Click this arrow to display the buttons that aren't currently visible.

# Use Ribbons

Many newer software programs, including Microsoft Office, use a ribbon interface that contains the most frequently used operations. A *ribbon* is typically located at the top of the window, beneath the title bar (and sometimes the menu bar). Ribbons often consist of multiple tabs; select a tab to see buttons and controls for related operations.

1. Click a tab to select that particular set of functions.

2. Click a button on the ribbon to select that operation.

### Display or Hide

If the ribbon isn't visible, click the down arrow at the far right side of the tabs. To hide the ribbon and its buttons, click the up arrow at the far right side of the ribbon.

# Finding and Installing Traditional Software Programs

As you learned in the previous chapter, you can purchase and download newer Windows apps online, from the Microsoft Store. Unfortunately, the Store does not offer traditional software programs; for these, you have to look elsewhere.

You can find traditional software programs at just about any consumer electronics store, office store, computer store, or mass merchant (such as Target or Walmart). You can also search online for traditional programs to download.

## Install Software from a Disc

Most software programs you purchase at retail come on either a CD or a DVD disc; these disks typically come with their own built-in installation utilities.

All you have to do is insert the program's disc into your computer's CD/DVD drive. The installation utility should run automatically.

**(1)** Insert the installation disc into your PC's CD or DVD drive.

**(2)** The program's installation utility should launch automatically. Follow the onscreen instructions to install the software.

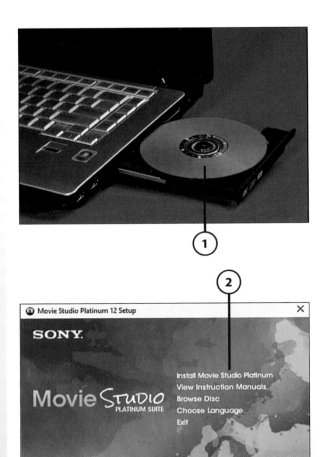

# Install Programs Online

Nowadays, many software publishers make their products available via download from the Internet. Some users like this because they can get their new programs immediately without having to make a trip to the store.

When you download a program from a major software publisher, the process is generally easy to follow. You probably have to read a page of do's and don'ts, agree to the publisher's licensing agreements, and then click a button to start the download. If you're purchasing a commercial program online, you also need to provide your credit card information, of course. Then, after you specify where (which folder on your hard disk) you want to save the downloaded file, the download begins.

(**1**) Open the website that offers the software you want; then click the buy or download link or button.

(**2**) If prompted to enter your name, email address, credit card number, or other payment information, do so; then follow the onscreen instructions to complete the download and install the software on your PC.

(**3**) When downloading from a free download site, such as Download.com (www.download.com), find and click the Download button; then follow the onscreen instructions to save and then run the installation file.

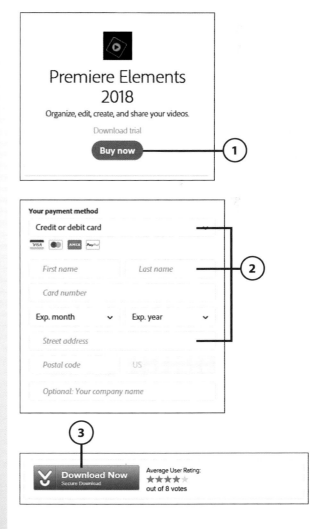

## It's Not All Good

### Download from Legitimate Sites Only

Limit your software downloads to reputable download sites and software publisher sites. Make sure the website has an address that begins with https:// (not just http://) and features a lock icon in the browser address box. This ensures that you're working over a secure Internet connection.

Another problem with programs downloaded from unofficial sites is that they might contain computer viruses or spyware (called *malicious software*, or *malware*), which can damage your computer. It's a lot safer to deal with official sites that regularly scan their offerings to ensure that they are not infected in this manner.

Even legitimate download sites might contain confusing advertisements that look like download links or buttons. Do not click these misleading links because you might end up downloading unwanted malware. Make sure you find the correct download link or button, and click it only.

And, when you're installing the software, be careful what options you click. Even some legitimate programs will attempt to install other unwanted software during their installation processes. (For example, when you're installing the Java software from www.java.com, you're prompted to install the Ask.com toolbar and other non-related items; it's easy to get tricked into approving these unnecessary and unwanted apps.) Read every onscreen message carefully, and only click to approve those items you want to install.

Public
(unsecured)
Wi-Fi hotspot

Private
(secured)
Wi-Fi network

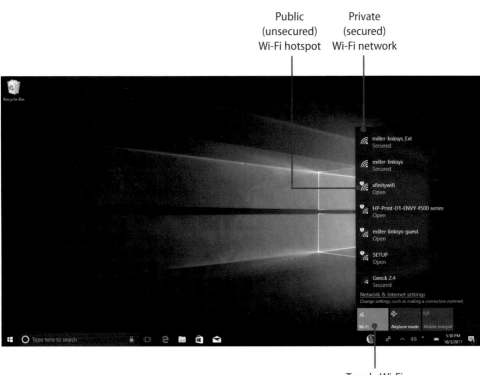

Toggle Wi-Fi
on and off

In this chapter, you find out how to connect to the Internet from your home network or at a public Wi-Fi hotspot.

→ Connecting to the Internet—and Your Home Network
→ Connecting to the Internet at a Wi-Fi Hotspot

# Connecting to the Internet—at Home or Away

Much of what you want to do with your new computer is found on the Internet. The Internet is a source of information, a conduit for shopping and other useful activities, a place to play games, and a tool for communicating with friends and family.

To get full use out of your new PC, then, you need to connect it to the Internet. You can connect to the Internet at home or away. All you need is access to a home network or, outside of your house, a Wi-Fi hotspot.

## Connecting to the Internet—and Your Home Network

To get Internet in your home, you need to contract with an *Internet service provider* (ISP). You can typically get Internet service from your cable company or from your phone company. Expect to pay somewhere between $25 and $50 a month.

Your ISP should set you up with a broadband *modem* that connects to the incoming cable or phone line. The modem takes the digital signals coming through the incoming line and converts them into a format that your computer can use.

In most cases, you connect your broadband modem to a *wireless router*. A router is a device that takes a single Internet signal and routes it to multiple devices; when you set up your router, following the manufacturer's instructions, you create a *wireless home network*. You connect your computer (as well as your smartphone, tablet, and other wireless devices) wirelessly to your router via a technology called Wi-Fi.

### Wireless Gateway

Some ISPs supply a *wireless gateway* that combines a broadband modem and wireless router in a single unit. This makes for easier connection and setup—you have one less cable to run and one less device to configure.

## Connect to Your Home Network

After your modem and wireless router are set up, you've created a wireless home network. You can then connect your PC to your wireless router—and access the Internet.

1. In the notification area of the taskbar, click the Connections icon to display the Connections panel.

### Connections Icon

If no network is currently connected, the Connections icon should be labeled Not Connected—Connections Are Available.

2. Click your wireless network; this expands the panel for this network.

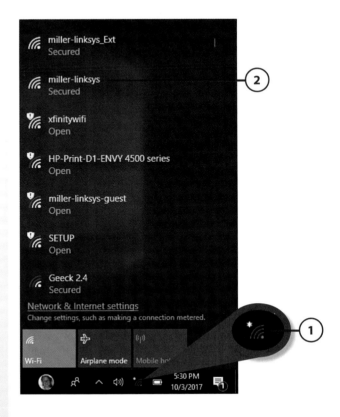

**3** To connect automatically to this network in the future, check the Connect Automatically box.

## Connect Automatically

When you're connecting to your home network, it's a good idea to enable the Connect Automatically feature. This lets your computer connect to your network without additional prompting or interaction on your part.

**4** Click Connect.

**5** When prompted, enter the password (called the *network security key*) for your network.

**6** Click Next.

**7** When the next screen appears, click Yes to allow your computer to be discovered by other PCs and devices on your home network. You're now connected to your wireless router and should have access to the Internet.

## One-Button Connect

If the wireless router on your network supports "one-button wireless setup" (based on the Wi-Fi Protected Setup, or WPS, technology), you might be prompted to press the "connect" or WPS button on the router to connect. This is much faster than going through the entire process outlined here.

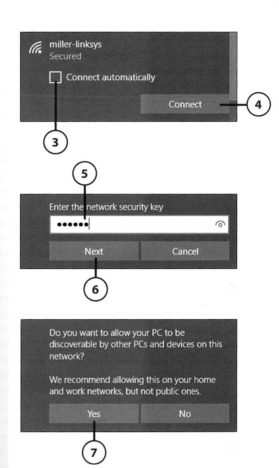

# Access Other Computers on Your Network

Once your computer is connected to your home network, you can access the content on other computers on the same network.

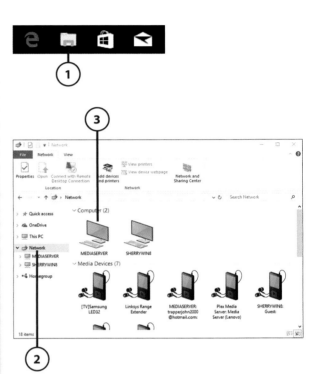

( 1 ) Click the File Explorer icon on the taskbar to open File Explorer.

( 2 ) Click Network in the navigation pane. This displays all the computers and devices connected to your network.

( 3 ) Double-click the computer you want to access.

( 4 ) Windows displays the shared folders on the selected computer. Double-click a folder to view that folder's content.

## Sharing Content

You can access content only on other computers that have been configured as shareable—that is, the computer owner has enabled sharing for that particular folder or type of content.

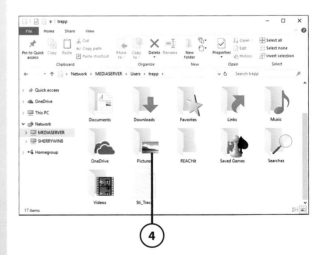

## >>>Go Further

## HOMEGROUPS

Windows also offers another way to network, in the form of what the company calls *home-groups*. A homegroup is a kind of simplified network that enables you to automatically share files and printers between other computers connected to the same homegroup; once you get a homegroup set up, you can connect other computers by sharing the homegroup password.

Homegroups were first introduced with Windows 7 as a way to make home networking easier. Back then not every network device easily connected to every other device, and networking was often a hit-or-miss kind of thing. Homegroups (theoretically) simplified all of this, at least for computers running Windows 7 (and up).

Not surprisingly, the networking world has changed tremendously since the days of Windows 7. Today's more advanced wireless routers make connecting a new computer to your network pretty much a plug-and-play operation. This means that you don't need to set up a homegroup to connect to other computers on your network; in fact, homegroup setup today is arguably more complex than connecting to a home network normally.

For that reason, Microsoft no longer puts homegroups front and center in its networking offer-ings. In fact, you have to look long and hard to find the homegroup options in Windows 10; they're still there, but pretty much deprecated. (You may still see a Homegroup icon in File Explorer; if you're connected to a homegroup, click this to view content on other homegroup computers.)

So when you're connecting your computer to your home network today, just do it the normal way and don't worry about the homegroup option. That's the simplest way to go.

# Connecting to the Internet at a Wi-Fi Hotspot

The nice thing about the Internet is that it's virtually everywhere. This means you can connect to the Internet even when you're away from home. All you need to do is find a wireless connection, called a *Wi-Fi hotspot*. Fortunately, most cof-feehouses, libraries, hotels, fast-food restaurants, and public spaces offer Wi-Fi hotspots—often for free.

## Connect to a Wi-Fi Hotspot

When you're near a Wi-Fi hotspot, your PC should automatically pick up the wireless signal. Just make sure your computer's Wi-Fi adapter is turned on (it should be, by default), and then get ready to connect.

1. On the taskbar, click the Connections button to display the Connections pane.

2. You now see a list of available wireless networks. An open or public network has a warning shield next to the Wi-Fi icon. Click the network to which you want to connect.

3. This expands the section for that network; click Connect to connect to the selected hotspot.

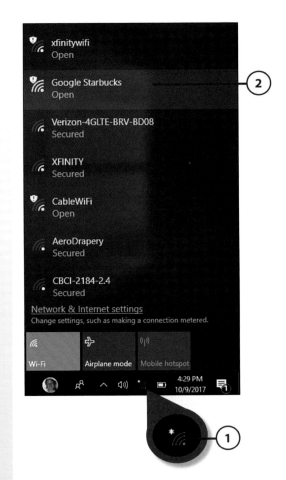

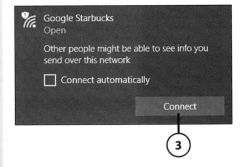

( **4** ) If the hotspot has free public access, you can open your web browser and surf normally. If the hotspot requires a password, payment, or other logon procedure, Windows should automatically open your web browser and display the hotspot's logon page. Enter the appropriate information to begin surfing.

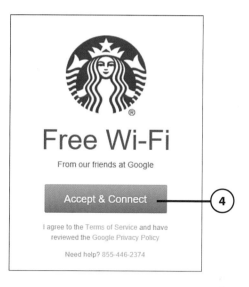

## It's Not All Good

### Unsecured Networks

Most public Wi-Fi hotspots are unsecured, which means that the information you send over these networks could be intercepted by others. For your security, you should avoid sending personal or financial information over unsecured public Wi-Fi hotspots. (To be safe, that means no online banking or shopping in public.)

## >>>Go Further

## AIRPLANE MODE

If you're using your notebook or tablet on an airplane and don't want to use the plane's wireless Internet service (if available), you can switch to Window's special Airplane mode so that you can use your computer while in the air.

To switch into Airplane mode, click the Connection button on the taskbar to open the Connections pane, and then click to activate the Airplane Mode tile. (It turns blue when activated.) You can switch off Airplane mode when your plane lands.

If the plane you're on offers Wi-Fi service (many now do), you don't have to bother with Airplane mode. Instead, just connect to the plane's wireless network as you would to any Wi-Fi hotspot. You might have to pay for it, but it enables you to use the Internet while you're en route—which is a great way to spend long trips!

Microsoft Edge browser

Google Chrome browser

In this chapter, you find out how to use a web browser to browse and search pages on the World Wide Web.

→ Understanding the Web
→ Using Microsoft Edge
→ Using Google Chrome
→ Searching the Internet
→ Searching—and More—with Cortana

# Browsing and Searching the Web

Now that you've connected to the Internet, either at home or via a public wireless hotspot, it's time to get busy. The World Wide Web is a particular part of the Internet with all sorts of cool content and useful services, and you surf the Web with a piece of software called a *web browser*.

Windows 10 includes a new web browser, called *Microsoft Edge*. But you can use other browsers if you like, such as the popular Google Chrome or Microsoft's older Internet Explorer.

What do you do with your web browser? Browse the Web, of course—as well as search it for fun and useful information.

## Understanding the Web

Before you can surf the Web, you need to understand a little bit about how it works.

Information on the World Wide Web is presented in pages. A *web page* is similar to a page in a book, made up of text and graphics. A web page differs from a book page, however, in that it can include other elements, such as audio and video as well as links to other web pages.

It's this linking to other web pages that makes the Web such a dynamic way to present information. A *link* on a web page can point to another web page on the same site or to another site. Most links are included as part of a web page's text and are technically called *hypertext links*, or just *hyperlinks*. (If a link is part of a graphic, it's called a *graphic link*.) These links are usually in a different color from the rest of the text and often are underlined; when you click a link, you're taken directly to the linked page.

Web pages reside at a website. A *website* is nothing more than a collection of web pages (each in its own computer file) residing on a host computer. The host computer is connected full time to the Internet so that you can access the site—and its web pages—any time you access the Internet. The main page at a website is called the *home page*, and it often serves as an opening screen that provides a brief overview and menu of everything you can find at that site. The address of a web page is called a URL, which stands for *uniform resource locator*. Most URLs start with http://, add www., continue with the name of the site, and end with .com, .org, or .net.

---

### No http://

You can normally leave off the http:// when you enter an address into your web browser. In most cases, you can even leave off the www. and just start with the domain part of the address.

---

## >>>Go Further

## DIFFERENT TYPES OF ADDRESSES

Don't confuse a web page address with an email address, or with a traditional street address. They're not the same.

As noted previously, a web page address has three parts, each separated by a period. A web page address typically starts with a **www** and ends with a **com** or **org**, and there are no spaces in it. You should only enter web page addresses into the Address box in your web browser.

An email address consists of two parts, separated by an "at" sign (@). The first part of the address is your personal name, and the last part is your email provider's domain. A typical email address looks something like this: **yourname@email.com**. You use email addresses to send emails to your friends and family; you do *not* enter email addresses into the Address box in your web browser.

Of course, you still have a street address that describes where you physically live. You don't use your street address for either web browsing or email online; it's solely for postal mail, and for putting on the front of your house or apartment.

# Using Microsoft Edge

Microsoft includes a new web browser in Windows 10, called Microsoft Edge. This browser replaces the aging Internet Explorer, which you might have used previously because it was included with older versions of Windows. Edge is a truly modern browser, designed to run quickly and efficiently, and it offers enhanced functionality to users.

## Open and Browse Web Pages

You launch Microsoft Edge from either the taskbar or the Start menu. Once launched, you can use Edge to visit any page on the Web.

**1** Click near the top of the browser window to display the Address box.

**2** Start to type a web page address into the Address box.

**3** As you type, Edge displays a list of suggested pages. Click one of these pages or finish entering the web page address and press Enter.

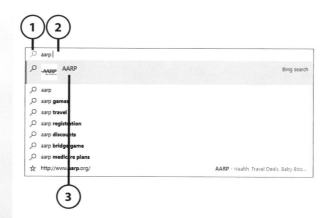

**4** To return to the previous web page, click the Back (left arrow) button beside the Address box.

**5** To move forward again, click the Forward (right arrow) button.

**6** To reload or refresh the current page, click the Refresh button.

**7** Pages on the Web are linked via clickable hyperlinks, typically presented with colored or underlined text. Click on a link to display the linked-to page.

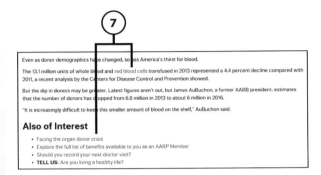

Even as donor demographics have changed, so has America's thirst for blood.

The 13.1 million units of whole blood and red blood cells transfused in 2013 represented a 4.4 percent decline compared with 2011, a recent analysis by the Centers for Disease Control and Prevention showed.

But the dip in donors may be greater. Latest figures aren't out, but James AuBuchon, a former AABB president, estimates that the number of donors has dropped from 6.8 million in 2013 to about 6 million in 2016.

"It is increasingly difficult to keep this smaller amount of blood on the shelf," AuBuchon said.

**Also of Interest**

- Facing the organ donor crisis
- Explore the full list of benefits available to you as an AARP Member
- Should you record your next doctor visit?
- **TELL US:** Are you living a healthy life?

## >>>Go Further
## LARGER TYPE

If the text on a given web page is too small for you to read, Microsoft Edge lets you zoom in to (or out of) the page. Click the More Actions (three dots) button, go to the Zoom section, and click + to enlarge the page (or click – to make the page smaller).

## Work with Tabs

Most web browsers, including Microsoft Edge, let you display multiple web pages as separate tabs, and thus easily switch between web pages. This is useful when you want to reference different pages or want to run web-based applications in the background.

**1** To open a new tab, click the + next to the last open tab. (Alternatively, press Ctrl+T on your computer keyboard.)

(2) To switch tabs, click the tab you want to view.

(3) Click the X on the current tab to close it.

(4) Click the down arrow to view thumbnails of all currently open tabs.

(5) Click a tab to open that web page.

(6) Click the up arrow to return to normal tab view.

(7) To set the current group of tabs aside for future use, click the Set These Tabs Aside icon.

(8) To view tabs you've set aside, click the Tabs You've Set Aside icon.

(9) Click a thumbnail to reopen that tab.

(10) Click Restore Tabs to add the set aside tabs to your current browser view.

## Save Favorite Pages

All web browsers let you save or bookmark your favorite web pages. In Microsoft Edge, you do this by adding pages to the Favorites list.

(1) Navigate to the web page you want to add to your Favorites list and then click the Favorites (star) icon in the Address box.

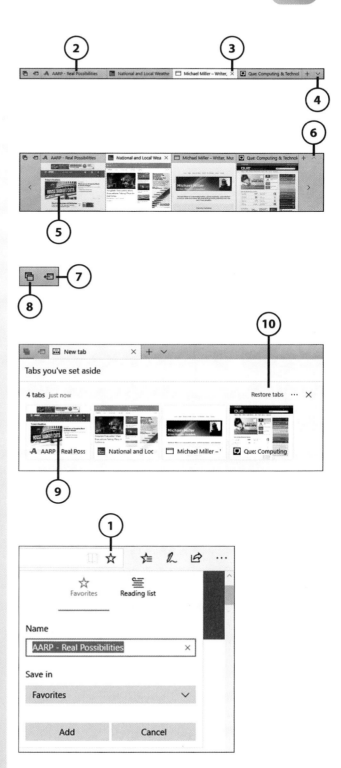

**②** Click to select the Favorites tab.

**③** Confirm or enter a name for this page.

**④** Favorites can be organized in folders. Pull down the Save In list to determine where you want to save this favorite.

**⑤** Click the Add button.

### Revisit History

To view a list of pages you've recently visited, click the Hub (star with three lines) button and select the History (timer) tab. Click the page you want to revisit.

## Save Multiple Tabs as Favorites

Sometimes you open a series of tabs that you'd like to return to in the future. (I do this all the time when I'm working and using multiple websites as references.) The Windows 10 Fall Creators Update lets you save all your open tabs as a single favorite so you can open that collection of tabs with a single click.

**①** Open all the tabs you want to save then right-click any of the tabs.

**②** Click Add Tabs to Favorites.

**③** Your open tabs are now added to the Favorites panel. Click that item to reopen the selected tabs.

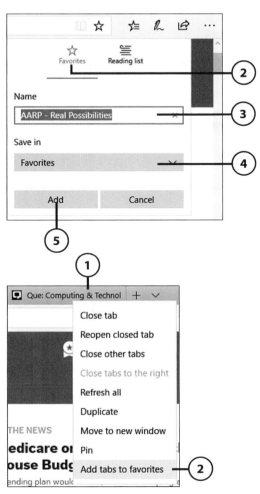

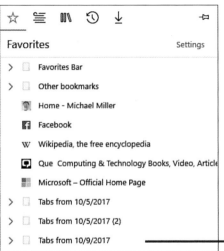

# Return to a Favorite Page

To return to a page or set of tabs you've saved as a favorite, open the Favorites list and make a selection.

1. Click the Hub button to display the Hub panel.

2. Click the Favorites (star) tab to display your Favorites list.

3. Click the page or set of tabs you want to revisit.

## Favorites Bar

For even faster access to your favorite pages, display the Favorites bar at the top of the browser window beneath the Address bar. Click the More Actions button and select Settings to display the Settings page; then click "on" the Show the Favorites Bar control.

# Set Your Start Page

Microsoft Edge lets you set a Start page that automatically opens whenever you launch the browser. Edge's default Start page displays a list of your Top Sites and a Bing Search box; you can, however, select any page on the Web as your Start page.

1. Click the More Actions (three-dot) button.

2. Click Settings to display the Settings pane.

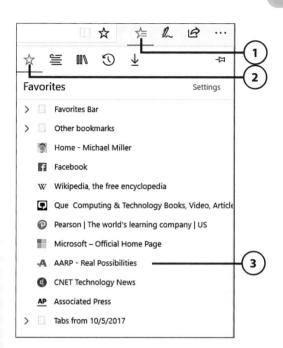

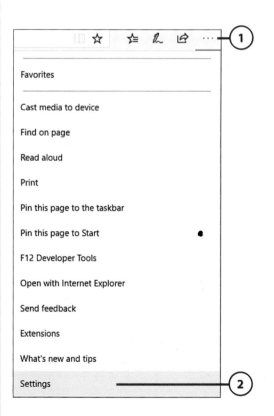

③ Pull down the Open Microsoft Edge With list and select A Specific Page or Pages.

④ Enter the URL of the page you want into the Enter a URL box.

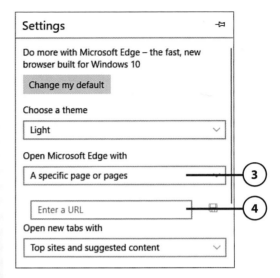

## Browse in Private

If you want to browse anonymously, without any traces of your history recorded, activate Edge's *InPrivate Browsing mode* in a new browser window. With InPrivate Browsing, no history is kept of the pages you visit, so no one can track where you've been.

① Click the More Actions button.

② Select New InPrivate Window.

③ A new InPrivate Edge window opens, ready to accept any URL you input.

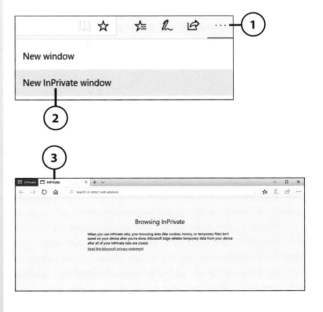

# Read a Page in Reading View

Some web pages are overly cluttered with advertisements and other distracting elements. You can get rid of these visual distractions by activating Edge's Reading view—which also increases the size of the text on the page, making it even easier to read.

In Reading view, all the unnecessary items are removed, so all you see is the main text and accompanying pictures. In addition, the onscreen text is significantly larger in Reading view, and there's more "white space" all around. The result is, perhaps, the best way to view web pages if you have even slight vision difficulties.

## Not All Pages

Not all web pages are available in Reading view. If the page can't be viewed in Reading view, the Reading View button is grayed out.

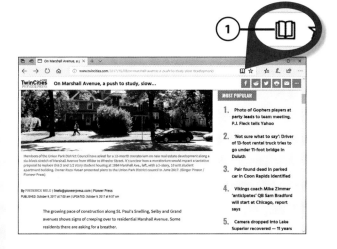

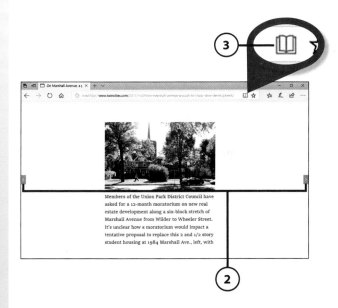

( **1** ) Navigate to the page you want to read; then click the Reading View button on the Edge toolbar.

( **2** ) This removes the unnecessary elements, increases the text size, and makes reading easier. Scroll right and left through the pages of the article by clicking the right and left arrows.

( **3** ) Click the Reading View button again to return to normal view.

# Print a Web Page

From time to time, you might run across a web page with important information you want to keep for posterity. While you can make this page a favorite, of course, you can also print it out on your computer's printer.

1. Click the More Actions button.

2. Click Print to display the Print window.

3. Click the Printer list and select your printer.

4. Click the Copies list and select how many copies you want to print.

5. Click the Pages list and select which pages you want to print (all or a range of pages).

6. Click the Print button to print a copy of this page.

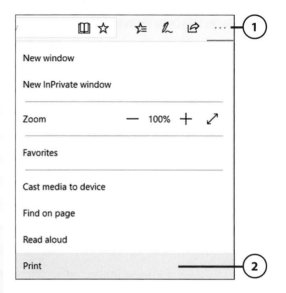

## >>>Go Further

### WEB NOTES

If you're doing research on the Web, you might want to mark up a given web page with notes, highlights, and such. You can do this with Edge's Web Notes tool.

To use the Web Notes tool, click the Add Notes (pencil) button to display the Web Notes toolbar. You can then use the appropriate markup tool to make your notes. Remember to click Save when you're done to save your notes!

# Using Google Chrome

Microsoft Edge isn't the only web browser you can use to surf the Internet. Several other browsers are available that are popular with users of all ages.

Prior to Windows 10 and Microsoft Edge, Microsoft made available the Internet Explorer browser. In fact, Internet Explorer is still available to Windows 10 users, although Edge is faster and more versatile.

While Edge is becoming more popular, the most-used browser today is Google Chrome. Like other web browsers, Google Chrome is free for anyone to use. To download Chrome to your PC, go to www.google.com/chrome and click the Download Chrome button. Follow the onscreen instructions from there to complete the installation.

### Other Browsers

Other popular web browsers include Mozilla Firefox (www.mozilla.org/firefox) and Apple Safari (www.apple.com/safari).

## Open and Browse Web Pages

Google Chrome's interface features many of the same elements found in Microsoft Edge. You enter web addresses into what Google calls the *Omnibox*—Chrome's version of Edge's Address box.

① Position your curser into the Omnibox at the top of the browser window.

② Begin typing the web page address (URL) into the Omnibox.

③ As you type, Google suggests both possible queries and web pages you are likely to visit. Select the page you want from the drop-down list or finish typing your URL and press Enter. Google Chrome navigates to and displays the page you entered.

④ To refresh the current web page, click the Reload This Page button to the left of the Omnibox.

⑤ To return to the previously viewed page, click the Back button.

⑥ To move forward again, click the Forward button.

**>>>Go Further**

## LARGER TYPE

Just as you can with Microsoft Edge, Chrome lets you zoom in to (or out of) a web page to make the text larger and easier to read. Click the Customize and Control (three dots) button at the top-right corner of the window, go to the Zoom section, and click + to enlarge the page (or click – to make the page smaller).

## Work with Tabs

Like Microsoft Edge, Google Chrome makes good use of tabbed browsing. You can display multiple web pages in multiple tabs, all located in a tab row at the top of the browser window.

**1** To open a new tab, click the small partial tab at the far right of the row of open tabs. (Alternatively, press Ctrl+T on your computer keyboard.) The new tab opens to the right of the currently open tabs.

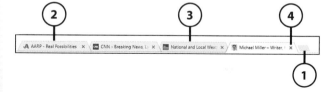

### Open a Link in a New Tab

You can open any link on a web page in a new tab by right-clicking the link and selecting Open Link as a New Tab.

**2** To switch to a different tab, click it.

**3** To change the order of open tabs, click and drag a tab into a new location in the tab row.

**4** To close a tab, click the X on that tab.

# Bookmark Your Favorite Pages

In Google Chrome, you keep track of your favorite web pages via the use of bookmarks. It's easy to create a bookmark for any web page you're viewing.

1. Navigate to a given web page and then click the Bookmark This Page (star) icon in the Omnibox.

2. Chrome displays the Bookmark Added dialog box. Edit the name of the bookmark if you want.

3. Bookmarks can be organized in folders. Pull down the Folder list to determine where you want to save this bookmark.

4. Click the Done button to close the dialog box.

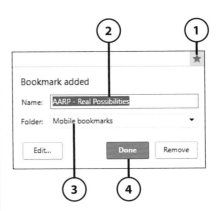

# Return to a Bookmarked Page

Returning to a bookmarked page is as easy as clicking that bookmark. There are two places you can find bookmarks in Chrome.

1. Click the Customize and Control button and then click Bookmarks.

2. This displays (along with other items) all the bookmarks you've created. Click a bookmark to return to that page.

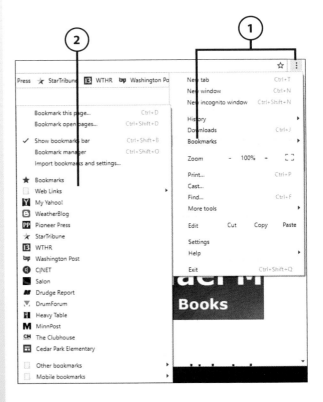

**(3)** Alternatively, display a bookmarks bar beneath the Omnibox by clicking the Customize and Control button, selecting Bookmarks, and then checking Show Bookmarks Bar.

**(4)** Click any bookmark on the Bookmarks Bar to display that page.

# Set Your Home Page

By default, Chrome displays its New Tab page as its home page. This page includes links to recently viewed web pages as well as the bookmarks bar.

If you prefer, you can specify any other web page as the browser's home page. All you need to know is the URL of that page.

**(1)** Click the Customize and Control button.

**(2)** Select Settings.

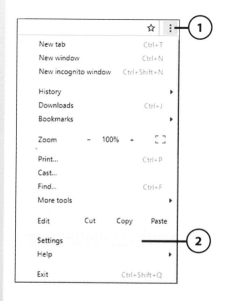

**3** In the Appearance section, make sure that Show Home Button switch is in the "on" position.

**4** Select Enter Custom Web Address.

**5** Enter the URL of the page you want as your home page.

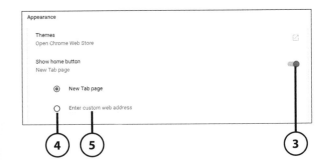

## Browse Anonymously in Incognito Mode

If you want or need to keep your browsing private, Google Chrome offers what it calls *Incognito mode*, which is very similar to Edge's InPrivate browsing. In Incognito mode (actually, a separate browser window), the pages you visit aren't saved to your browser's history file, cookies aren't saved, and your activity is basically done without any record being kept.

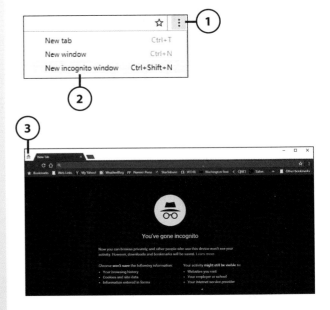

**1** Click the Customize and Control button.

**2** Select New Incognito Window.

**3** This opens a new browser window with a reverse color scheme and a little spy icon in the upper-left corner, next to the first tab. When you're done with your private browsing, just close the Incognito window and no one will be the wiser.

## Print a Web Page

Find a web page you want to print out for future reference? It's easy to print that page from within Chrome.

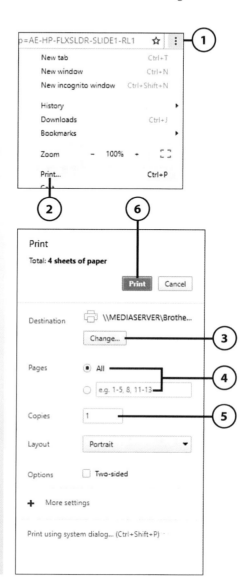

① Navigate to the desired page and click the Customize and Control button.

② Click Print to open the Print panel.

③ Make sure the desired printer is selected in the Destination section; if not, click Change and select a different printer.

④ In the Pages section, select how much of the web page you want to print. To print the entire page, select All. To print just part of a page, enter a page number or page range into the box.

⑤ In the Copies section, click the control to select how many copies to print.

⑥ Click the Print button to print the page.

# Searching the Internet

There is so much information on the Web—so many web pages—that it's sometimes difficult to find exactly what you're looking for. The best way to find just about anything on the Internet is to search for it, using a *web search engine*.

# Search Google

The most popular search engine today is Google (www.google.com), which indexes billions of individual web pages. Google is easy to use and returns extremely accurate results.

1. From within your web browser, enter **www.google.com** into the Address box or Omnibox and then press Enter. This opens Google's main search page.

2. Enter one or more keywords into the Search box.

3. Press Enter or click the Google Search button.

4. When the results are displayed, go to the result you want to view and then click the link for that result. This displays the selected web page within your web browser.

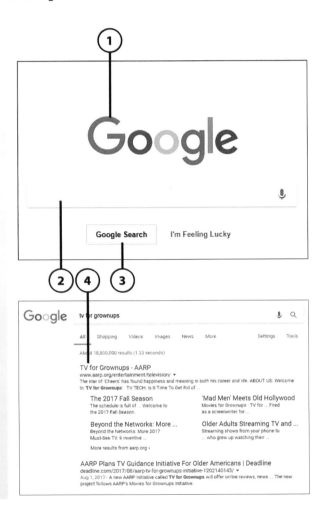

>>>*Go Further*

## FINE-TUNE YOUR SEARCH RESULTS

Google lets you fine-tune your search results to display only certain types of results. Use the links at the top of Google's search results page to display only Images, Maps, Shopping, or News results—or click Search Tools for further refinements.

## Search Bing

Microsoft's search engine is called Bing (www.bing.com). It works pretty much like Google, and Microsoft would very much like you to use it.

( 1 ) From within your web browser, enter www.bing.com into the Address box or Omnibox and press Enter. This opens Bing's main search page.

( 2 ) Enter one or more keywords into the Search box.

( 3 ) Press Enter or click the Search (magnifying glass) button.

( 4 ) When the results are displayed, click any page link to view that page.

# >>>Go Further
## REFINING YOUR SEARCH

No doubt you'll be using Google or Bing to search for various topics of interest specific to people of your age. You want to see results tailored to your age-specific needs, not general results of less interest and value to you.

In some cases, the topic itself defines age-appropriate results. For example, if you search for **retirement communities**, the results you see should link to pages that contain the information for which you're looking.

In other instances, your search query might be more general, and so it will return more general (and less age-specific) results. For example, searching for **Florida vacations** is going to bring up a lot of Mickey Mouse stuff of interest to youngsters and families, but not necessarily the snowbird-related information you were looking for.

In these instances, you can narrow your search results by including the word "seniors" in your query. In the vacation instance, change your query to search for **Florida vacations for seniors** and you'll be much more satisfied with the results. Same thing if you're searching for quilting clubs (**quilting clubs for seniors**), life insurance (**life insurance for seniors**), or comfortable clothing (**comfortable clothing for seniors**); adding a word or two to your main query makes all the difference.

# Searching—and More—with Cortana

Windows 10 includes an intelligent virtual assistant, called *Cortana*, that can help you search for files on your computer and information on the Web. You can query Cortana by typing into the Search box on the taskbar, with voice commands (by speaking into your computer's microphone), or from within the Edge browser.

Interestingly, the more you use Cortana, the more it will learn about you and display information you find useful. You can use Cortana to track weather conditions, traffic conditions, stock prices, airline flights, and more.

## Search with Cortana

You can use Cortana to search for information on the Web or to search for files on your computer. All searches utilize the Type Here to Search box on the left side of the Windows taskbar.

1. Click within the Type Here to Search box in the taskbar and begin typing your query.

(2) As you type, Cortana displays items that match your query in the results pane. This might include apps and files on your computer, as well as results from the Web. Click an item to display or open it.

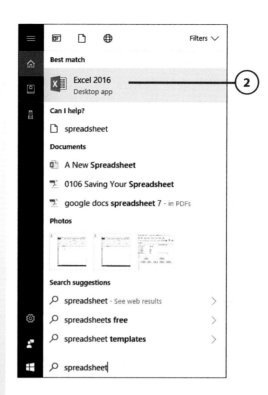

## Voice Commands

If your computer has a built-in microphone, or if you have a microphone connected to your computer, you can control Cortana with voice commands. Click the microphone within the Cortana Search box or say, "Hey, Cortana" into your computer's microphone, followed by whatever it is you want to ask.

# View News and Other Information

As Cortana learns about you (through the items you view and search for), it displays information it deems relevant—news items, stock prices, weather conditions, and such.

(1) Click within the Search box to display the Cortana pane.

(2) Reminders, tips, and other relevant items are displayed. Click an item to view it in your web browser.

(3) To view more items of interest, click I've Got More for You.

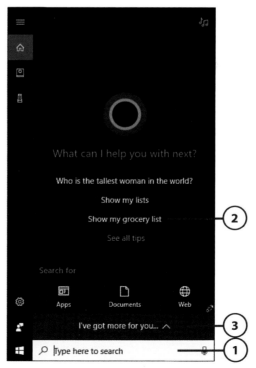

**(4)** You now see suggested new stories, weather reports, and more. Click an item to view it in your web browser or the relevant app.

## Personalized Content

To personalize the content Cortana displays, click the Notebook icon and then click the content you wish to customize.

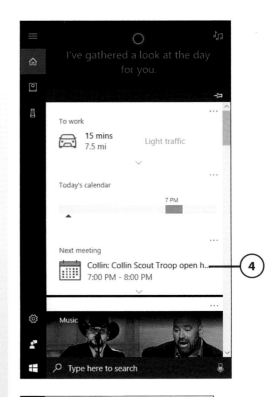

## Set a Reminder

You can use Cortana to remind you of events and deadlines.

**(1)** Click within the Search box to display the Cortana pane.

**(2)** Click the Notebook icon to display the Notebook tab.

**(3)** Click Reminders to see all your reminders.

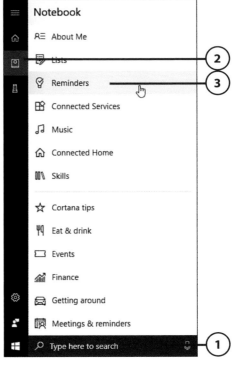

**4** Click a reminder to view more details

**5** Click the + (Add) button to add a new reminder.

**6** Enter the reminder where it says Remember To.

**7** To add a location to this reminder, click Place and then enter that location.

**8** To set a time for this reminder, click Time and then enter the desired time.

**9** Click the Save button.

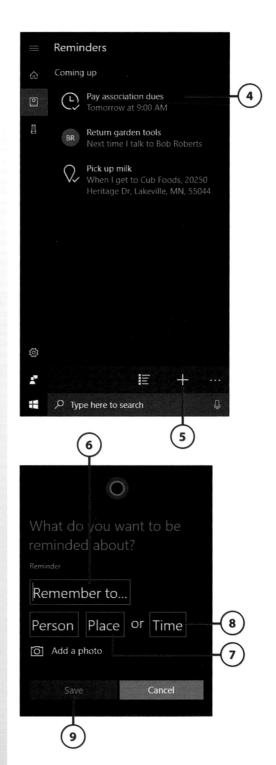

## Search Cortana from Within Edge

You can also use Cortana to display more information about a given topic from within the Edge browser. Cortana uses Bing to search the Web; then it displays its results in a pane within the Edge browser.

1. From within the Edge browser, highlight the word or phrase on a web page.

2. Right-click and select Ask Cortana.

3. You now see a Cortana pane within Edge displaying additional information. Click any item to view more information.

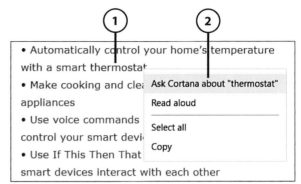

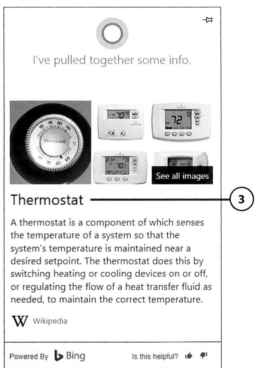

## Do Even More with Cortana

Cortana can do a lot more than just display news stories and reminders. You can ask Cortana all manner of things to find useful—and fun!—information. Cortana can even perform important operations on your computer and over the Internet. All you have to do is ask—no typing necessary.

Here's a sampling of what you can ask Cortana:

- Perform basic Windows operations by saying something like "Restart Windows" or "Shut down my computer."
- Configure Windows settings by saying something like "Turn on Wi-Fi" or "Turn off Bluetooth."
- Open an app or software program by saying "Launch <program name>."
- Open a web page by saying "Open <website name>."
- Ask about the weather by saying "What's the weather forecast?"
- Have Cortana read the latest news headlines by saying "Show me the news."
- Find a sports score by saying something like "What was the score of last night's Yankees game?"
- Write an email message by saying "Write an email to <contact name> saying <text of message>."
- See emails from a given person by saying "Show me emails from <contact name>."
- Perform simple calculations by saying something like "What's 4 plus 5?" or "What's 27 divided by 3?"
- Perform conversions by saying something like "What is ten miles in kilometers?" or "How many ounces in a pound?"
- Find out about scheduled events in your calendar by asking "What's on my schedule for today?" or "When is my doctor appointment?"
- Add an appointment to your calendar by saying something like "Add neighborhood meeting to Friday at 6 p.m."
- Set up a reminder by saying something like "Remind me to call Rhonda tomorrow at noon."
- Set an alarm by saying "Set an alarm for <time>."
- Search for files on your computer by saying something like "Find pictures from last week" or "Find documents from June 2012."
- Search for files by name by saying "Find a document called <filename>."

- Search the Internet for information by saying something like "How far is it to New York City?" "How old is Oprah Winfrey?" or "When is the next full moon?"

- Identify a currently playing song by asking "What is this song?"

- Play a particular song/artist/album/genre by saying "Play 'Brown Sugar'" or "Play music by Bob Dylan" or "Play *The White Album*" or "Play some country music."

- Define a word by saying "What is the definition of <word>?"

- Translate a word or phrase into another language by asking "How do you say <word or phrase> in <language>?"

- Track a package by saying "Where are my packages?"

And there's a lot more than that. When in doubt, just say "Hey, Cortana" and ask away. You never know what Cortana knows!

Amazon
(www.amazon.com)

Lowe's
(www.lowes.com)

Macy's
(www.macys.com)

Target
(www.target.com)

Walmart
(www.walmart.com)

In this chapter, you learn how to safely shop online.

13

# Shopping Safely Online

Online shopping is a practical alternative for people who find real-world shopping inconvenient, at best. Almost every brick-and-mortar store has an online storefront, offering a similar, if not expanded, selection. And there are plenty of bargains to be had online, too—if you know where to look.

## How to Shop Online Safely

Shopping online is every bit as safe as shopping at your local retail store. The big online retailers are just as reputable as traditional retailers, offering safe payment, fast shipping, and responsive service.

# Shop Safely

Some consumers are wary about buying items online, but online shopping can be every bit as safe as shopping at a traditional brick-and-mortar retailer—as long as you take the proper precautions.

( **1** ) Make sure the online retailer prominently displays its contact information and offers multiple ways to connect. You want to be able to email, call, tweet, or chat with the retailer if something goes wrong.

( **2** ) Look for the site's return policy and satisfaction guarantee. You want to be assured that you'll be taken care of if you don't like what you ordered.

( **3** ) A reputable site should tell you whether an item is in stock and how long it will take to ship— before you place your order.

( **4** ) For the best protection, pay by major credit card. (You can always dispute your charges with the credit card company if something goes wrong and the retailer won't make it good.)

( **5** ) Make sure the retailer uses a secure server for its checkout process. Look in the Address box for the letters https:// (not the normal http://) before the URL; you should also see the "lock" symbol before or after the address. If the checkout process is not secure, do not proceed with payment.

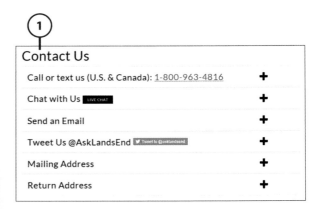

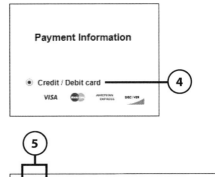

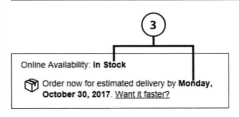

## CREDIT CARD PROTECTIONS

The safest way to shop online is to pay via credit card because credit card purchases are protected by federal law. In essence, you have the right to dispute certain charges, and your liability for unauthorized transactions is limited to $50.

In addition, some card issuers offer a supplemental guarantee that says you're not responsible for *any* unauthorized charges made online. (Make sure that you read your card's statement of terms to determine the company's exact liability policy.)

# Purchasing from Online Retailers

If you've never shopped online before, you're probably wondering just what to expect. Shopping over the Internet is actually easy; all you need is your computer and a credit card—and a fast connection to the Internet!

The online shopping experience is similar from retailer to retailer. You typically proceed through a multiple-step process from discovery to ordering to checkout and payment. We'll examine each of these steps separately.

## Discover Online Retailers

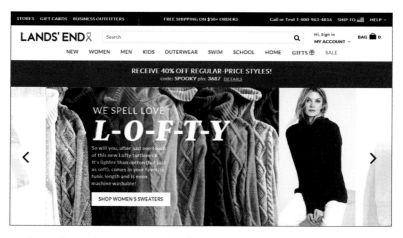

The first step in online shopping is finding where you want to shop. Most major retailers, such as The Home Depot (www.homedepot.com), Kohl's (www.kohls.com),

Macy's (www.macys.com), Office Depot (www.officedepot.com), Target (www.target.com), and Walmart (www.walmart.com), have their own websites you can use to shop online. Most catalog merchants, such as Coldwater Creek (www.coldwatercreek.com), L.L.Bean (www.llbean.com), and Land's End (www.landsend.com), also have their own websites for online ordering.

In addition, there are many online-only retailers that offer a variety of merchandise. These are companies without physical stores; they conduct all their business online and then ship merchandise direct to buyers. These range from smaller niche retailers to larger full-service sites, such as Amazon.com (www.amazon.com), Overstock.com (www.overstock.com), and Wayfair (www.wayfair.com).

In short, you should find no shortage of places to shop online. If worse comes to worst, you can use Google to search for merchants that sell the specific items you're interested in.

## Search or Browse for Merchandise

WOMEN'S
SWEATERS

Lands' End / Women's
/ **Sweaters**

CATEGORIES

Cardigans
Pullovers
Cashmere
Business Uniforms

SIZE RANGE                         —

| Regular | Plus | Petite |

| Tall |

After you've determined where to shop, you need to browse through different product categories on that site or use the site's search feature to find a specific product.

Browsing product categories online is similar to browsing through the departments of a retail store. You typically click a link to access a major product category, and then click further links to view subcategories within the main category. For example, the main category might be Clothing; the subcategories might be Men's, Women's, and Children's clothing. If you click the Men's link, you might see a list of further subcategories: Outerwear, Shirts, Pants, and the like. Just keep clicking until you reach the type of item that you're looking for.

Searching for products is often a faster way to find what you're looking for if you have something specific in mind. For example, if you're looking for a women's leather jacket, you can enter the words **women's leather jacket** into the site's search box and get a list of specific items that match those criteria.

The only problem with searching is that you might not know exactly what it is you're looking for; if this describes your situation, you're probably better off browsing. But if you *do* know what you want—and you don't want to deal with lots of irrelevant items—then searching is the faster option.

## Examine the Product

Whether you browse or search, you'll probably end up looking at a list of different products on a web page. These listings typically feature one-line descriptions of each item—in most cases, not nearly enough information for you to make an informed purchase.

The thing to do now is to click the link for the item you're particularly interested in. This should display a dedicated product page, complete with a picture and full description of the item. This is where you can read more about the item you selected. Some product pages include different views of the item, pictures of the item in different colors or sizes, links to additional information, customer reviews, and maybe even a list of optional accessories that go along with the item.

If you like what you see, you can proceed to the ordering stage. If you want to look at other items, just click your browser's Back button to return to the larger product listing.

## Make a Purchase

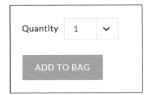

Somewhere on each product description page should be a button labeled Purchase, Buy Now, Add to Cart, Add to Bag, or something similar. This is how you make the actual purchase: by clicking that "buy" button. You don't order the product just by looking at the product description; you have to manually click the "buy" button to place your order.

When you click the "buy" button, that particular item is added to your *shopping cart*. That's right, the online retailer provides you with a virtual shopping cart that functions just like a real-world shopping cart. Each item you choose to purchase is added to your virtual shopping cart.

---

### In-Stock Notification

The better online retailers tell you either on the product description page or during the checkout process whether an item is in stock. Look for this information to help you decide how to group your items for shipment.

---

After you've ordered a product and placed it in your shopping cart, you can choose to shop for other products on that site or proceed to the site's *checkout*.

It's important to note that when you place an item in your shopping cart, you haven't actually completed the purchase yet. You can keep shopping (and adding more items to your shopping cart) as long as you want.

You can even decide to abandon your shopping cart and not purchase anything at this time. All you have to do is leave the website, and you won't be charged for anything. It's the equivalent of leaving your shopping cart at a real-world retailer and walking out the front door; you don't actually buy anything until you walk through the checkout line. (Although, with some sites, the items remain in your shopping cart—so they'll be there waiting for you the next time you shop!)

## Check Out and Pay

To finalize your purchase, you have to visit the store's checkout. This is like the checkout line at a traditional retail store; you take your virtual shopping cart through the checkout, get your purchases totaled, and then pay for what you're buying.

The checkout at an online retailer typically consists of one or more web pages with forms you have to fill out. If you've visited the retailer before, the site might remember some of your personal information from your previous visit. Otherwise, you have to enter your name, address, and phone number, as well as the address you want to ship the merchandise to (if it's different from your billing address). You also have to pay for the merchandise, typically by entering a credit card number.

The checkout provides one last opportunity for you to change your order. You can delete items you decide not to buy or change quantities on any item. At some merchants, you can even opt to have your items gift-wrapped and sent to someone as a present. You should be able to find all these options somewhere in the checkout process.

You might also have the option of selecting different types of shipping for your order. Many merchants offer both regular and expedited shipping—the latter for an additional charge.

Another option at some retailers is to group all items for reduced shipping cost. (The alternative is to ship items individually as they become available.) Grouping items is attractive cost-wise, but you can get burned if one of the items is out of stock or not yet available; you could end up waiting weeks or months for those items that could have been shipped immediately.

After you've entered all the appropriate information, you're asked to place your order. This typically means clicking a button that says "Place Your Order" or something similar. You might even see a second screen asking you whether you *really* want to place your order, just in case you have second thoughts.

After you place your order, you see a confirmation screen, typically displaying your order number. Write down this number or print this page; you need to refer to this number if you have to contact customer service. Most online merchants also send you a confirmation message, including this same information, via email.

That's all there is to it. You shop, examine the product, place an order, proceed to checkout, and pay. It's that easy!

# Finding Bargains Online

If you have no preference as to which online retailers to shop, you can use a *price comparison site* to help find the best merchandise and pricing online. These sites let you search for specific products and then sort and filter the results in a number of different ways.

# Discover Price Comparison Sites

Many of the price comparison sites include customer reviews of both the products and the available merchants. Some even let you perform side-by-side comparisons of multiple products, which is great if you haven't yet made up your mind as to what you want to buy.

**1** Google Shopping (www.google.com/shopping) differs from the other sites in that it searches retailer sites with its own search engine, and doesn't rely on paid listings for its results. Google also shows items available in local stores, if you can't wait for that item to be shipped.

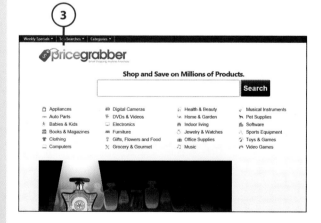

**2** NexTag (www.nextag.com) is great for comparing prices from multiple retailers. It also offers a robust selection of customer product reviews, so you can see what other consumers thought of an item before you decide to buy.

**3** PriceGrabber (www.pricegrabber.com) lets you shop by department or search for specific products.

**4** Shopping.com (www.shopping.com) compares pricing on a multitude of products from numerous retailers.

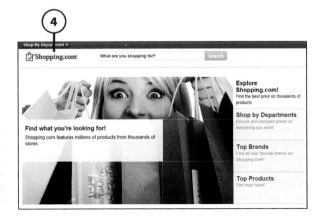

# Using Craigslist

When you're looking to buy something locally, you can often find great bargains on Craigslist (www.craigslist.org), an online classified advertising site. Browse the ads until you find what you want, and then arrange with the seller to make the purchase.

## Other Services

The Craigslist site isn't just for buying and selling merchandise. You can also use Craigslist to look for or offer services, jobs, and housing.

# Buy Items on Craigslist

Listings on Craigslist are just like traditional newspaper classified ads. All transactions are between you and the seller; Craigslist is just the "middleman." That means that when you purchase an item from a Craigslist seller, expect to pick up the item in person and pay in cash.

1. Open your web browser and go to www.craigslist.org. Craigslist should automatically recognize your location; if not, click the name of your city in the far right column.

2. Go to the For Sale section and click the category you're looking for.

3. Click the link or picture for the item you're interested in.

4. Read the item details; then click the Reply button to email the seller and express your interest.

## Contacting the Seller

When you contact the seller via email, let him know you're interested in the item and would like to see it in person. The seller should reply with a suggested time and place to view and possibly purchase the item.

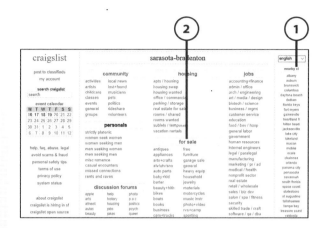

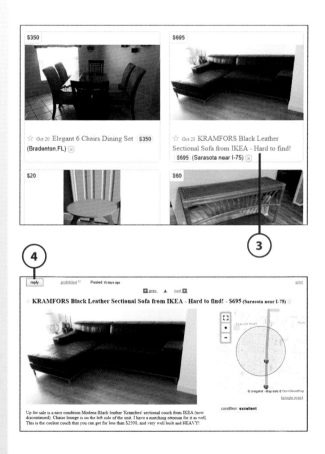

## It's Not All Good

**Buyer Beware**

Just as with traditional classified ads, Craigslist offers no buyer protections. Plug in anything electric or electronic and test its capabilities, thoroughly inspect items in good lighting and from all angles, and make sure the product is exactly want you want *before* handing over any money.

## Sell Items on Craigslist

The Craigslist site is also a great place to sell items you want to get rid of. Just place an ad and wait for potential buyers to contact you!

**1** From the Craigslist site, click the Post to Classifieds link.

**2** Click the type of ad you want to place—typically For Sale by Owner.

**3** Click the category that best fits what you're selling. (If necessary, click through to an appropriate subcategory.)

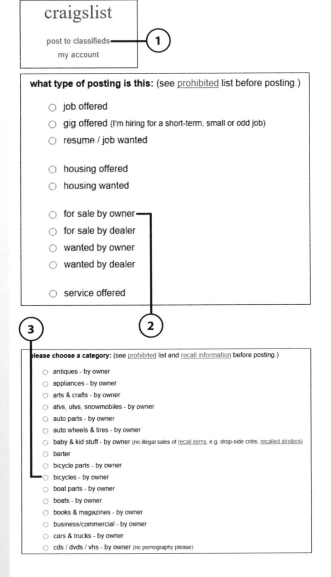

**4** Enter the necessary details about what you're selling, including the listing title, asking price, and description, along with your contact information; then scroll to the bottom of the page and click Continue.

**5** You are now prompted to add pictures of your item. (Items sell better if buyers can see what's for sale, although such photos are optional.) Click the Add Images button to select digital photos of your item.

**6** Click the Done with Images button.

**7** Confirm the listing details and then click the Publish button to finalize the listing.

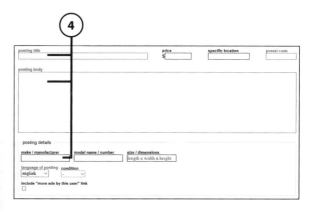

## It's Not All Good

### Safety First

Make sure someone else is with you before you invite potential buyers into your home to look at the item you have for sale—or if you go to a seller's house to buy something. It's always better to arrange to meet buyers at a safe neutral (and public) location.

AARP
(www.aarp.org)

All Recipes
(www.allrecipes.com)

Ancestry
(www.ancestry.com)

KAYAK
(www.kayak.com)

WebMD
(www.webmd.com)

14

# Discovering Useful Websites

The Internet offers a ton of useful and interesting resources for people of all ages. Whether you're looking for community news, healthcare information, or shopping bargains, you can find it online—using your Windows PC.

## Reading Local and Community News Online

The Internet has become a primary source of news in today's digital world. We might have grown up reading newspapers and magazines, but readers today are more likely to get their news and information online. In fact, most newspapers and magazines have their own online editions—often readable for free.

# Find Local News

You can find numerous sources of local news online, from your local newspaper to websites devoted solely to community news.

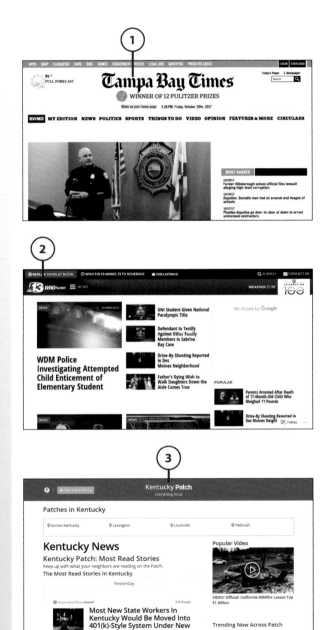

**1** One of the best sources of local news is your local newspaper. Use Google or Bing to search for your local newspaper online, or go to the US Newspaper List (www.usnpl.com) for a list of newspapers nationwide.

**2** Many local television and radio stations also have websites with up-to-date local news, sports, and weather information. Search Google or Bing for radio and TV station sites in your area. (For example, to search for TV stations in Orlando, query **Orlando tv stations**.)

**3** Patch (www.patch.com) is a consortium of neighborhood news websites. Enter the name of your town or your ZIP Code to view news and information gathered locally by neighborhood correspondents. Patch is available for more than 1,200 communities in all 50 states (plus the District of Columbia).

## Online Subscriptions

Many local newspapers have free Internet editions, although some charge for online access. You might get free or discounted online access as part of your print subscription, however, so ask about available options. Some paid newspaper sites also let you view a limited number of articles at no charge, even without a subscription.

>>>*Go Further*

## KEEPING IN TOUCH WHEREVER YOU ARE

You're not limited to reading the local news from where you currently reside. If you're vacationing elsewhere, doing the snowbird thing during the winter, or just curious about what's happening where you grew up, you can use the Internet to access those local news sites from wherever you happen to be.

For example, if your current home is in Minnesota but you winter in Florida, use Google to search for your local Minneapolis newspaper or television station, and then read your northern news while you're sunning in the South. Likewise, if you grew up in Indiana but now live in Arizona, there's nothing stopping you from reading the *Indianapolis Star* online in your web browser.

You can even read news from other countries online. If your family has Irish roots, for example, just search Google for newspapers in Ireland, and keep in touch from around the globe.

## Find Local Weather

Many local news sites also provide local weather reports. Also, several national weather sites provide local forecasts.

1. The Weather Channel's website (www.weather.com) is one of the most detailed in terms of local weather forecasts and conditions. You can view hourly, daily, weekly, and long-term forecasts, as well as view current conditions on an interactive radar map.

( **2** ) AccuWeather (www.accuweather.
com) is another popular general
weather website. Enter your
location for local conditions and
forecasts.

# Exploring Travel Opportunities Online

If you like to travel, there is a tremendous amount of travel-related information
and services online that you can use to plan your next trip.

## Research a Destination

Before you make a trip, find out more
about where you're going. The Internet
has pretty much replaced traditional
travel guidebooks as a source for information about key destinations.

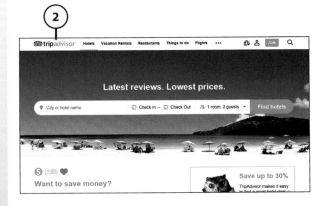

( **1** ) Most of the traditional printed
guidebooks have travel-oriented
websites, with lots of free
information. Check out the sites
for Fodor's (www.fodors.com),
Frommer's (www.frommers.
com), and Lonely Planet (www.
lonelyplanet.com).

( **2** ) When you want reviews of hotels,
restaurants, and other destinations,
check out TripAdvisor (www.
tripadvisor.com). You can link
directly from the site's user reviews
to make reservations, if you like.

**3** The travel section on the AARP website (travel.aarp.org) offers a variety of information and advice for travelers. You can find destination guides, tips and articles, and even member discounts. The site also offers online flight, hotel, rental car, and cruise ship booking, powered by Expedia.

## Make Reservations

You can't beat the Internet for making flight and hotel reservations, from the comfort of your living room. Just log on, enter the required information, and reserve away!

**1** You can make flight reservations directly from the websites of major carriers. Some of the most popular airline sites include American Airlines (www.aa.com), Delta (www.delta.com), Southwest (www.southwest.com), and United (www.united.com).

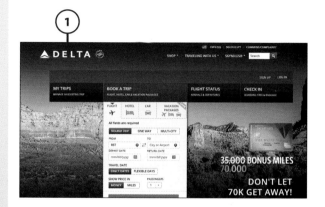

( 2 ) You can make hotel reservations directly at the websites of most big hotel chains. Some of the most popular chains include Choice Hotels (www.choicehotels.com for Comfort Inn, Quality Inn, Clarion, and EconoLodge), Hilton (www.hilton.com for Doubletree, Embassy Suites, Hampton Inn, Homewood Suites, and Hilton), Hyatt (www.hyatt.com for Hyatt and Hyatt Place), and Marriott (www.marriott.com for Courtyard, Fairfield Inn and Suites, Marriott, Residence Inn, Springhill Suites, and TownPlace Suites); use Google to search for other hotels you like.

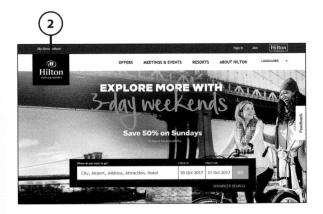

( 3 ) You can use several general travel sites to research destinations and book hotel rooms, rental cars, cruises, and flights. These sites include Expedia (www.expedia.com), KAYAK (www.kayak.com), Orbitz (www.orbitz.com), and Travelocity (www.travelocity.com).

# Discovering Recipes Online

The Internet is a great resource for home cooks. It's easy to search Google for your favorite recipes, or browse sites that contain nothing but recipes. The most popular sites have tools that allow you to file recipes in your own personal recipe box so you can save them for later. Virtually all of these recipes can be printed, with some sites offering nutritional information, shopping lists, and color photographs of the final results.

# Find Tasty Recipes

Can't remember the ingredients you need for a particular dish? Want to explore new tastes? Then check out some of the most popular recipe sites online; great food is just a click away!

1. All Recipes (www.allrecipes.com) is a general recipe site. It also offers how-to videos that lead you step by step through your favorite recipes and cooking techniques.

2. Epicurious (www.epicurious.com) is a community for serious home cooks. Browse this site for recipes, food-related articles, and cooking guides.

3. Want to cook like the famous chefs you see on TV? Then check out the all-star recipes on the Food Network's website (www. foodnetwork.com); whether you're into Guy Fieri, Bobby Flay, or Rachel Ray, you'll find their recipes here.

4. My Recipes (www.myrecipes.com) offers more than 50,000 recipes for all kinds of meals. Search or browse for what you want.

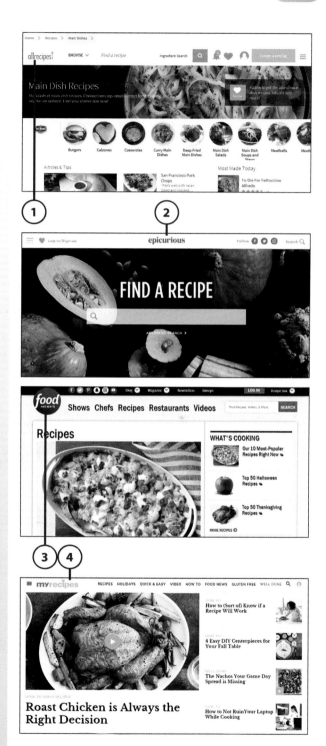

# Finding Healthcare Information Online

Health is a big concern for people of any age, but becomes even more important as we get older. Fortunately, the Internet is a great source of healthcare information and services. AARP (www.aarp.org) is one great resource for healthcare information on a variety of topics, including medical conditions, medications, and insurance. Whether you need to research a particular medical condition, make a doctor's appointment, or fill a prescription, you can do it online.

## Research Medical Conditions

Have a new ache or pain? Stubborn cough? Just not feeling right? Turn to these websites to research all sorts of medical conditions, before you call your doctor.

1. WebMD (www.webmd.com) is one of the most popular websites for researching all sorts of ailments and conditions. The site features sections for specific health conditions, drugs and supplements, and living healthy—and also includes a symptom checker.

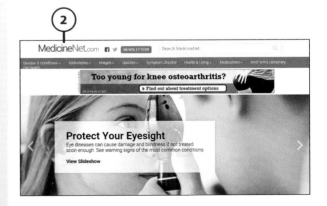

2. MedicineNet.com (www.medicinenet.com) features health news and information, including a huge database of diseases and conditions, along with an online symptom checker.

**(3)** The National Institute on Aging (part of the National Institutes of Health) offers an informative website (www.nia.nih.gov), with stories, videos, and other information specifically geared for an older audience.

# Find a Doctor

Looking for a new doctor? You can find one online.

**(1)** Find a Doctor (www.findadoctor.com) lets you search for physicians by specialty and location, and then schedule an appointment—all online.

**(2)** The American Medical Association maintains a comprehensive database on more than 814,000 licensed doctors nationwide. The AMA's DoctorFinder site (https://apps.ama-assn.org/doctorfinder) lets you search this database for a doctor near you.

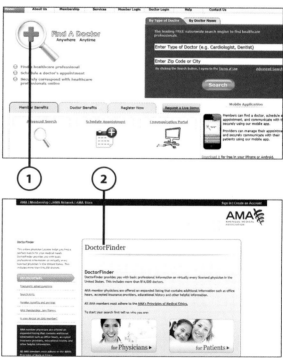

**(3)** When you're looking for physicians and healthcare professionals who are enrolled in the Medicare program, use Medicare's official Physician Compare site (www.medicare.gov/physiciancompare).

## >>>*Go Further*

## APPOINTMENTS AND RECORDS ONLINE

Many (but not all) doctors and clinics let you schedule future appointments online. Some even let you access your medical records via secure websites.

Check with your doctor or clinic to see what web-based services they offer. You'll probably need to set up a secure account, complete with username and password, so that only you can access your records. Once the account is set up, it's then easy to track your lab results and long-term progress via your computer and the Internet.

## Order Prescription Drugs

You can fill your prescriptions at your local pharmacy or use one of a number of online prescription services. And your local pharmacy probably has a website that makes ordering easier!

1. The big national pharmacy chains have their own websites for filling your prescriptions so that you can pick them up at your local store. You can order online from CVS (www.cvs.com), Rite Aid (www. riteaid.com), Walgreens (www. walgreens.com) and other major pharmacies.

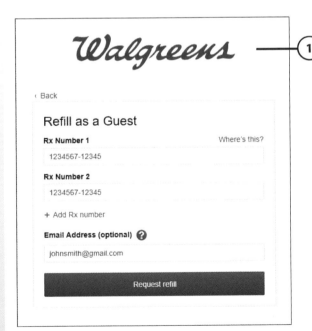

( **2** ) Several "virtual pharmacies" on the Web let you order prescription drugs and have them delivered to your door, via the mail. The most popular include Express Scripts (www.express-scripts.com), Familymeds (www.familymeds. com), HealthWarehouse (www. healthwarehouse.com), and RXdirect (www.rx-direct.com). You need to have your doctor fax or email your prescriptions to get started.

## Insurance Plans

Check with your health insurance company to see which online pharmacies are covered under your specific insurance plan.

# Obtaining Legal Advice Online

The Internet will never replace a licensed attorney, but you can still find lots of legal advice online. Whether you need help with estate planning or anticipate a nasty guardianship fight, the Web is a great place to start, but make sure to check anything you see online with a lawyer about your personal circumstances.

# Find Legal Advice and Services

When you need legal advice, there are a few general sites to start with. You can also search Google for legal services in your state or city.

1. With LawHelp.org (www. lawhelp.org), you can search for legal advice and services by state. There's a special section just for seniors, covering wills and trusts, guardianship and conservatorship, nursing homes and assisted living, elder abuse and exploitation, and other issues of interest to older Americans.

2. LegalAdvice.com (www. legaladvice.com) enables you to ask questions of legal professionals, as well as search past answers.

3. Justice in Aging (www. justiceinaging.org) is an advocacy organization providing legal services to low-income seniors nationwide. Although the site does not provide specific legal advice, it does include links to several organizations that do.

# Managing Your Finances Online

Thanks to the Internet, you can do your banking and bill paying online—as well as manage all your other financial activities, too.

# Do Your Banking and Pay Your Bills

When it comes to managing your banking activities, you have two choices. You can use your bank's website or an online financial management site, such as Mint.

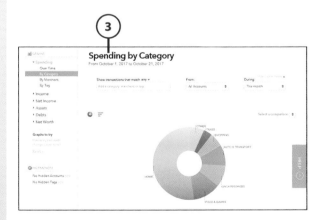

(1) Most banks have their own websites, from which you can view and reconcile your checking and saving accounts, transfer funds between accounts, and even pay your bills online. You typically need your bank account numbers, personal identification numbers (PINs), and other personal data to create your account; after you log on, each activity is no more than a few clicks away.

(2) Your credit card companies also have their own websites. After you sign up and sign in, you can review past transactions, make payments, and more.

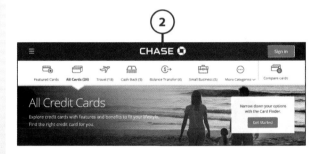

(3) If you want to manage all your financial transactions in one place, consider signing up for Mint (www.mint.com). Mint is a personal finance site where you can enter all your online accounts (banking, credit cards—you name it) and view your daily activities online. You can use Mint to pay bills, transfer funds, and perform other essential tasks—as well as review your income and expenditures over time.

## It's Not All Good

**Safety First**

When you're dealing with websites that contain sensitive information, such as banks and other financial sites, make sure you sign out of the site when you're done using it. You don't want some other user of your computer to be able to access your personal information, just because you left the site open on your PC.

It's also a good idea not to do your online banking in public, over a public Wi-Fi hotspot. Wait until you get home and you're on your private Wi-Fi network.

In addition, make sure you create a super secure password for all the banking and financial sites you use. Make sure it's long and complex and unguessable—and create different passwords for each site. You don't want strangers accessing your computer and getting into your bank accounts online.

## Track Your Investments

If you have a number of investments—in stocks, mutual funds, IRAs, or 401(k) plans—you can track their performance online, in real time. A number of websites offer both investment tracking and financial news and advice.

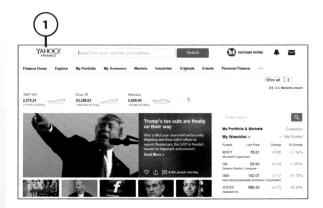

1 Yahoo! Finance (finance.yahoo.com) is the most popular financial website today. It's loaded with tons of financial news and opinion, and lets you track your own portfolio online.

(2) CNN Money (money.cnn.com) is the online home of both *Fortune* and *Money* magazines. In addition to some of the best financial news and opinion on the Web, you can also use the site to create a watch list of your personal investments, and then track your investments over time.

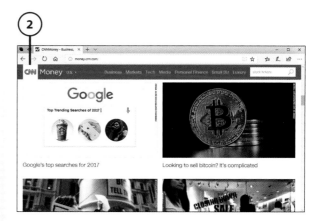

(3) The Motley Fool (www.fool.com) has more opinion and advice than competing financial sites, and is both fun and useful. Plus, of course, you can create your own watch list to track your investments.

### Finance App

The Windows Money app is another good way to track your investments and read financial news. Learn more in Chapter 9, "Using Windows 10 Apps."

# Discovering Organizations Online

Many prominent organizations for people over age 50 have sites on the Web. These websites typically offer news, services, and useful advice.

# Browse Useful Organizations

Organizations that serve people 50-plus use the Web to provide news and information.

(1) AARP has more than 37 million members, and AARP's website (www.aarp.org) offers useful information about health, work and jobs, retirement, money, family, entertainment, food, travel, caregiving, and more.

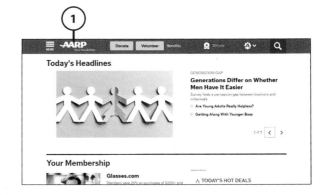

(2) The Canadian Snowbird Association (CSA) is a Canadian organization for retirees who travel south for the winter. The CSA website (www.snowbirds. org) offers news and other information of interest to snowbirds, including travel insurance, currency exchange rates, and tax forms.

(3) The Senior Job Bank (www. seniorjobbank.org) brings together interested employers with qualified older job seekers. It's a great place to find full- or part-time work near you.

# >>>Go Further

## RESEARCH YOUR ROOTS

One of the most popular online activities for users of all ages is researching your family roots. There are several big genealogy sites online that let you research and create family trees, often linking your personal data to that of other users to fill in the blanks going back generations.

The most popular genealogy site today is Ancestry (www.ancestry.com). The site claims to host more than 20 billion historical records and 90 million family trees. It's a good first stop if you're interested.

Other popular genealogy sites include FamilySearch (www.familysearch.org), Find My Past (www.findmypast.com), and Genealogy.org (www.genealogy.org). Some of these sites are free (or have free levels); others offer monthly subscription access. Check out a few of these sites and see which fit your interests—and your budget.

Windows Defender
Security Center

# Protecting Yourself Online

While most sites on the Internet are safe, there are some unscrupulous operators waiting to prey on unsuspecting users. You can, however, take steps to protect yourself when you're online. You need to be able to identify the most common online threats and scams and know how to avoid becoming a victim.

## Protecting Against Identity Theft and Phishing Schemes

Online predators want your personal information—your real name, address, online usernames and passwords, bank account numbers, and the like. It's called *identity theft*, and it's a way for a con artist to impersonate you—both online and in the real world. If your personal data falls into the hands of identity thieves, it can be used to hack into your online accounts, make unauthorized charges on your credit card, and maybe even drain your bank account.

Identity theft is a major issue. According to Javelin Strategy and Research, $16 billion was stolen from more than 15 million victims of identity theft in 2016. A typical case of identity theft costs the average victim more than $1,000.

Criminals have many ways to obtain your personal information. Almost all involve tricking you, in some way or another, into providing this information of your own free will. Your challenge is to avoid being tricked.

## Avoiding Phishing Scams

Online, identity thieves often use a technique called *phishing* to trick you into disclosing valuable personal information. It's called that because the other party is "fishing" for your personal information, typically via fake email messages and websites.

*It's Not All Good*

### Phishing Means Phony

A phishing scam typically starts with a phony email message that appears to be from a legitimate source, such as your bank, the postal service, PayPal, or other official institution. This email purports to contain important information that you can see if you click the enclosed link. That's where the bad stuff starts.

If you click the link in the phishing email, you're taken to a fake website masquerading as the real site, complete with logos and official-looking text. You're encouraged to enter your personal information into the forms on this fake web page; when you do so, your information is sent to the scammer, and you're now a victim of identity theft.

How can you avoid falling victim to a phishing scam? There are several things you can do:

- Look at the sender's email address. Most phishing emails come from an address different from the one indicated by the (fake) sender. (For example, in an email that's supposedly from FedEx, the email address 619.RFX@ jacksonville.com would be suspicious; you'd expect an email from FedEx to look something like ***address*@fedex.com**.)

- Mouse over any links in the email. In a phishing email, the URL for the link will not match up with the link text or the (fake) sender's supposed website.

- Look for poor grammar and misspellings. Many phishing schemes come from outside the U.S. by scammers who don't speak English as their first language. As such, you're likely to find questionable phrasing and unprofessional text— not what you'd expect from your bank or other professional institution.

- If you receive an unexpected email, no matter the apparent source, do *not* click any of the links in the email. If you think there's a legitimate issue from a given website, go to that site manually in your web browser and access your account from there.

- Some phishing messages include attached files that you are urged to click to display a document or image. Do *not* click or open any of these attachments; they might contain malware that can steal personal information or damage your computer. (Read more about malware later in this chapter.)

---

### Phishing Filters

Many web browsers—including Google Chrome and Microsoft Edge—offer some built-in protection against phishing scams, in the form of filters that alert you to potential phishing sites. If you click a bad link or attempt to visit a known or suspected phishing site, the browser displays a warning message. Do not enter information into these suspected phishing sites—return to your home page instead!

---

# Keeping Your Private Information Private

Identity theft can happen any time you make private information public. This has become a special issue on social networks, such as Facebook, where users tend to forget that everything they post is publicly visible.

Many Facebook users not only post personal information in their status updates, but also include sensitive data in their personal profiles. Javelin Strategy and Research found that 68% of people with public social media profiles shared their birthday information, 63% shared the name of their high schools, 18% shared their phone numbers, and 12% shared their pet's names.

None of this might sound dangerous, until you realize that all of these items are the type of personal information many companies use for the "secret questions" their websites use to reset users' passwords. A fraudster armed with this publicly visible information could log on to your account on a banking website, for example, reset your password (to a new one he provides), and thus gain access to your banking accounts.

The solution to this problem, of course, is to enter as little personal information as possible when you're online. For example, you don't need to—and shouldn't—include your street address or phone number in a comment or reply to an online news article. Don't give the bad guys anything they can use against you!

Follow these tips:

- Unless absolutely necessary, do not enter your personal contact information (home address, phone number, and so on) into your social media profile.

- Do not post or enter your birthdate, children's names, pet's names, and the like—anything that could be used to reset your passwords at various websites.

- Do not post status updates that indicate your current location—especially if you're away from home. That's grist for both physical stalkers and home burglars.

## It's Not All Good

**Corporate Data Breaches**

As careful as you may be in protecting your own personal information, the fact remains that many big companies collect information about you—and that information is not always secure. Many big-time hackers target large corporations—retailers, banks, financial firms—in search of data to steal, which can then be used to perpetrate identity theft and other crimes.

The largest such data breach, as these attacks are called, occurred at Equifax, the big credit reporting bureau. Cybercriminals hacked into Equifax in mid-2017 and accessed more than 145 million personal records, including names, birth dates, addresses, Social

Security numbers, and driver's license numbers. This is a major, major breach, with implications for almost half of all Americans.

What can you do when your personal data is accessed by cybercriminals? Most companies that have been hacked will offer ways to check on your personal data, including offering free credit monitoring for a period of time. You can also consider putting a credit freeze on your accounts, so that unauthorized persons cannot open new accounts in your name. You should also manually monitor the transactions in your bank and credit card accounts, so that you're immediately aware if something is amiss.

Unfortunately, there's not much you can do to prevent this sort of situation from happening; that responsibility lies in the hands of those storing your data. Unless you go completely off the grid, your personal data is going to be available to various companies online, and anything online (or even offline) can be hacked. We can hope that the big data companies get better at protecting our data, but until then we just have to be alert to what happens if or when these criminal attacks occur.

# Hiding Personal Information on Facebook

Too many Facebook users of all ages make all their personal information totally public—visible to all users, friends or not. Fortunately, you can configure Facebook's privacy settings to keep your private information private.

---

### Facebook
Learn more about using the Facebook social network in Chapter 18, "Connecting with Facebook and Pinterest."

---

( 1 )  Click your name in the Facebook toolbar to open your personal profile page.

**2** Click the Edit Profile button.

**3** Click the Edit (pencil) button for the information you want to make private.

**4** Mouse over the item you want to change and then click the Privacy button for that item.

**5** Click the Privacy button and select Friends to make this information visible only to people on your friends list—or click Only Me to completely hide this information from others.

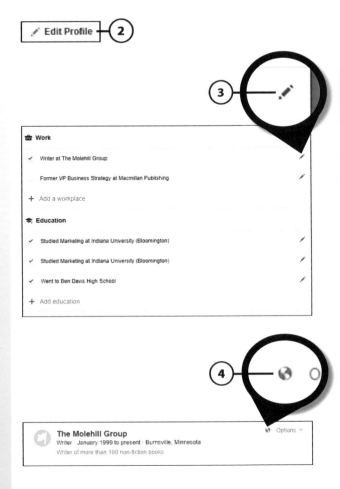

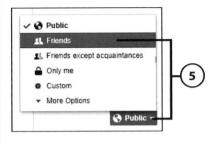

# Keeping Your Facebook Posts Private

You can configure Facebook to hide your status updates from anyone not on your friends list. You can also configure the privacy settings for each individual post you make on Facebook. This way, you can post more personal information only to select friends, and hide it from the general public.

1. Click the Help button on the Facebook Toolbar to display the pull-down menu.

2. Click Privacy Shortcuts.

3. Select Who Can See My Stuff? to expand the pull-down menu.

4. Pull down the Who Can See My Future Posts? list and select Friends.

5. To change who can see any individual status update, create a new post, click the Privacy button, and make a new selection: Public or Friends.

## Custom Privacy

To hide posts from select individuals, select Custom in the Privacy list and then enter the names of people you don't want to share with. Finish by clicking Save Changes.

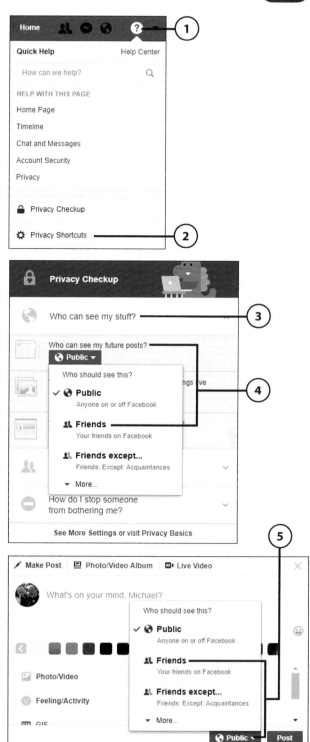

# Protecting Against Online Fraud

Identity theft isn't the only kind of online fraud you might encounter. Con artists are especially creative in concocting schemes that can defraud unsuspecting victims of thousands of dollars.

Most of these scams start with an email message that promises something for nothing. Maybe the message tells you that you've won a lottery, or you are asked to help someone in a foreign country deposit funds in a U.S. bank account. You might even receive requests from people purporting to be far-off relatives who need some cash to bail them out of some sort of trouble.

The common factor in these scams is that you're eventually asked to either send money (typically via wire transfer) or provide your bank account information—with which the scammers can drain your money faster than you can imagine. If you're naive or gullible enough, the damage can be considerable.

Protecting yourself from the huge number of these online scams is both difficult and simple. The difficulty comes from the sheer number of scams and their amazing variety. The simplicity comes from the fact that the best way to deal with any such scam is to use common sense—and ignore it.

---

### Scams Are Not Spam

You can't rely on your email program's spam filter to stop scam emails. Spam and scams are two different things, even if they're both unwanted. Although some scam messages are stopped by spam filters, many messages get through the filter and land in your inbox, just as if they were legitimate messages—which, of course, they aren't.

---

## Identifying Online Scams

Most online fraud is easily detectible by the simple fact that it arrives in your email inbox out of the blue and seems too good to be true. So if you get an unsolicited offer that promises great riches, you know to hit the Delete key—pronto.

You can train yourself to recognize scam emails at a glance. That's because most scam messages have one or more of the following characteristics in common:

- The email does not address you personally by name; your name doesn't appear anywhere in the body of the message.

- You don't know the person who sent you the message; the message was totally unsolicited.

- The message is rife with spelling and grammatical errors. (Scammers frequently operate from foreign countries and do not speak English as their first language.) Conversely, the text of the message might seem overly formal, as if written by someone not familiar with everyday English.

- You are promised large sums of money for little or no effort on your part.

- You are asked to provide your bank account number, credit card number, or other personal information—or are asked to provide money upfront for various fees, or to pay the cost of expediting the process.

## It's Not All Good

### Tech Support Scams

Here's another scam that's going the rounds. You get a phone call from someone purporting to be from "Windows" or "Windows Technical Support." (But never Microsoft; they never use the real company's name.) This person, typically speaking in fractured English, tells you he's received notice that your computer or version of Windows has been infected with viruses and that he can walk you through the steps to correct the problem.

The problem is that there isn't any problem; the person calling you has no knowledge or connection to your computer, and if you go along with it, you're about to be scammed. The person on the other end of the phone may have you open up a Windows tool called the Event Viewer to "show" you that you're under attack; you'll then see all the typical behind-the-scenes Windows alerts and warnings that look scary but are really quite normal. Once the person has convinced you that you have a problem, you're then conned into paying for and downloading purported anti-malware or tech support software that, in reality, places real spyware and viruses on your computer. This malware might even require you to pay more and more, over time, for additional "fixes."

If you receive this type of phone call, just hang up. It's a dangerous scam that all too many people fall for. Don't be a victim!

## Avoiding Online Fraud

Recognizing a scam email is just one way to reduce your risk of getting conned online. Here are some more tips you can employ:

- Familiarize yourself with the common types of online scams—and if a message in your inbox resembles any of these common scams, delete it.

- Ignore all unsolicited emails, of any type. No stranger will send you a legitimate offer via email; it just doesn't happen. When you receive an unsolicited offer via email, delete it.

- Don't give in to greed. If an offer sounds too good to be true, it is; there are no true "get rich quick" schemes.

- Never provide any personal information—including credit card numbers, your Social Security number, and the like—via email. If such information is legitimately needed, you can call the company yourself or visit their official website to provide the information directly.

### >>>Go Further
### WHAT TO DO IF YOU'VE BEEN SCAMMED

What should you do if you think you've been the victim of an email fraud? There are a few steps you can take to minimize the damage:

- If the fraud involved transmittal of your credit card information, contact your credit card company to halt all unauthorized payments—and to limit your liability to the first $50.

- If you think your bank accounts have been compromised, contact your bank to put a freeze on your checking and savings accounts—and open new accounts, if necessary.

- Contact one of the three major credit-reporting bureaus to see if stolen personal information has been used to open new credit accounts—or max out your existing accounts. The three major bureaus are Equifax (www.equifax.com), Experian (www.experian.com), and TransUnion (www.transunion.com).

- Contact your local law enforcement authorities—fraud is illegal, and it should be reported as a crime.

- Report the fraud to your state attorney general's office.

- File a complaint with the Federal Trade Commission (FTC) via the form located at www.ftc-complaintassistant.gov.

- Contact any or all of the following consumer-oriented websites: Better Business Bureau (www.bbb.org), Internet Crime Complaint Center (www.ic3.gov), National Consumers League (NCL) (www.nclnet.org), and the NCL's Fraud Center (www.fraud.org).

Above all, don't provide any additional information or money to the scammers. As soon as you suspect you've been had, halt all contact and cut off all access to your bank and credit card accounts. Sometimes the best you can hope for is to minimize your losses.

# Protecting Against Computer Viruses and Other Malware

Any malicious software installed on your computer is dubbed *malware*. The two primary types of malware are *computer viruses* and *spyware*.

A computer virus is a malicious software program designed to do damage to your computer system by deleting files or even taking over your PC to launch attacks on other systems. A virus attacks your computer when you launch an infected software program, launching a "payload" that oftentimes is catastrophic.

Even more pernicious than computer viruses is the proliferation of spyware. A spyware program installs itself on your computer and then surreptitiously sends information about the way you use your PC to some interested third party. Spyware typically gets installed in the background when you're installing another program, and is almost as bad as being infected with a computer virus. Some spyware programs will even hijack your computer and launch pop-up windows and advertisements when you visit certain web pages. If there's spyware on your computer, you definitely want to get rid of it.

# Protecting Against Malware

You can do several things to avoid having your PC infected with malware. It's all about smart and safe computing.

- Don't open email attachments from people you don't know—or even from people you do know, if you aren't expecting them. That's because some malware can hijack the address book on an infected PC, thus sending out infected email that the owner isn't even aware of. Just looking at an email message won't harm anything; the damage comes when you open a file attached to the email.

- Download files only from reliable file archive websites, such as Download.com (download.cnet.com) and Softpedia (www.softpedia.com). Do not download files you find on sites you don't know.

- Don't access or download files from music and video file-sharing and BitTorrent networks, which are notoriously virus and spyware ridden. Instead, download music and movies from legitimate sites, such as the iTunes Store and Amazon MP3 Store.

---

### BitTorrent

BitTorrent is a technology that enables the sharing of large files between individual computers on the Internet. Today, BitTorrent is typically used to illegally share pirated music and movie files.

---

- Because viruses and spyware can also be transmitted via physical storage media, share USB drives, CDs, DVDs, and files only with users you know and trust.

- Use anti-malware software, such as Windows Defender, to identify and remove viruses and spyware from your system.

# Using Anti-Malware Software

Windows 10 comes with its own antivirus utility built in. It's called Windows Defender, and it tells you the last time your system was scanned, whether any threats have been detected, and more security-related information.

Of course, you're not locked into using Microsoft's anti-malware solution. Several third-party antivirus programs are available, including the following:

- AVG Internet Security (www.avg.com)
- Avira Antivirus (www.avira.com)
- Iobit Malware Fighter (www.iobit.com)
- McAfee Internet Security (www.mcafee.com)
- Norton Security (us.norton.com)
- Trend Micro Titanium (www.trendmicro.com)

If you just purchased a new PC, it might come with a trial version of one of these third-party antivirus programs preinstalled. That's fine, but know that you'll be nagged to pay for the full version after the 90-day trial. You can do this if you want, but you don't need to; remember, you have Windows Defender built in to Windows, and it's both free and very effective.

By the way, if you want to get rid of the trial version of one of these antivirus programs, open the Settings window, click Apps, then click Apps & Features. Select the program you want to get rid of and then click Uninstall. This will get rid of all the "upgrade" nagging from the program in question.

Whichever anti-malware solution you employ, make sure you update it on a regular basis. These updates include information on the very latest viruses and spyware, and are invaluable for protecting your system from new threats. (Windows Defender is configured to update itself automatically—so there's nothing you have to do manually.)

## It's Not All Good

**Kaspersky Lab**

When working with anti-malware tools you might encounter software from a company called Kaspersky Lab. This firm is based in Russia and, although it has a long history of use worldwide, it has been accused of contributing to the alleged Russian interference in our country's 2016 elections. The charges are serious enough that the U.S. Department of Homeland Security has banned Kaspersky products from all government departments.

As such, I can no longer recommend using Kaspersky's anti-malware products. If you have any Kaspersky utilities installed on your computer, I recommend uninstalling them and switching to tools from a different vendor.

## Using the Windows Defender Security Center

The easiest way to protect your computer from malware is with Windows 10's built-in Windows Defender app. In most instances you don't have to access the app at all; it's enabled and configured automatically. You can, however, view your security settings (and change any settings you want) from the new Windows Defender Security Center.

(1) Click the Notification icon in the taskbar and click All Settings to open the Settings tool.

(2) Click Update & Security.

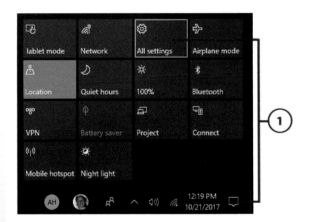

**3** Select the Windows Defender tab.

**4** Click Open Windows Defender Security Center.

**5** The Home tab is selected by default. You see that your PC is being protected and when the last scan occurred. Any issues you need to address are highlighted here.

**6** Click Virus & Threat Protection to change Windows Defender settings.

**7** Click Device Performance & Health to view information about the health of your computer.

**8** Click Firewall & Network Protection to configure Windows Firewall settings.

**9** Click App & Browser Control to configure SmartScreen protection for the Edge browser and Windows apps.

**10** Click Family Options to configure parental controls on your computer.

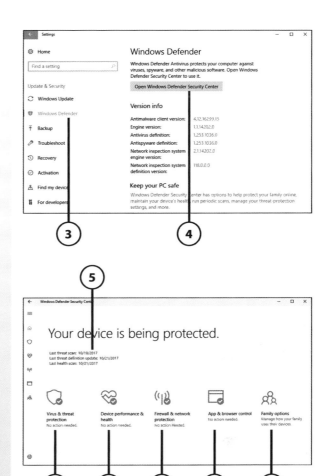

## Protecting Against Ransomware

There's a relatively new type of malware making the rounds that takes your computer hostage and won't let you access your files until you pay the hacker a monetary ransom. While this *ransomware* is typically targeted at large institutions (who can afford paying a large ransom), it sometimes hits individual PCs, with devastating results.

Fortunately, the Windows 10 Fall Creators Update offers protection from ransomware, via what Microsoft calls controlled folder access. Activating this option keeps unauthorized applications, including ransomware, from accessing your computer's files and folders. You need to enable this option manually, as it's not automatically enabled in Windows 10.

**( 1 )** From the Windows Defender Security Center, click Virus & Threat Protection.

**( 2 )** Click Virus & Threat Protection Settings.

**( 3 )** Scroll down and click "on" Controlled Folder Access.

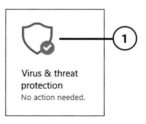

Virus & threat protection
No action needed.

 Virus & threat protection settings
No action needed.

Controlled folder access

Protect your files and folders from unauthorized changed by unfriendly applications.

 On

Protected folders
Allow an app through Controlled folder access

# Protecting Against Online Attacks and Intrusions

Connecting to the Internet is a two-way street—not only can your PC access other computers online, but other computers can also access your PC. So, unless you take proper precautions, malicious hackers can read your private data, damage your system hardware and software, and even use your system (via remote control) to cause damage to other computers.

## Zombie Computers

When a computer is controlled by remote control to attack other computers or send out reams of spam, that computer is said to be a *zombie*. A collection of zombie computers is called a *botnet*.

## Employing a Firewall

You protect your system against outside attack by blocking the path of attack with a firewall. A *firewall* is a software program that forms a virtual barrier between your computer and the Internet. The firewall selectively filters the data that is passed between both ends of the connection and protects your system against outside attack.

Fortunately, Windows includes its own built-in firewall utility. The Windows Firewall is activated by default and is, for most users, more than enough protection against computer attacks. (You can configure or disable the Windows Firewall from the Windows Defender Security Center.)

If you want even more protection, employ a third-party firewall program. Most of these programs are more robust and offer more protection than the Windows built-in firewall. The best of these programs include McAfee Total Protection (www.mcafee.com), Norton Security (us.norton.com), and ZoneAlarm Free Firewall (www.zonelabs.com).

## >>>Go Further

## ARE UPDATES LEGIT?

From time to time, you will inevitably be pestered to "update" something on your computer. This might be an update to Windows itself, or to one of the programs you have installed, or some such.

Should you click "yes" when asked to install one of these updates? Or is this just another way to install malware on your system?

Although most updates are legitimate and necessary (they typically contain important bug fixes), some are just another way for the bad guys to install bad stuff on your system. This is especially so if the "update" notice is for a program or service you've never heard about and don't even have installed on your PC.

That said, if it's Windows that's asking you to approve the update, you should do it. Microsoft beams out updates to Windows over the Internet on a regular basis, and these *patches* (as they're called) help to keep your system in tip-top running condition. The same thing with updates to legitimate software programs; these updates sometimes add new functionality to the apps you use on a day-to-day basis.

(This includes updates to Java and Flash, two behind-the-scenes technologies that help to power the web pages you visit. They're both legitimate and need periodic updating.)

So here's the rule: If it's an update to Windows or a program that you know and use on a regular basis, approve it. If it's an update to a program you don't use or don't know, then don't approve it. When in doubt, play it safe.

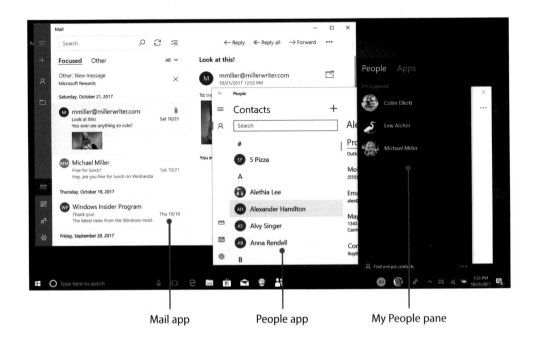

Mail app    People app    My People pane

# Emailing Family and Friends

When it comes to keeping in touch with the people you know and love, the easiest way to do so is via electronic mail, otherwise known as *email*. An email message is like a regular letter, except that it's composed electronically and delivered almost immediately via the Internet. You can use email to send both text messages and computer files (such as digital photos) to pretty much anyone with an Internet connection.

One of the easiest ways to send and receive email from your new PC is to use the Windows Mail app. You can also send and receive email in your web browser, using a web-based email service such as Gmail or Yahoo! Mail. Either approach is good and lets you create, send, and read email messages from all your friends and family.

## Using the Windows Mail App

Windows 10 includes a built-in Mail app for sending and receiving email messages. By default, the Mail app manages email from any Microsoft email service linked to your Microsoft Account, including Outlook.com and the older Hotmail. This means you'll see Outlook and Hotmail messages in your Mail Inbox and will be able to easily send emails from your Hotmail or Outlook account.

## Set Up Your Email Account

By default, the Mail app sends and receives messages from the email account associated with your Microsoft account. You can, however, configure Mail to work with other email accounts, if you have them. You launch the Mail app from the Windows taskbar or Start menu.

### Account Types

The Mail app lets you add Outlook.com (including Hotmail addresses), AOL, Google (Gmail), and Yahoo! Mail accounts. You can also set up other email accounts, such as those from your Internet Service Provider or employer, using EAS or IMAP.

1. From within the Mail app, click the Settings button to display the Settings pane.

2. Click Manage Accounts to display the Manage Accounts pane.

3. Click Add Account to display the Choose an Account window.

**4** Click the type of account you want to add.

**5** Enter the requested information. (This will be different for different services, but typically includes your email address and password.)

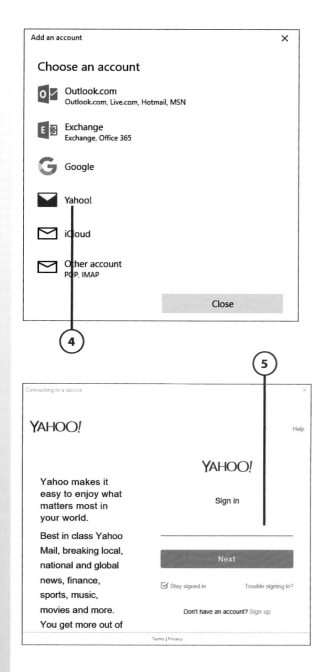

(6) Click the Sign In button.

## Switching Accounts

To view the Inbox of another email account, click the name of that account in the Accounts section of the folders pane.

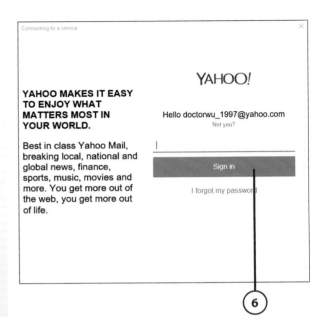

**YAHOO!**

**YAHOO MAKES IT EASY TO ENJOY WHAT MATTERS MOST IN YOUR WORLD.**

Hello doctorwu_1997@yahoo.com
Not you?

Best in class Yahoo Mail, breaking local, national and global news, finance, sports, music, movies and more. You get more out of the web, you get more out of life.

Sign in

I forgot my password

# View Incoming Messages

All email messages sent to you from others are stored in the Inbox of the Mail app. Unread messages are displayed in bold.

### Resize the Window

By default, the Mail app launches in a squarish window. In this configuration, you only see two panes; when you click a message in the message pane, the content of that message then replaces the message pane. If you resize the window so that it's wider, or simply click the Maximize button to display the window full-screen, you'll see three panes, with a new content pane to the right of the message pane. In this configuration, when you click a message in the message pane, its contents display automatically in the content pane.

( 1 ) In the folder pane, click the email account you want to use. (If you have multiple accounts, that is.)

( 2 ) Click the message you want to view; the contents of that message are now displayed in the Mail window.

( 3 ) If the message has a photo attached, click the default thumbnail to view a thumbnail image of the photo. (To download a photo or other file to your computer, right-click the item and select Download.)

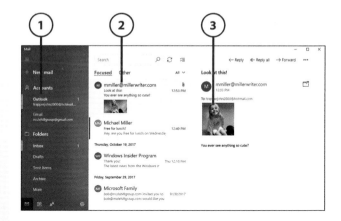

## It's Not All Good

### Download Danger

Be cautious when downloading and opening files attached to email messages. This type of file attachment is how computer viruses are often spread; opening a file that contains a virus automatically infects your computer.

You should only download attachments that you're expecting from people you know. Never open an attachment from a stranger. Never open an attachment you're not expecting. When in doubt, just ignore the attachment. That's the safest way to proceed.

## Reply to a Message

Replying to an email message is as easy as clicking a button and typing your reply.

( 1 ) From an open message, click Reply at the top of screen. The contents change to a reply screen, with the sender's email address already added to the To field.

### Reply All

If the original message was sent to multiple recipients (including you), you have the Reply All option, which sends your reply to everyone who received the original message. Don't click this option by mistake if you only want to reply to the original sender!

( 2 ) Enter your reply at the top of the message; the bottom of the message "quotes" the original message.

( 3 ) Click Send when you're ready to send the message.

## Send a New Message

Composing a new message is similar to replying to a message. The big difference is that you have to manually enter the recipient's email address.

( 1 ) Click + New Mail at the top of the folders pane to display the new message.

① ← Reply   ≪ Reply all   → Forward   •••

②   ③

Format   Insert   Options   🗑 Discard   ▷ Send

A   ≡¶   Heading 1   ∨   ↺ Undo

From: trapperjohn2000@hotmail.com

To: Michael Miller;   👤 Cc & Bcc

RE: Free for lunch?

My name is Michael Miller and this is my signature

**From:** Michael Miller
**Sent:** Saturday, October 21, 2017 12:49 PM
**To:** Michael Miller
**Subject:** Free for lunch?

Hey, are you free for lunch on Wednesday? I could meet you at noon at Carbones, be good to catch up on things. Let me know!

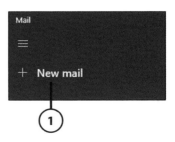

Mail

≡

+ New mail

①

( **2** ) Click within the To field and begin entering the name or email address of the message's recipient.

( **3** ) If the name you type matches any in your contact list, Mail displays those names; select the person you want to email. (If there are no matches, continue entering the person's email address manually.)

( **4** ) Click the Subject field and type a subject for this message.

( **5** ) Click within the main body of the message area and type your message.

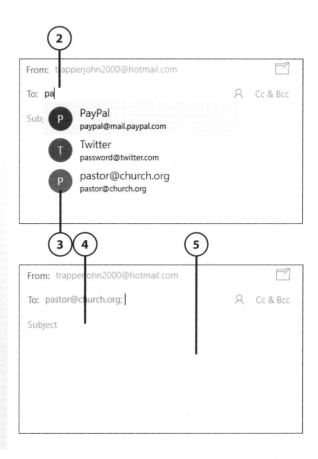

### Formatting Your Message

Click the Format tab to apply Font, Bold, Italic, and other formatting to your message text.

> ### >>>Go Further
> ## COPYING OTHER RECIPIENTS
>
> You can also send carbon copies (Cc) and "blind" carbon copies (Bcc) to additional recipients. Just click Cc & Bcc at the right of the To field to display the Cc and Bcc fields; then enter the appropriate email addresses.
>
> A Bcc differs from a Cc in that the additional recipients remain invisible to the other recipients. Use Cc when you want everyone to see everybody else; use Bcc when you want to keep other recipients private.

(6) To send a file, such as a digital photo, along with this message, click the Insert tab, click Files, and then select the file.

(7) Click Send to send the message and its attachment.

## It's Not All Good

### Don't Insert Picture

The Insert tab includes an option to insert a picture (the Pictures button). In spite of the compelling name, do *not* use this option to insert a picture. This option places the picture, full-size, in line with the text in your document. This is confusing for recipients, makes it difficult to view the picture and read the accompanying text, and also makes it more difficult for recipients to download the picture if they want. The better approach is to use the Attach Files option, which attaches the picture as a file to your message.

### Large Files

Be careful when sending extra-large files (2MB or more) via email. Files of this size, such as large digital photos or home videos, can take a long time to upload—and just as long for the recipient to download when received.

## Move a Message to Another Folder

New messages are stored in the Mail app's Inbox, which is actually a folder. Mail uses other folders, too; there are folders for Outbox (messages waiting to be sent), Drafts, Junk (spam), Sent, Stored Messages, and Trash. For better organization, you can easily move messages from one folder to another.

( 1 ) From within the messages pane, right-click the message you want to move; then click Move. This displays the Move To pane.

( 2 ) Click the destination folder (where you want to move the message). The message is now moved to that folder.

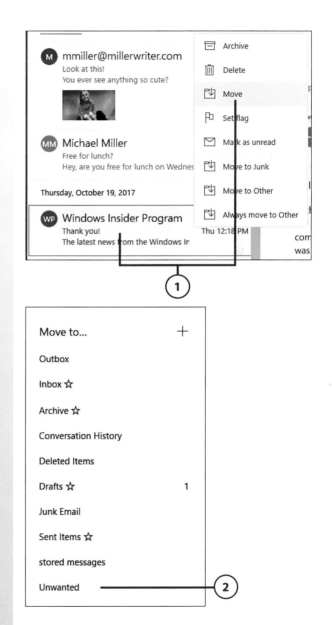

>>>*Go Further*

## ACCESS YOUR EMAIL FROM ANYWHERE

If you have a Microsoft email account (with an **@outlook.com**, **@live.com**, or **@hotmail. com** address) you can check and send email from any computer, smartphone, or tablet, even when you're at work or away from home. All you have to do is use your device's web browser to go to the Outlook website at **www.outlook.com**.

From the site's main page, click Sign In and then enter your email address and password. You'll see all the messages in your inbox and other folders. As in the Mail app, click a message header to view the message contents, and click New Message to create and send a new message. You can sign in from anywhere!

# Using Gmail

In addition to the email account you were given when you signed up for your home Internet service, you can add other email accounts you might have with various web-based email services. These services, such as Gmail and Yahoo! Mail, let you send and receive email from any computer connected to the Internet, via your web browser. They're ideal if you travel a lot or maintain two homes in different locations. (Snowbirds rejoice!!)

## Receive and Reply to Messages

Google's Gmail is the most popular web-based email service today. You can use any web browser to access your Gmail account, and send and receive email from any connected computer, tablet, or smartphone.

To sign up for a new account (it's free), use your web browser to go to mail. google.com, where you can set up a new account with an email address and a password. You can then send and receive email from any computer, just by signing in to your Google Account.

1. Gmail organizes your email into types, each with its own tab: Primary, Social (messages from Facebook, Google+, and similar social networks), and Promotions (advertising messages). Most of your messages will be the Primary tab, so click that or another tab you want to view.

2. Click the Inbox link to display all incoming messages.

3. Click the header for the message you want to view.

4. To download an attached folder or file, mouse over the item and then click the Download or Save to Drive icon. (Save to Drive saves the file to Google Drive, Google's online storage service.)

5. To reply to an open message, click Reply.

6. Enter your reply text in the message window.

7. Click Send when done.

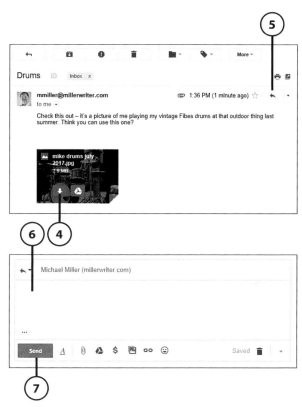

## Send a New Message

New messages you send are composed in a New Message pane that appears at the bottom-right corner of the Gmail window.

1. Click Compose from any Gmail page to display the New Message pane.

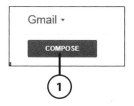

( 2 ) Enter the email address of the recipient(s) in the To box. (Google might offer some suggestions, based on your contacts list and previous activity; click a name to select it.)

( 3 ) Enter a subject in the Subject box.

( 4 ) Move your cursor to the main message area and type your message.

( 5 ) To attach a file to a message, click the Attach Files (paper clip) icon, navigate to and select the file you want to attach, and then click the Open button.

( 6 ) Send the message by clicking the Send button.

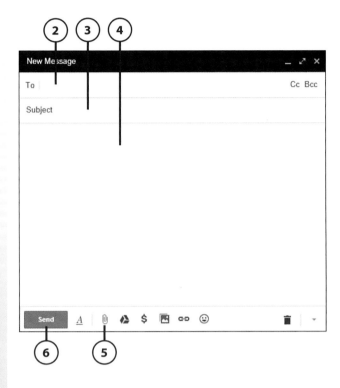

## Managing Your Contacts with the People App

The people you email regularly are known as *contacts*. When someone is in your contacts list, it's easy to send her an email; all you have to do is pick her name from the list instead of entering her email address manually.

In Windows 10, all your contacts are managed from the People app. This app connects to the Microsoft account you used to create your Windows account so that all the contacts from your main email account are automatically added. It can also connect to your other email accounts, including Gmail and Outlook.com. The People app serves as the central hub for everyone you interact with online.

### First-Time Use

The first time you launch the People app, you're prompted to add your Microsoft Account to the app, and to add your contacts from those accounts as well. Do so by entering your email address and password. You can later add other email accounts to the app.

# View Your Contacts

The People app centralizes all your contacts in one place, and it even combines a person's information from multiple sources. So if a given person is a Facebook friend and is also in your email contacts list, his Facebook information and his email address appear in the People app. Launch the People app from the Windows Start menu.

## Expand the Window

By the default, the People app appears in a narrow window that displays only a single pane of information—initially, your contacts list. It's more useful to display two panes in the app, so that you can view the contacts list and the selected contact at the same time. Use your mouse to manually widen the window until both panes are displayed, or just click the Maximize button to display the window full-screen.

1. Click a person's name to view that person's contact information.

2. Click the person's email address to send this person an email in the Windows Mail app.

3. Click Map to view where this person lives.

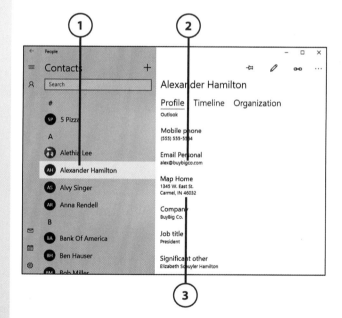

## Add a New Contact

When you find someone you know online, you can add that person as a contact in the People app.

**1** Click the + to display the New Contact pane.

**2** If you have more than one email account connected to the People app, pull down the Save To and select which account you want to use to send email to this person.

**3** Enter the person's full name into the Name box.

**4** Optionally, enter the person's mobile phone number into the Mobile Phone box.

**5** Optionally, enter the person's email address into the Personal Email box.

**6** To include additional email addresses, phone numbers, street addresses, or other information for this person, click + Email, + Phone, + Address, or + Other and enter the necessary information.

**7** Click Save when done.

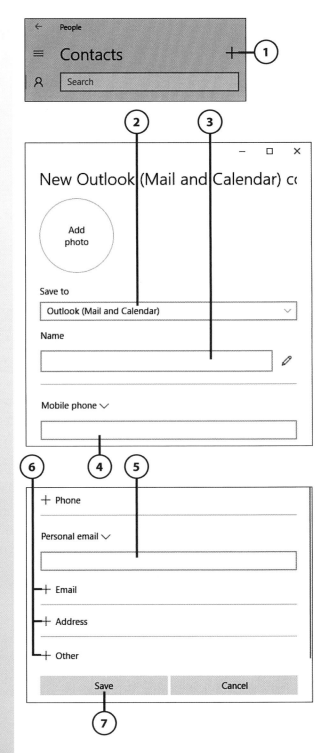

# >>>Go Further

## OPTIONAL AND ADDITIONAL INFORMATION

Many of the fields available when you create a new contact are optional. For example, you don't have to enter a person's company information if you don't want to.

You can also add more information than is first apparent. For example, you can enter additional phone numbers (for work, home, mobile, and the like) by clicking the + under the Phone box. It's the same thing if you want to enter additional email addresses, street addresses, companies, and other information; just click the appropriate + sign and enter the necessary information.

## Use My People

The Windows 10 Fall Creators Update adds a new tool for managing your contacts. My People lets you add icons for your favorite contacts to the Windows taskbar; you can then message those people directly from the taskbar.

( 1 ) Click the People icon in the taskbar's notification area to open the My People pane.

( 2 ) Select the People tab to view suggested favorites.

( 3 ) Click the Apps tab to open the People, Mail, or Skype apps.

( 4 ) Click Find and Pin Contacts to display all your contacts.

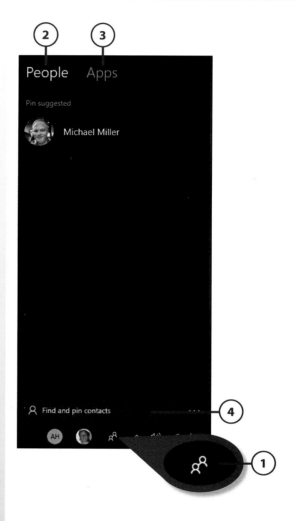

(5) Click the contact you want to add to your taskbar.

(6) Click a person's icon on the taskbar to view the My People pane for that individual.

(7) Click People to view that person's contact and other information.

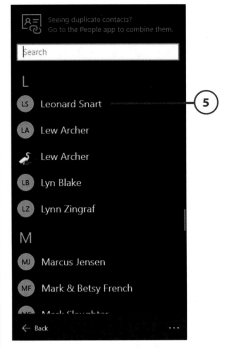

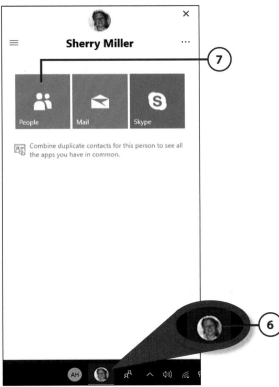

**8** Click the back arrow to return to this person's My People pane.

**9** Click Mail to send that person an email.

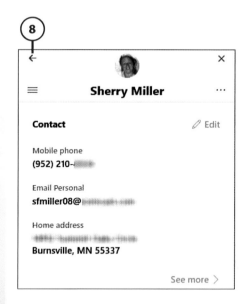

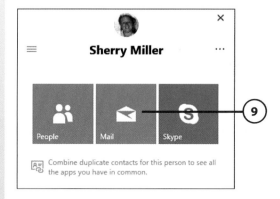

**10** Previous email messages are displayed here. Click a message to read it.

**11** Click the + to create and send a new email message.

**12** Your email address and those of the recipient are already filled in.

**13** Enter the subject of the message.

**14** Type the message.

**15** Click the Send icon to send the email.

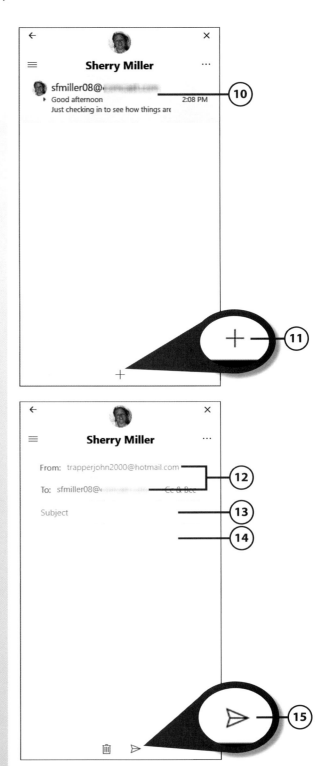

**16** Click Skype to initiate a Skype conversation with that person.

**17** Enter a text message into the field at the bottom of the Skype pane. *Or…*

**18** Click the Phone icon to initiate a voice call. *Or…*

**19** Click the Video icon to initiate a video call.

**20** Click the X to close the My People pane for this person.

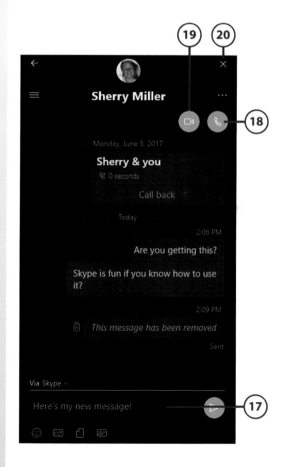

Skype app

Person you're talking to

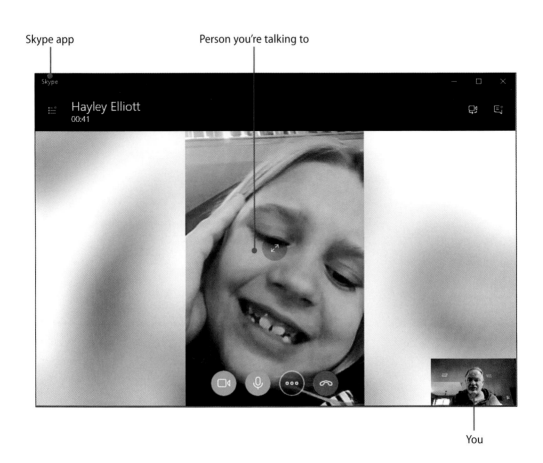

Hayley Elliott
00:41

You

In this chapter, you discover how to use Skype to talk one-on-one with friends and family members, and how to send and receive text messages on your computer.

→ Using the Skype App
→ Communicating with Skype
→ Sending and Receiving Text Messages on Your PC

# Video Calling and Text Messaging

Your Windows 10 computer is a versatile communications device. Not only can you use your PC to send and receive emails, as you learned in the previous chapter, you can also use your computer to make voice and video calls to other computer users—and send and receive text messages via your mobile phone.

## Using the Skype App

You may often find yourself far away from the people you love. Just because you're far away, however, doesn't mean that you can't stay in touch—on a face-to-face basis.

When you want to talk to your family members and other loved ones, Microsoft's Skype service is what you need. Skype lets you participate in text chats, voice calls, and even video calls with friends, family, and co-workers. Use Windows 10's Skype app to do all your communicating—right on your computer!

## Choose Your Service

Skype is a service that enables subscribers to connect with one another over the Internet, in real time. You can use Skype to conduct one-on-one text chats, audio conversations, and video chats.

Before you use Skype, you need to either create a new Skype account or sign in with your existing Microsoft account. The basic Skype service is free and lets you make one-on-one voice and video calls to other Skype users. To call non-Skype landline and cell phones, you can choose to pay 2.3 cents per minute, or subscribe to the North American Unlimited plan to get unlimited calling for $6.99/month. (Rates and plans are higher for calls outside of North America.)

### Skype and Microsoft

Formerly an independent company, Skype was acquired by eBay in 2005 and then by Microsoft in 2011. Skype currently has more than 650 million users worldwide.

## Get to Know the Skype App

To use Skype to communicate with others, you can use Skype's traditional desktop application (available from www.skype.com) or the Skype app included with Windows 10. This chapter focuses on the Windows 10 Skype app.

You launch the Skype app from the Windows Start menu. Just click Start and then click Skype.

## Add a Contact

Before you call someone with Skype, you have to add that person to your Skype contacts list. You can easily add your existing contacts to Skype or find others who are Skype users.

1. From within the Skype app, click the Contacts button to display the Contacts pane.

**( 2 )** Select the Contacts tab. Any contacts you've already added are displayed here.

**( 3 )** To search for a specific person on Skype, enter his or her name into the Search box.

## Bots

In addition to communicating with real people, Skype lets you connect to various virtual robots, or *bots*. Bots can do many useful things, including search for news and play games with you. To view and add bots to your contacts, select the Bots tab in the Contacts pane.

**( 4 )** Skype displays people who match your query in both your local address book and publicly on Skype.

**( 5 )** Click the name of the person you want to contact. A new message to this person open.

**( 6 )** Type a message to this person.

**( 7 )** Click Send. The person you selected now receives a request to become your Skype contact. If he accepts your request, you'll be added to each other's contact lists.

## Accepting Contact Requests

Just as you can request someone to be your contact, other people can send contact requests to you. You have the option of accepting or declining any such request. Make sure it's someone you know before you accept.

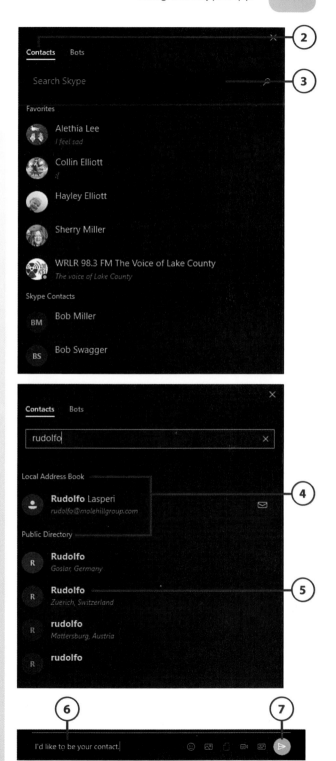

# Communicating with Skype

The whole point of Skype is to let you talk to friends and family. You can use the Skype app to make voice-only calls or to make video calls—which are great for seeing your loved ones, face to face. Or, if you prefer texting, you can use Skype to conduct text-based chats. How you communicate is totally up to you.

## Make a Video Call

To conduct a video call, both you and the person you want to talk to must have webcams built in to or connected to your PCs. In addition, you both must be connected to the Internet for the duration of the call.

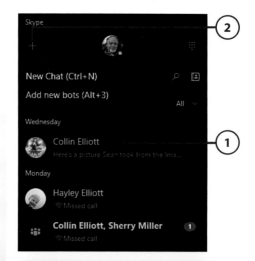

( 1 ) The main screen of the Skype app displays your recent video, audio, and text conversations in the left panel. To resume a previous conversation, click the person's name.

( 2 ) Click the New (+) button and select New Chat to start a new conversation. This displays the New Conversation pane.

( 3 ) Click to select the person you want to chat with, or enter that person's name into the Type a Name box.

( 4 ) Click the Start button. You now see a text conversation with this person.

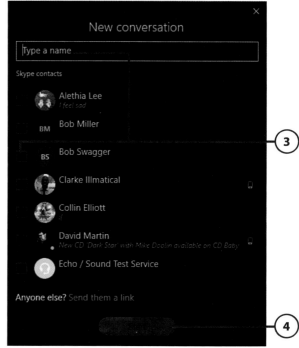

**5** Click the Video Call (camera) icon.

**6** Skype now calls this person. When she answers the call, her live picture appears in the main part of the screen. (Your live picture appears smaller, in the lower-right corner.) Start talking!

**7** When you're done talking, mouse over the screen to display the control buttons then click the red "hang up" button to end the call.

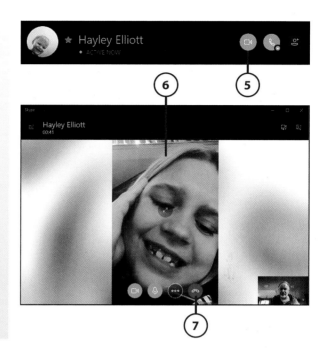

# >>>Go Further
## WEBCAMS

Most notebook PCs have webcams built in. You can use your notebook's built-in webcam to make video calls with Skype. Because the webcam includes a built-in microphone, you can also use it to make voice calls.

If your PC doesn't have a built-in webcam, you can purchase and connect an external webcam to make Skype video calls. Webcams are manufactured and sold by Logitech and other companies, and they connect to your PC via USB. They're inexpensive (as low as $30 or so) and sit on top of your monitor. After you've connected it, just smile into the webcam and start talking.

## Make a Voice Call

If you don't have a webcam attached to your computer, or if you'd rather talk to a person without seeing him, you can use Skype to make a voice call. To do this, you both need microphones and speakers attached to your PC, or you can use a USB headset with a built-in microphone.

(1) Start a new or reopen an existing conversation, as described in the previous task.

(2) Click the Call (phone) icon (NOT the Video Call icon).

(3) When the other person answers the call, you're ready to start talking.

(4) Click the red "hang up" button to end the call.

## Conduct a Text Chat

If you'd rather just text message a friend, Skype is good for that, too.

(1) Start a new or reopen an existing conversation, as described in the previous task.

(2) Type your message into the Type a Message field at the bottom of the conversation pane.

(3) Click the smiley face icon to insert emoji.

(4) Click the picture icon to insert a picture.

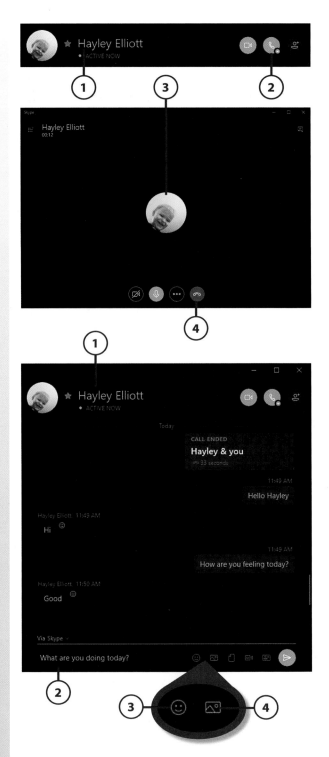

5. Click the Send icon to send your message.

6. Your message and the other person's responses are displayed one after another in the conversation pane.

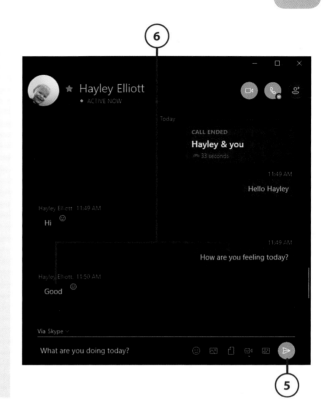

# Sending and Receiving Text Messages on Your PC

The Fall Creators Update for Windows 10 adds a very nifty and useful feature. You can now synchronize your personal computer to your cell phone and send and receive text messages from your PC. (And it's a lot easier to type texts on your big computer keyboard than it is on the tiny one on your smartphone!)

## Link Your Phone to Your PC

For your phone and computer to share text messages and other data, you first have to install Microsoft's Cortana app on your phone. (Windows uses the Cortana utility to manage the exchange of messages and information.) You can find the Cortana app in your phone's app store; it's free.

Once you've installed the Cortana app on your phone, you need to link your Windows 10 computer with your phone. You do this by configuring both your computer and the Cortana app on your phone. (The following instructions are for the Android version of the Cortana app; the iPhone version is similar but slightly different.)

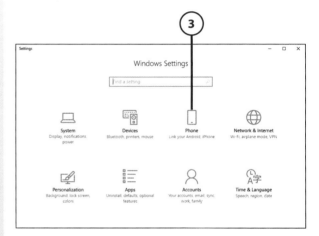

( 1 ) On your computer, click the Notifications icon on the taskbar to open the Action Center.

( 2 ) Click All Settings to display the Settings tool.

( 3 ) Click Phone.

( 4 ) Any phones you've previously linked are listed here. To link a new phone, click Add a Phone.

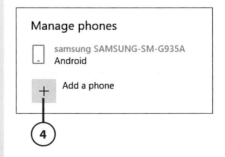

**5** When prompted, enter your phone number.

**6** Click Send.

**7** Microsoft sends a text to your phone. Tap the link in this text to display the Microsoft Cortana app in your phone's app store.

**8** Tap Install to download and install the Microsoft Cortana app on your phone.

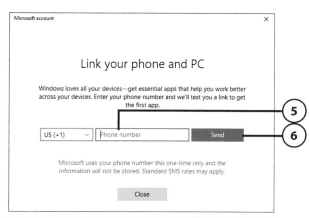

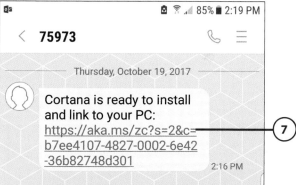

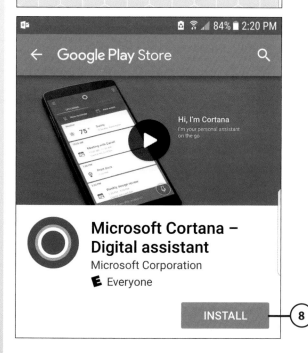

**9** Open the Cortana app on your phone.

**10** When you see the sign in screen, tap to select your Windows account. (If your account is not listed, tap Add an Account and follow the onscreen instructions.)

**11** When you're prompted to allow Cortana to access your phone's location, tap Allow.

**12** When you're prompted to allow Cortana to access media files on your phone, tap Allow.

**13** When you're prompted to allow Cortana to access your calendar, tap Allow.

**9**

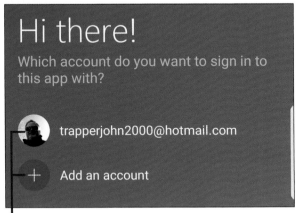

# Hi there!

Which account do you want to sign in to this app with?

trapperjohn2000@hotmail.com

+ Add an account

**10**

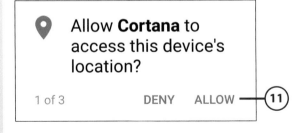

Allow **Cortana** to access this device's location?

1 of 3 · DENY · ALLOW — **11**

Allow **Cortana** to access photos, media, and files on your device?

2 of 3 · DENY · ALLOW — **12**

Allow **Cortana** to access your calendar?

3 of 3 · DENY · ALLOW — **13**

**14** You're now prompted to add Cortana to your phone's lock screen. You don't have to do this; tap either Add Cortana to My Lock Screen or No, Thanks.

**15** You're prompted to use Cortana as your phone's default assistant. You don't have to if you don't want to; this doesn't affect the linking to your computer. (For example, if you have an iPhone you might prefer to continue using the Siri assistant.) Tap either Add Cortana as Default Assistant or No, Thanks.

**16** From the home screen of the Cortana app, tap the Menu (three-line) icon to open the Menu pane.

**17** Tap Settings to display the Settings screen.

**18** Tap Cross Device.

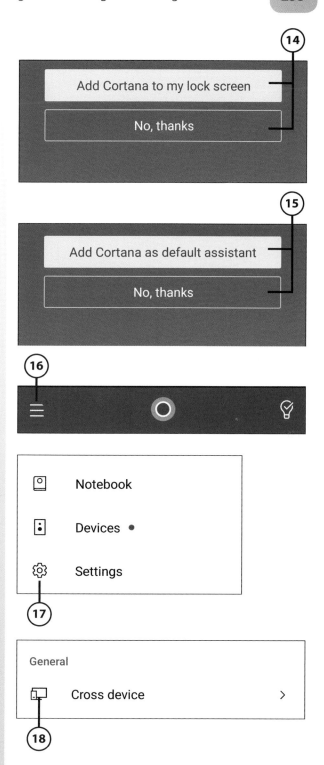

**19** The first time you access the Cross Device screen you're prompted to let Cortana make and manage phone calls. Tap Allow.

**20** You're asked to allow Cortana to access your phone's contacts. Tap Allow.

**21** You're asked to allow Cortana to send and view text (SMS) messages. Tap Allow.

**22** Change any of these settings by tapping "on" or "off" those notifications you want to receive on your PC—Missed Call Notifications, Incoming Message Notifications, Low Battery Notifications, and/or App Notifications Sync. Make sure that Incoming Message Notifications is turned on; you need this to send and receive texts on your computer.

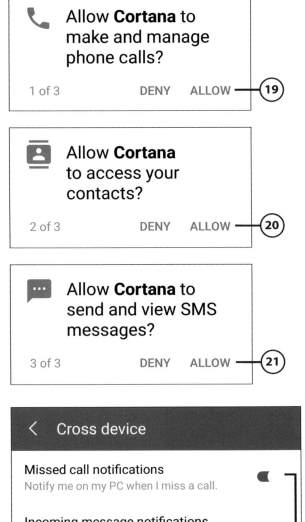

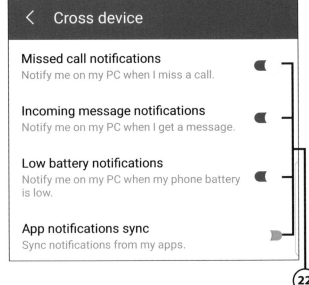

## Receive Texts on Your PC

Once the Cortana app on your phone is linked to your Windows 10 computer, you will receive all the texts you receive on your phone in Windows 10. New texts appear as notifications on the right side of the desktop and within the Action Center.

**1** If you see an alert notification for this text, type your reply into the Reply box.

**2** Click the Send arrow.

**3** To view other texts, click the Notifications icon on the taskbar to open the Action Center.

**4** Recently received texts are displayed here.

**5** To remove a text from the Action Center, click Dismiss.

**6** Enter a reply to a text within the Reply box.

**7** Click the Send arrow to send the text.

## Send New Texts from Your PC

You use Cortana to send new SMS text messages from your computer.

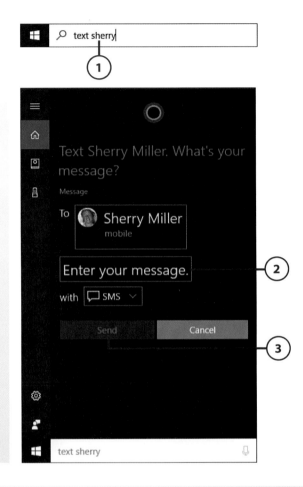

1. Click within the Type Here to Search box in the taskbar and enter **text [name]**. Replace [name] with the name of someone in your contacts list. For example, to text John Brown, enter **text john brown**.

2. Enter the text of your message in the Cortana panel.

3. Tap Send.

Facebook

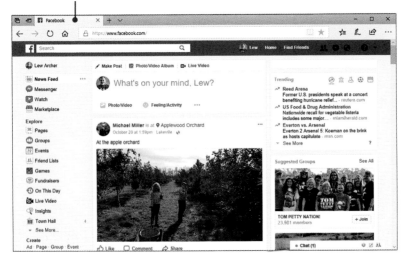

Pinterest

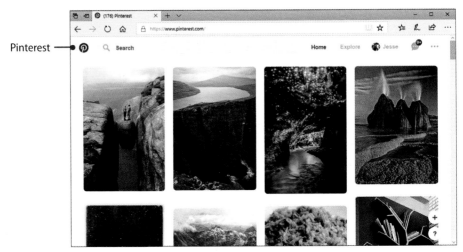

In this chapter, you find out how to use
Facebook and other social networks to connect
with friends and family.

→ Sharing with Friends and Family on Facebook
→ Pinning Items of Interest to Pinterest

18

# Connecting with Facebook and Pinterest

When you want to keep track of what friends and family are up to and
keep them up to date on your activities, there's no better place to do it
than Facebook. Facebook is a *social network*, which is a website that lets
you easily share your activities with people you know. Write one post,
and it's seen by hundreds of your online "friends." It's the easiest way I
know to connect with almost everyone you know.

Facebook isn't the only social network on the Internet, however. Other
social media, such as Pinterest and Twitter, target particular types of
users. You might find yourself using social media other than Facebook to
keep in touch with friends and family.

## Sharing with Friends and Family on Facebook

A social network is a website community that enables users to connect
with and share their thoughts and activities with one another. Think

of it as an online network of friends and family, including former schoolmates, coworkers, and neighbors.

The largest and most popular social network today is Facebook, with more than 2 billion active users worldwide each month. Although Facebook started life as a social network for college students, it has since expanded its membership lists, and it is now the preferred social network for more mature users. (In fact, the fastest growing segment of Facebook users are those aged 45 and older.)

## Sign Up for Facebook

To use Facebook, you have to sign up for an account and enter some personal information. Fortunately, signing up for an account is both easy and free.

**1** Launch your web browser and go to the Facebook home page at www.facebook.com.

**2** If you already have a Facebook account and have recently accessed the site on this computer, click your name or picture.

**3** If you have a Facebook account but haven't accessed it on this computer, enter your email address and password, and then click the Log In button.

**4** If you're new to Facebook, go to the Create a New Account section and enter your first and last name into the First Name and Last Name boxes.

**5** Enter your email address or mobile phone number into the Mobile Number or Email box.

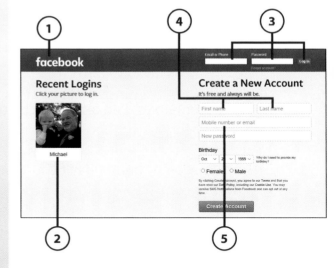

**6** Enter your desired password into the New Password box.

**7** Use the Birthday controls to enter your month, day, and year of birth.

**8** Check your gender (Female or Male).

**9** Click the Create Account button. If you signed up with your email address, Facebook sends you an email message asking you to confirm your new Facebook account; when you receive this email, click the link to proceed. If you signed up with your phone number, you get a text message with a Facebook code; enter this code on the log-in page to confirm your account.

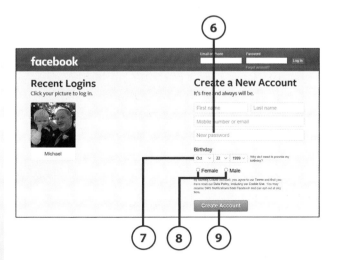

## Additional Information

After you've created your Facebook account, you're prompted to enter additional personal information and then search for friends. You can do both of these things now or later, as you want.

# Discover New—and Old—Friends on Facebook

To connect with someone on Facebook, you must become mutual *friends*. A Facebook friend can be a real friend, or a family member, colleague, acquaintance, you name it. When you add someone to your Facebook friends list, he sees everything you post—and you see everything he posts.

The easiest way to find friends on Facebook is to let Facebook find them for you—based on the information you provided for your personal profile. The more Facebook knows about you, especially in terms of where you've worked and gone to school, the more friends it can find.

( 1 ) Log in to your Facebook account and click the Friend Requests button on the Facebook toolbar.

( 2 ) The pull-down menu lists any friend requests you've received, and offers a number of friend suggestions from Facebook ("People You May Know"). To add one of these people to your friends list, click the Yes button.

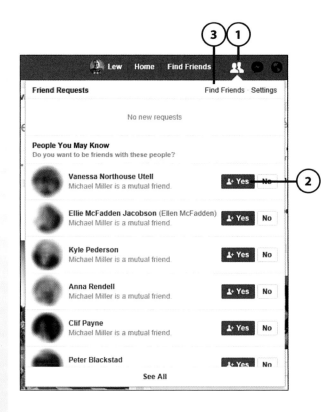

## Suggested Friends

The people Facebook suggests as friends are typically people who went to the same schools you did, worked at the same companies you did, or are friends of your current friends.

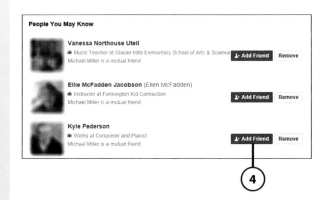

( 3 ) To continue searching for friends, click Find Friends at the top of the menu to display your Friends page.

( 4 ) Scroll down the page to view other suggested friends from Facebook in the People You May Know section. Click the Add Friend button for any person you'd like to add as a friend.

**( 5 )** To find people in your email contacts list who are also members of Facebook, go to the Add Personal Contacts section at the top of the Friends page. Click the email service you use, enter any requested information (typically your email address and password), and then click the Find Friends button.

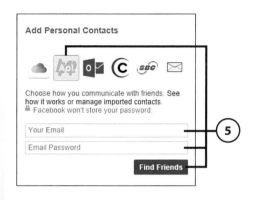

**( 6 )** To search directly for any old friends who might be on Facebook, go to the Search for Friends section and enter a person's name into the Name box.

**( 7 )** Fine-tune your search by using the controls in the Search for Friends section. For example, you can filter the results by current city, hometown, and school.

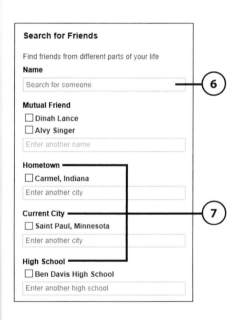

**( 8 )** The results of your search appear in the People You May Know section. If your friend is listed, click the Add Friend button to send him a friend request.

## Friend Requests

Facebook doesn't automatically add a person to your friends list. Instead, that person receives an invitation to be your friend; she can accept or reject the invitation. To accept or reject any friend requests you've received, click the Friend Request button on the Facebook toolbar. (And don't worry; if you reject a request, that person won't be notified.)

## >>>Go Further

### HOW MANY FRIENDS?

By the time you get to our age you've made the acquaintance of thousands of people through school, work, neighborhood activities, and the like—not to mention all the many members of your immediate and extended family. Do you really want to keep in touch with all these people via Facebook?

The answer is probably "no." Sure, there are some folks you're close to and want to stay close to, but there are others who you didn't like that much way back then, and probably won't like any better today. The reality is that you don't have to make everyone you've ever known a Facebook friend; you don't even have to put every member of your family on your friends list.

Facebook is great for getting back in touch with all the people you've cared about over the years, true friends and trusted family members. Not every acquaintance you've ever made falls into that category. So don't get carried away with adding more names to your Facebook friends list; the more "friends" you have, the more updates you have to keep track of in your News Feed. Too many friends can be overwhelming.

In particular, you might want to avoid having Facebook cull through your email contacts list for possible friends. Just because you've sent a few emails to someone in the past doesn't mean you want to be informed of all her thoughts and activities every blasted day on Facebook. Be proactive about making friends on Facebook, and choose only those you want to hear from on a regular basis.

## Post a Status Update

To let your family and friends know what you've been up to, you need to post what Facebook calls a status update. Every status update you make is broadcast to everyone on your friends list, displayed in the News Feed on their home pages. A basic status update is text only, but you can also include photos, videos, and links to other web pages in your posts.

① Click Home on the Facebook tool-bar to return to your home page.

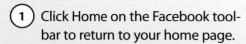

( 2 ) Click within the Status box at the top of the page. The box expands to offer more options.

( 3 ) Type within the box to enter your message.

( 4 ) If you're with someone else and want to mention them in the post, click Tag Friends and enter that person's name.

( 5 ) If you want to include your current location in your post, click Check In and select a place from the suggested list or enter the city or place where you are.

( 6 ) To include a picture or video with your post, click Photo/Video to display the Open dialog box; then select the photos or videos to include.

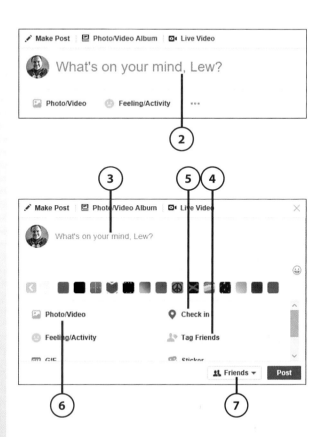

## Sharing Photos

Facebook has become the Web's most popular site for sharing photos. To learn more about photo sharing on Facebook, see Chapter 19, "Storing and Sharing Your Pictures and Movies."

( 7 ) To determine who can read this post, click the Privacy button and make a selection.

## Who Sees Your Posts?

You can opt to make any post Public (meaning anyone can read it), visible only to your Friends, visible only to yourself (Only Me), or Custom (you select individuals who can and can't view it).

**8** To include a link to another web page, enter that page's URL in your status update.

**9** Facebook should recognize the link and display an image from that page.

**10** When you're ready to post your update, click the Post button.

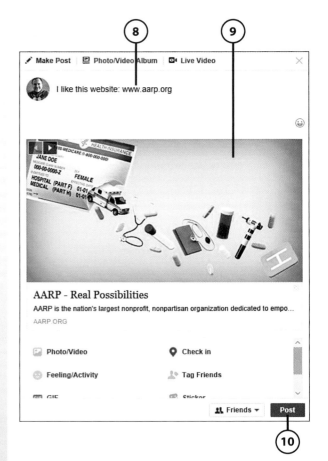

## Find Out What Your Friends Are Up To

Your home page on Facebook displays a News Feed of status updates made by people on your friends list. The newest and/or most popular posts are at the top; scroll down through the list to read older posts.

**1** Click Home on the Facebook toolbar to return to your home page.

**2** Your friends' posts are displayed in the News Feed in the middle of the page. To leave your own comments about a post, click Comment and then enter your text into the resulting text box.

**3** To "like" a post, click Like.

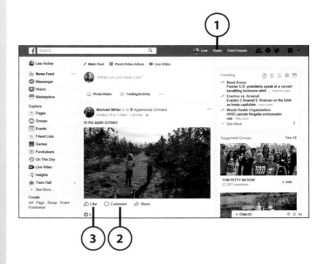

**4** If a post includes a link to another web page, that link appears beneath the post, along with a brief description of the page. Click the link to open the other page in your web browser.

**5** If a post includes one or more photos, click the photo to view it in a larger onscreen lightbox.

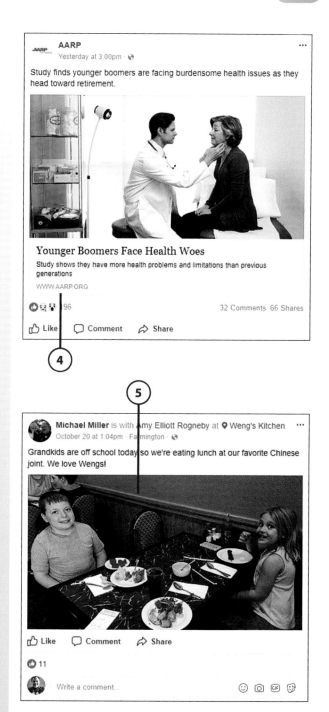

**6** If a post includes a video, playback should start automatically. (If not, click the Play button.) Click the volume control to unmute the sound.

**7** Click the Pause button to pause the video; the button turns into a Play button. Click the Play button to resume playback.

# Explore Your Friends' Profiles

If you want to know what an old friend has been up to, you can do so by visiting that person's Facebook profile page. This page includes personal information about a member, a "timeline" of that person's posts and major life events, and all the photos and videos that person has posted.

**1** Click a person's name anywhere on the Facebook site to display his or her profile page.

**2** View key personal information by clicking About.

**3** View a list of this person's friends by clicking Friends.

**4** View your friend's photos by clicking Photos.

**5** View a person's status updates in reverse chronological order (newest first) in the right-hand column on the Timeline.

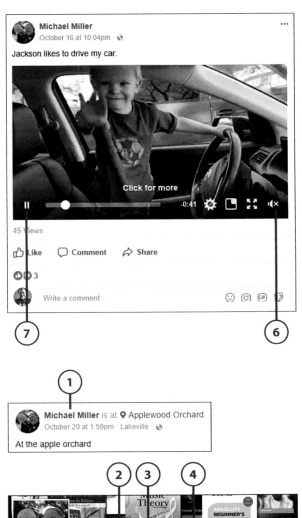

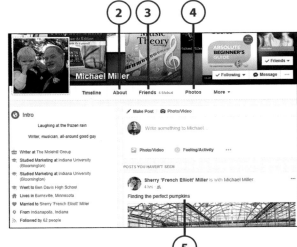

# Pinning Items of Interest to Pinterest

Facebook isn't the only social network that might be of interest to you. Pinterest (www.pinterest.com) is a newer social network with particular appeal to middle-aged and older women—although there is a growing number of male users, too.

Unlike Facebook, which lets you post text-based status updates, Pinterest is all about images. The site consists of a collection of virtual online "boards" that people use to share pictures they find interesting. Users save or "pin" photos and other images to their personal boards, and then they share their pins with online friends.

You can pin images of anything—clothing, furniture, recipes, do-it-yourself projects, and the like. Your Pinterest friends can then "repin" your images to their boards—and on and on.

## Joining Pinterest

Like other social media sites, Pinterest is free to join and use. You can join with your email address or by using your Facebook account login.

## Create a New Board

Pinterest lets you create any number of boards, each dedicated to specific topics. If you're into quilting, you can create a Quilting board; if you're into radio-controlled airplanes, you can create an RC Airplanes board with pictures of your favorite craft.

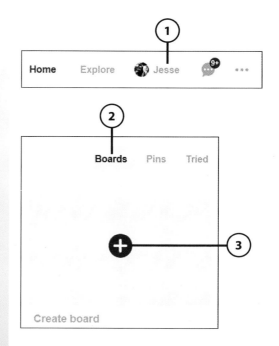

1. From the top-right corner of the Pinterest home page (www.pinterest.com), click your picture or profile icon to display your profile page.

2. Click Boards to select the Boards tab.

3. Click Create Board (+) to display the Create Board panel.

**4** Enter the name for this board into the Name box.

**5** Click the Create button.

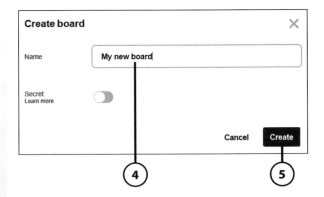

## Find and Save Interesting Items

Some people say that Pinterest is a little like a refrigerator covered with magnets holding up tons of photos and drawings. You can find lots of interesting items pinned from other users—and then save them to your own personal boards.

**1** Enter the name of something you're interested in into the Search box at the top of any Pinterest page and then press Enter. Pinterest displays pins that match your query.

**2** Mouse over the item you want to save and click the Save button. The Choose Board panel displays.

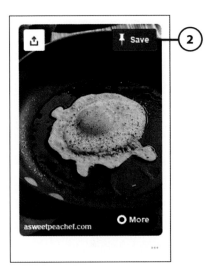

**3** Accept the existing description or click the pencil icon to add your own in the Description box.

**4** Click the board you want to pin to. This pins the item to that board.

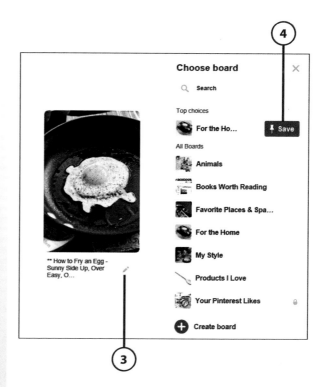

## Save an Item from a Web Page

You can also pin images you find on nearly any web page. It's as easy as copying and pasting the page's web address.

**1** From Pinterest's main page, click the + button in the lower-right corner.

**2** Click Save from a Website.

**3** Enter the web address (URL) of the page you want to pin.

**4** Click the Next button.

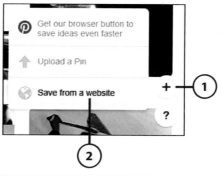

(5) Pinterest displays all images found on the selected web page. Mouse over the image you want to pin and click the Save button to open the Choose Board panel.

(6) Accept the current item description or click the pencil icon to enter your own description into the Description box.

(7) Click the board to which you want to pin this image. The item is now pinned to that board.

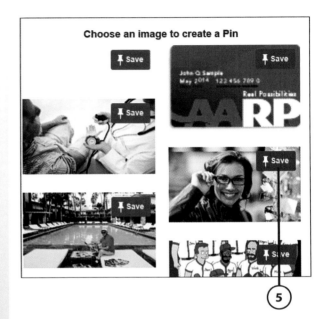

## Pin It Button

Pinning a page is even easier if the page displays its own Pin It button. Just click the button, select an image from the page, and you're good to go.

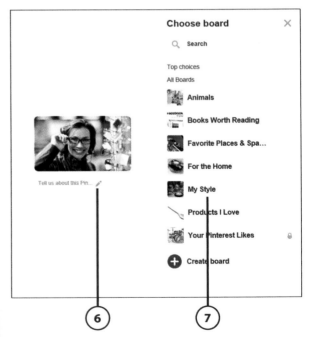

# >>>Go Further

## SAVE A PAGE FROM YOUR WEB BROWSER

It's even easier to pin an image from a web page if you install Pinterest's Browser Button in your web browser. When you click the + button and then select Pin from a Website, you see a link to get the Pinterest Browser Button. Click this link and you're taken to a page that describes the button. Click the Get Our Browser Button button, and the button will be installed in your web browser—typically in the toolbar or next to the Address box.

When you next visit a web page that you'd like to pin from, click the Pinterest button in your browser. You'll see images from this web page; click the Pin It button for the image you want to pin and proceed from there.

## Find People to Follow

When you find someone who posts a lot of things you're interested in, you can follow that person on Pinterest. Following a person means that all of that person's new pins display on your Pinterest home page.

( **1** ) When you find a pin you like, click the name of the person who pinned it to see that person's personal page.

( **2** ) On the person's page, click Boards to see all of her boards.

( **3** ) Click the Follow button at the top of the page to follow all of this person's boards.

( **4** ) Alternatively, if you only want to follow pins for some of this person's boards, click the Follow buttons for the boards you want to follow.

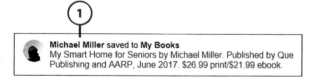

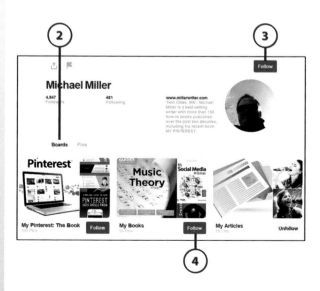

## >>>Go Further
## OTHER POPULAR SOCIAL MEDIA

Facebook and Pinterest are the two most popular social networks, but they aren't the only social networks out there. Other social media networks cater to different demographic groups—and might be worth considering if you want to connect to younger friends or family members.

The most popular of these other social networks are LinkedIn (www.linkedin.com), which targets business professionals and is good for business networking and job hunting, and Twitter (www.twitter.com), the social medium of choice for twenty- and thirty-somethings—and, most recently, politicians and celebrities.

All these social networks are free to use, and work in much the same fashion as does Facebook.

Windows Photos app

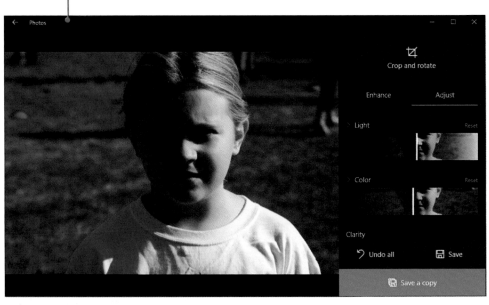

In this chapter, you find out how to transfer photos from your digital camera to your Windows PC, how to edit those photos, and how to share them online with friends and family.

→ Using Your Smartphone or Digital Camera with Your Windows PC
→ Viewing Photos and Videos on Your PC
→ Touching Up Your Photos
→ Turning Your Photos into Videos with Story Remix
→ Sharing Your Pictures and Videos Online

19

# Storing and Sharing Your Pictures and Movies

If you're like me, you take a lot of pictures and videos with your digital camera—pictures of places you've been and people you've met—and lots and lots of pictures of your family, especially your kids or grandkids. You need to store those photos someplace, and there's no place better than your Windows PC. What's more, you can use your computer to touch up your photos and share them with friends and family—online, over the Internet.

## Using Your Smartphone or Digital Camera with Your Windows PC

The first step in managing all your digital photos is to transfer those pictures from your digital camera or smartphone to your computer. There are a number of ways to do this.

# Transfer Photos from a Smartphone or Tablet

If you're like me, you take most of your photos with your smartphone or tablet. It's certainly more convenient to whip out your phone or tablet to take a quick picture than it is to lug around a digital camera everywhere you go.

Fortunately, it's easy to transfer photos from any smartphone or tablet to your PC. All you need is the connection cable supplied with your device.

## iCloud Backup

If you have an iPhone or iPad, you can configure your device to use Apple's iCloud online storage service to back up your photos and other data. With your device thus configured, the photos you take will automatically be transferred from your device to your home computer whenever your device is connected to your home Wi-Fi network.

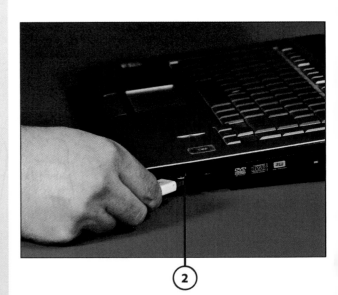

1. Connect one end of the supplied cable to your smartphone or tablet.

2. Connect the other end of the cable to a USB port on your PC.

## iTunes

If you have an iPhone or iPad, when you connect your device to your computer, the iTunes software will probably open automatically. Close it or just ignore it; you don't use iTunes to copy photos and videos.

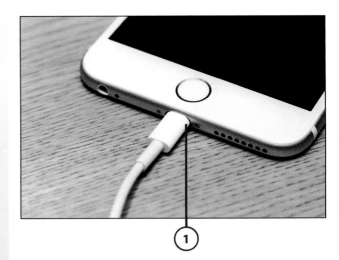

( **3** ) Click File Explorer on the taskbar or Start menu to open File Explorer.

( **4** ) Click the This PC icon in the navigation pane.

( **5** ) Click the icon for your smartphone or tablet, select the main folder (typically labeled DCIM or Pictures), and then select the appropriate subfolder to see your photos.

( **6** ) Hold down the Ctrl key and click each photo you want to transfer.

( **7** ) Select the Home tab, click the Copy To button, and then click Pictures.

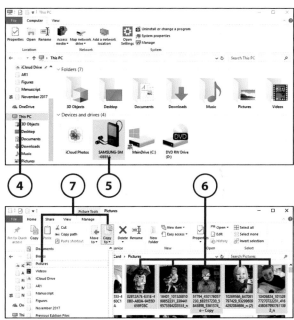

# Transfer Photos from a Memory Card

If you still use a digital camera to take photos, it's equally easy to transfer your pictures from your camera to your computer. The easiest way to do this is to use your camera's memory card.

## Connecting Your Camera Directly

You can also transfer photos by connecting your digital camera to your computer via USB. This is similar to connecting your phone or tablet to your PC; Windows should recognize when your camera is connected and automatically download the pictures in your camera, while displaying a dialog box that notifies you of what it's doing.

( **1** ) Turn off your digital camera and remove the flash memory card.

**(2)** Insert the memory card from your digital camera into the memory card slot on your PC.

## Copying Automatically

Windows might recognize that your memory card contains digital photos and start to download those photos automatically—no manual interaction necessary. Alternatively, you might get prompts from other apps, such as Photoshop Express and Picasa, to download your photos, depending on which programs you have installed on your computer.

**(3)** Click File Explorer on the taskbar or Start menu to open File Explorer.

**(4)** Click This PC in the navigation pane.

**(5)** Click the drive for your memory card reader, select the main folder (typically labeled DCIM), and then select the appropriate subfolder to see your photos.

## Different Folder Names

Some cameras might use a name other than DCIM for the main folder.

**(6)** Hold down the Ctrl key and click each photo you want to transfer.

**(7)** Select the Home tab, click Copy To, and then select Pictures.

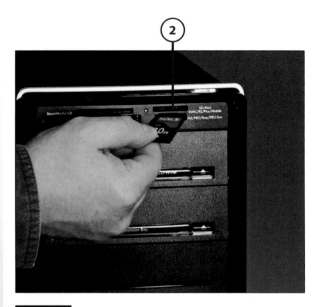

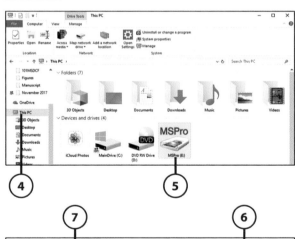

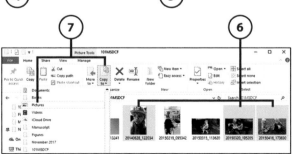

## Delete Your Photos

Once you've copied photos from your smartphone or camera to your computer, you can delete them from your device. If you don't delete them, your phone or camera storage fills up rather quickly. You can delete photos using the menus on your phone or camera, or choose to *move* photos from your device to your computer instead of copy them. (Moving deletes the originals; copying leaves the originals in place.) Just select the Move To option instead of the Copy To option in File Explorer.

# Viewing Photos and Videos on Your PC

Windows includes a built-in Photos app for viewing and editing photos stored on your PC. There's also a Videos app for viewing home movies you shoot with your camcorder or mobile device.

## View Your Photos

The Photos app is the hub for all your photo viewing and editing in Windows. It lets you navigate to and view all the photos stored on your PC. You launch the Photos app from the Start menu.

( 1 ) Within the Photos app, the Collection view is selected by default and photos are grouped by date taken. (To instead display pictures stored in specific folders on your computer's hard drive, click Folders.)

( 2 ) To change the size of the photos displayed, click either View Large, View Medium, or View Small.

( 3 ) To display a single photo large within the Photos app, click it.

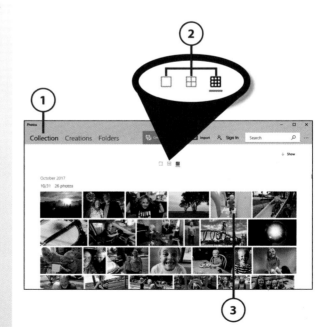

**4** To move to the next picture, click the right arrow on the screen or press the right-arrow key on your keyboard. To return to the previous picture, click the left arrow on the screen or press the left-arrow key your keyboard.

**5** To zoom into or out of the picture, click Zoom and then drag the slider right (to zoom in) or left (to zoom out).

**6** To view a slideshow of the pictures in this folder, starting with the current picture, click See More (three-dot icon) and then select Slideshow.

**7** Click Rotate to rotate the picture 90 degrees clockwise.

**8** Click Delete (or press the Del key on your keyboard) to delete the current picture.

**9** Click the back arrow to return to the previous screen.

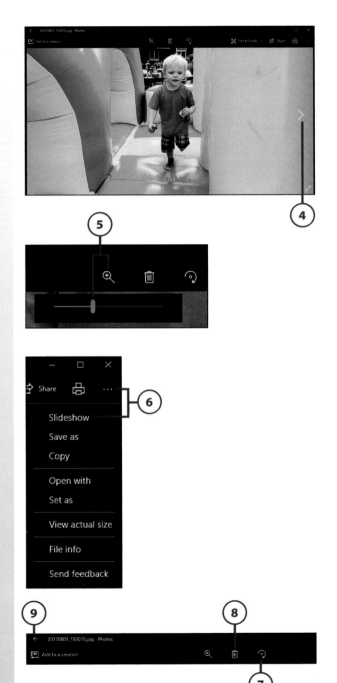

## >>>Go Further

## LOCK SCREEN AND BACKGROUND PICTURE

To use the current picture as the image on the Windows Lock screen, display the photo full screen, click See More, click Set As, and then click Set As Lock Screen. To set this picture as your desktop background, click See More, click Set As, and then click Set As Background.

## Create and View Photo Albums

The Windows 10 Fall Creators Update adds a new feature called *creations*. A creation can be a simple photo album, filled with photos you select, or a short video comprising your selected photos. Let's look first at how to create and view a photo album.

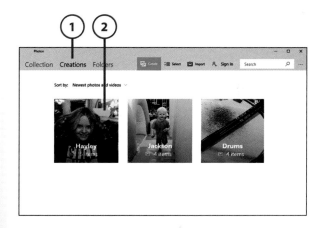

1. From within the Photos app, click Creations to display the Creations view.

2. All of your previously created albums (and Story Remixes— more on these later) are displayed here. Click an album to view the photos within.

3. To create a new album, click Create and then click Album.

4. Click to select the photos you want to include.

5. Click Add.

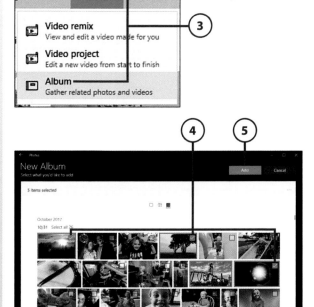

**6** Click "New Album" and type a new title.

**7** Click Done.

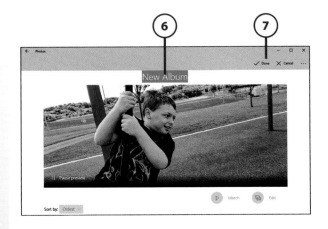

## OneDrive

By default, your photo albums are stored locally on your current PC. If you want your albums to be available to other devices via Microsoft's OneDrive cloud storage service, open an album, scroll to the bottom of the screen, and click Add to OneDrive.

# View Your Videos

To watch the videos you take with your camcorder or mobile device, you use a different app—the Movies & TV app. Launch this app from the Windows Start menu.

**1** From within the Movies & TV app, click the Personal tab.

**2** Navigate to and click the video you want to watch. (Click any folder to view the videos within.)

**3** Playback starts automatically. Mouse over the video to display the playback controls.

**4** Click the Pause button to pause playback; click the button again to resume playback.

**5** Click and drag the scrub (slider) control to move to a specific point within the video.

**6** Click the Fullscreen button to display the video full screen.

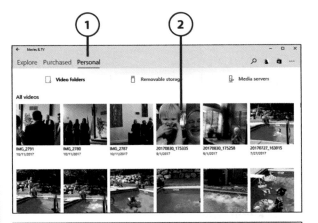

# Touching Up Your Photos

Not all your pictures turn out perfect. Maybe you need to crop a picture to high-light the important area. Maybe you need to brighten a dark picture, or darken a bright one. Or maybe you need to adjust the tint or color saturation.

Fortunately, the Windows Photos app lets you do this sort of basic photo editing. A better-looking photo is only a click or a tap away!

## Automatically Enhance a Photo

When you want to quickly touch up a photo, use the Photos app's Enhance tool. This tool applies a variety of automatic changes that may—or may not—make your picture look better.

1. From within the Photos app, navigate to and display the photo you want to edit.

2. Mouse over the photo to display the toolbar at the top of the screen and then click Edit & Create.

3. Click Edit. This displays your photo in editing view, along with the editing pane on the right.

4. Click the Enhance tab. (This may be selected by default.)

5. Click Enhance Your Photo.

6. The Photos app's automatic enhancement is applied at 50% strength. To decrease the amount of enhancement, click and drag the white line to the left. To increase the amount of enhancement, click and drag the white line to the right.

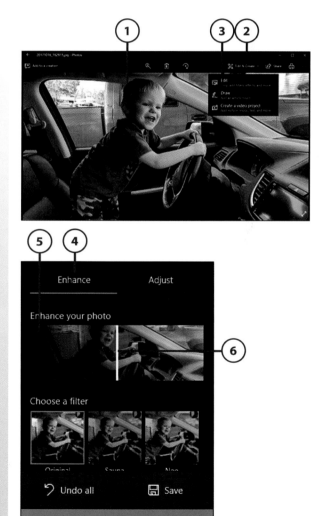

(7) Click Undo All to undo the enhancement.

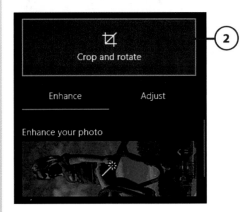

## Rotate a Photo

Is your picture sidewise? To turn a portrait into a landscape, or vice versa, use the Photos app's Rotate tool.

(1) Display the photo you want to edit, click Edit & Create, and then click Edit to enter editing view.

(2) Click Crop & Rotate.

3 Click Rotate to rotate the picture 90 degrees clockwise. Continue clicking to further rotate the picture.

4 To rotate in less than 90-degree increments, click and drag the Straightening control until the picture is in the desired position.

5 When you're done, click Done.

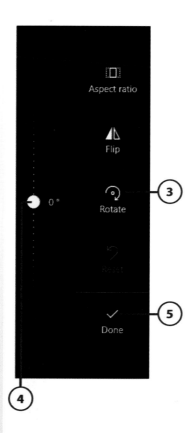

## Crop a Photo

Sometimes you don't get close enough to the subject for the best effect. When you want to zoom in closer, use the Photos app's Crop control to crop out the edges you don't want.

1 From the editing screen, click Crop and Rotate.

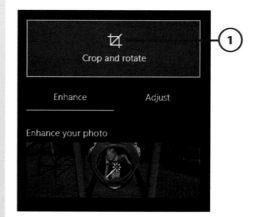

( 2 ) If you want to crop to a specific aspect ratio click Aspect Ratio and make a selection—Original, Custom, Square, 3:2, 4:3, 7:5, or 10:8.

( 3 ) Use your mouse to drag the corners of the white border until the picture appears as you like.

( 4 ) Click Done when you're finished.

## Apply a Filter

The Photos app includes several built-in filters you can apply to your pictures. Use filters to quickly and easily apply interesting effects to a photo.

( 1 ) From the editing screen, click to display the Enhance tab.

( 2 ) In the Choose a Filter section, click the filter you want to apply.

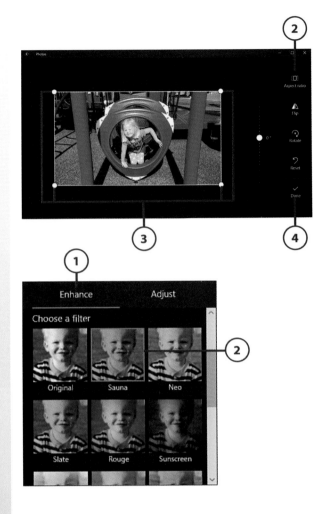

## Remove Red Eye

Red eye is caused when a camera's flash causes the subject's eyes to appear a devilish red. The Photos app lets you remove the red eye effect by changing the red color to black in the edited photo.

( 1 ) From the editing screen, select the Adjust tab.

( 2 ) Scroll down and click Red Eye. The cursor changes to display a translucent blue circle.

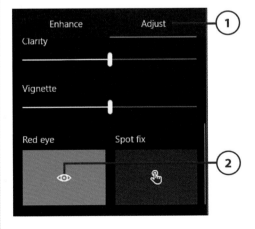

**3** Click the eye(s) you want to fix to remove the red eye effect.

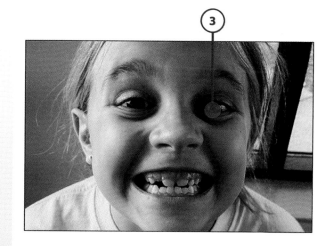

## Retouch a Photo

Does someone in your photo have a blemish or a loose hair? Is there a rough or scratched area in the photo you want to get rid of? Or does that cute baby in the picture have a bit of drool dripping down his chin? Use the Photos app's Retouch control to smooth out or remove blemishes from your photos.

**1** From the editing screen, click to select the Adjust tab.

**2** Scroll down and click Spot Fix. The cursor changes to include a translucent blue circle.

**3** Click the area you want to repair. The area is now repaired.

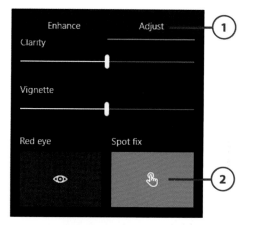

# Adjust Brightness and Contrast

When a photo is too dark or too light, use the Photos app's Light controls. The Contrast control increases or decreases the difference between the photo's darkest and lightest areas. The Exposure control increases or decreases the picture's exposure to make the overall picture lighter or darker. Use the Highlights control to bring out or hide detail in too-bright highlights; use the Shadows control to do the same in too-dark shadows.

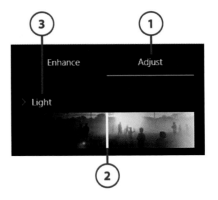

1. From the editing screen, click to select the Adjust tab.

2. In the Light section, click and drag the white line to the left to make the picture darker, or to the right to make the picture lighter.

3. To display additional brightness and contrast controls, click Light.

4. Click and drag the control for the item you want to adjust— Contrast, Exposure, Highlights, or Shadows.

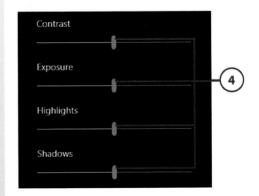

# Adjust Color and Tint

The Photos app lets you adjust various color-related settings.

( **1** ) From the editing screen, click to select the Adjust tab.

( **2** ) In the Color section, click and drag the white line to the left to decrease the color saturation for the picture, or to the right to increase the color saturation.

( **3** ) To display additional color-related controls, click Color.

( **4** ) Click and drag the Tint control to change the tinting of the picture.

( **5** ) Click and drag the Warmth control to the left to make the picture cooler (more blue) or to the right to make a warmer (more red) picture.

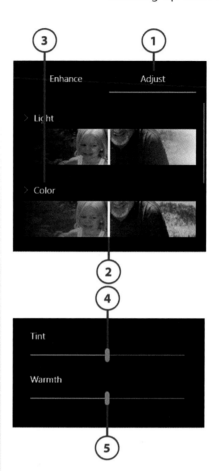

# Apply Other Effects

You can also use the Photos app to change the picture's focus or apply a vignette effect.

( **1** ) From the editing screen, click to select the Adjust tab.

( **2** ) Click and drag the Clarity control to the left to make the picture more blurry, or to the right to make it sharper.

( **3** ) Click and drag the Vignette control to the left to apply a white vignette around the picture, or to the right to apply a black vignette.

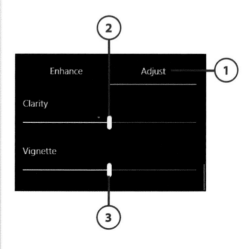

## Save Your Work

You can opt to save your changes to the original picture, or as a copy of that picture—which leaves the original unchanged.

① From the editing screen, click Save to save your changes to the original picture. *Or…*

② Click Save a Copy to save your changes to a new file, leaving the original file unchanged.

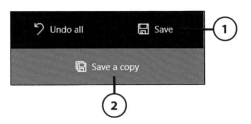

### Cancel Changes

If, when you're editing a photo, you decide you don't want to keep the changes you've made, click Undo All.

---

## >>>Go Further

### OTHER PHOTO-EDITING PROGRAMS

If you need to further edit your photos beyond what you can do in the Photos app, you need to install and use a more full-featured photo-editing program. These programs let you fix red eye, correct bad color and brightness, and perform additional touch-up functions.

Some of the more popular photo-editing programs include Adobe Photoshop Elements (www.adobe.com) and Corel PaintShop Pro (www.paintshoppro.com/en/products/paintshop-pro/). Both programs offer a variety of photo-editing tools, and sell for less than $100.

# Turning Your Photos into Videos with Story Remix

New to the Fall Creators Update is the ability to turn selected photos (and videos) into video slideshows, complete with fancy transitions and background music. This new feature is dubbed *Story Remix*, and it's a great way to make your photos even more entertaining.

## Create an Automatic Story Remix

The easiest way to create a Story Remix is to have the Windows Photos app do it for you. You select the photos (and videos) you want to include, and the Photos app does the rest.

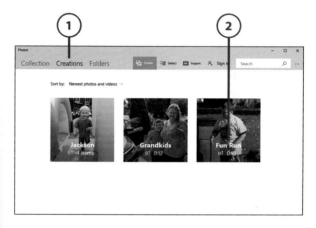

1. From within the Photos app, click Creations to display the Creations view.

2. All of your previously created Story Mixes (and albums) are displayed here. Click a Story Mix to view it.

3. To create a new Story Mix, click Create and then click Video Remix.

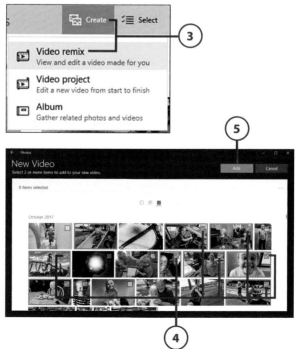

4. Click to select the photos and videos you want to include in this project.

5. Click Add.

(**6**) When prompted, enter a title for this project.

(**7**) Click Create Video.

(**8**) The app displays and plays the new video. Click Play to replay it.

(**9**) Click Remix It for Me if you want to change the style or background music in the video.

(**10**) Click Edit Video if you want to edit the video yourself.

(**11**) Click Close to save your work and return to the Creations screen.

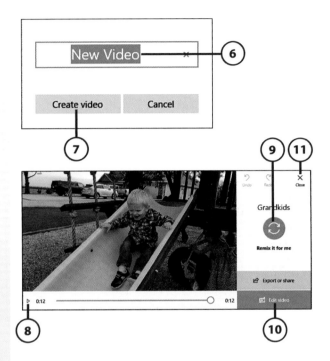

## Create a Customized Video Project

The automatic video Mix is easiest to work with, but you can also create customized videos from your photos and videos. In addition to choosing which items to include, you can determine the length of time each item is displayed, the background music used, which transitions you apply, and more.

(**1**) From the Creations view, click Create and then click Video Project.

(**2**) Click to select the photos and videos you want to include in this project.

(**3**) Click Add.

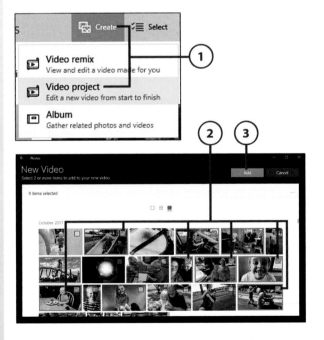

( 4 ) When prompted, enter a title for this project.

( 5 ) Click Create Video to open the video-editing screen.

( 6 ) Click Add Photos and Videos to add more items to this project.

( 7 ) Click Themes to apply a prepared visual theme to this project.

( 8 ) Click Music to choose which background music plays for this video.

( 9 ) Change the order of items in your project by clicking and dragging an item to a new position in the timeline.

( 10 ) Click an item to edit it.

( 11 ) Click Duration to change the length of time this item appears in the video.

( 12 ) Click Filters to apply a photo filter to this item.

( 13 ) Click Text to overlay words onto this item.

( 14 ) Click Motion to choose how this item appears onscreen.

( 15 ) Click the Play button to play this video.

( 16 ) Click Export or Share to save this file for sharing with others.

( 17 ) Click the back arrow to return to the Creations screen.

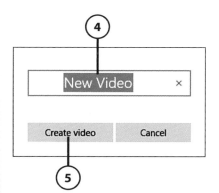

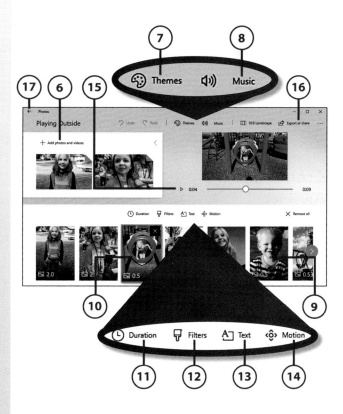

## Edit a Story Remix

You can always make changes to the Story Remixes you create. Editing is easy, whether you created an automatic or customized video.

1. From the Creations view, click the Story Mix you want to edit.

2. Click Edit or Edit Video to display the editing screen.

3. Make the changes you want; play back your new video to see how it looks.

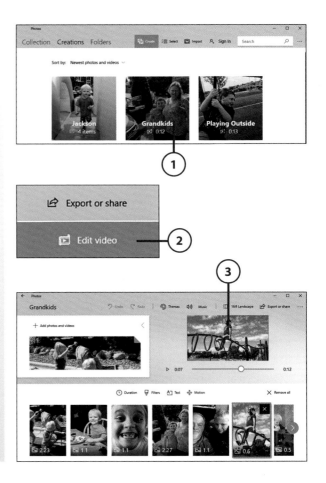

# Sharing Your Pictures and Videos Online

It's fun to look at all the digital pictures and videos (and Story Remixes!) you've stored on your PC, but it's even more fun to share those items with family and friends. Fortunately, the Internet makes it easy to share your favorite photos and videos online, so everyone can ooh and aah over your cute children or grandchildren.

# Sharing a Photo from the Photos App

If you're working from within the Photos app, Windows makes it easy to share any given photo a number of different ways.

1. Open the photo you want to share and then click Share.

2. Your favorite and most recent contacts are listed at the top of the Share panel. Click a person's icon to share with that person and then select how you want to share. *Or…*

3. Select the app you want to use to share. Depending on what you have installed on your computer, you can share via the Mail app, Facebook, Skype, Twitter, and more.

4. Follow the normal procedure for that app to select a recipient, add a text message, and send the photo.

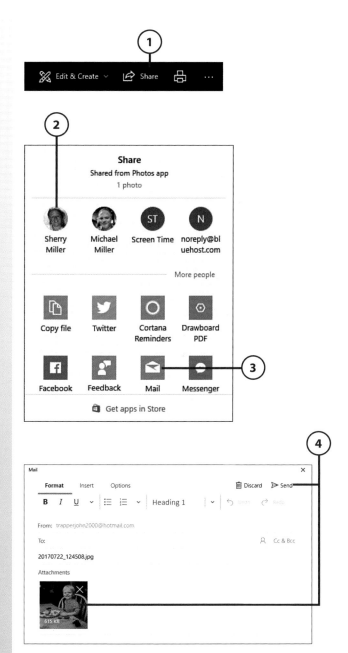

# Attach a Photo or Video in Windows Mail

If you're working within the Windows Mail app, you can use that app to send one or more photos and videos via email. You do this by attaching a picture or video file to an email message and then sending that item along with the message to your intended recipients. When a friend or family member opens your email, she can click to view the photo or video.

All email programs and services let you attach photo and video files to your messages. Let's look at how it's done in the Windows Mail app.

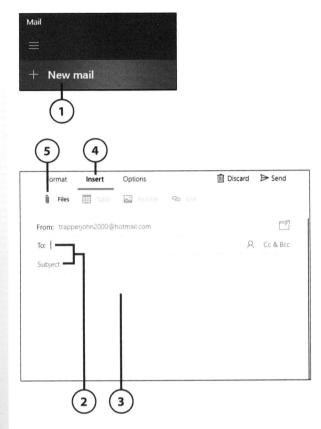

1. Launch the Mail app and then click + New Mail to open a new email message.

2. Enter the recipient and subject information as normal.

3. Enter any accompanying text into the message area.

4. Click the Insert tab.

5. Click Files and, when prompted, select the photo(s) or video(s) you want to share.

6. A thumbnail for the photo appears in your message; click Send to send the message to its recipients.

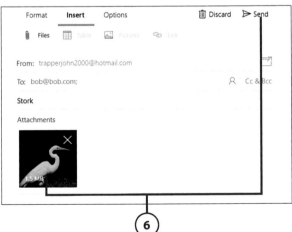

## Other Email Programs

Other email programs and services, such as Gmail and Yahoo! Mail, also let you attach photos and videos in a similar fashion.

# Upload Photos to a New Facebook Photo Album

Assuming that you and your friends and family are all on Facebook, you can use that social network as a photo sharing site. In fact, Facebook is the largest site for photo sharing on the Internet; you can easily upload photos that can then be viewed by all your Facebook friends.

## Facebook

Learn more about Facebook in Chapter 18, "Connecting with Facebook and Pinterest."

You can share individual or small groups of photos through individual status updates, as discussed in Chapter 18. You can also create photo albums, centered around specific events or topics, and then share those albums with your Facebook friends.

## Photo Requirements

Facebook lets you upload photos in the JPG, GIF, PNG, TIF, and BMP file formats. The maximum file size you can upload is 100MB. You're limited to 1,000 photos per album, but you can have an unlimited number of albums—which means you can upload an unlimited number of photos.

( 1 ) Go to your Facebook profile page and click Photos.

( 2 ) Click Create Album.

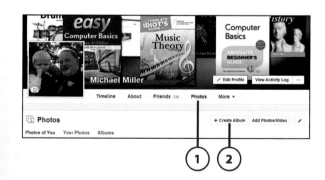

**(3)** From the Open dialog box, navigate to and select the photos you want to upload.

**(4)** Click the Open button. The Create Album pane opens.

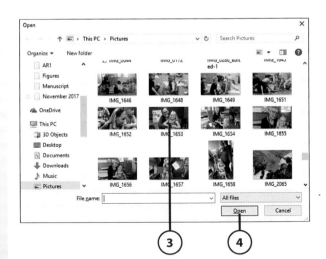

## Selecting Multiple Photos

You can upload more than one photo at a time. Hold down the Ctrl key while clicking files to select multiple files.

**(5)** Click Untitled Album and enter the desired album title.

**(6)** Click Say Something About This Album and enter an album description.

**(7)** To enter a geographic location for all the photos in this album, go to the Location box and enter a location.

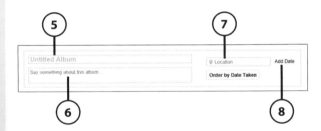

**(8)** To add a common date to all the photos in this album, click Add Date and select a date from the pop-up box. (If you don't do this, all the photos will be stamped with their original individual dates.)

## Optional Information

All the information you can add to a photo album is entirely optional; you can add as much or as little as you like. You don't even have to add a title—if you don't, Facebook uses the title Untitled Album.

**9** To determine who can view the photos in this album, click the Privacy button and make a selection—Public, Friends, Only Me, or Custom.

**10** Click the Post Photos button when done.

**11** You might be prompted to "tag" individuals in the photos you've posted. You can accept the recommended name tags, click the X to delete any individual tag, or, if no tag is applied, enter the individual's name manually.

**12** Click Save Tags when you're done tagging.

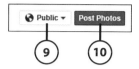

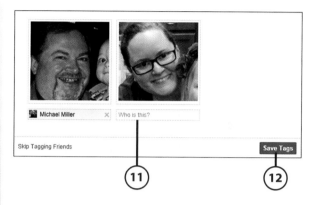

## High-Quality Photos

For the best possible picture quality for anyone downloading or printing your photos, check the High Quality option to upload and store your photos at their original resolution. Note, however, that it takes longer to upload high-quality photos than those in standard quality.

# Upload Pictures to an Existing Facebook Photo Album

After you've created a photo album, you can easily upload more photos to that album; you don't have to create a new album every time you want to upload new photos.

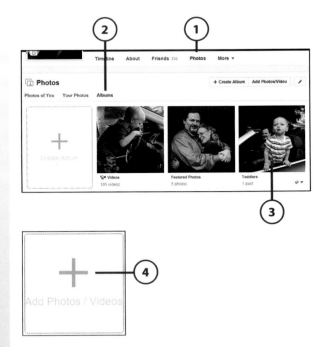

1. From your profile page, click Photos to display your Photos page.

2. Click Albums to display your photo albums.

3. Click to open the album to which you want to add new photos.

4. Click the Add Photos/Videos (+) tile and, when prompted, select the photos to upload.

5. The photos you selected are displayed in a new pane. Add any information you want about a given photo—location, date, information, and the like. You can also tag people in each photo.

6. Click the Post Photos button.

## Uploading Videos to Facebook

Although you can upload a video directly to the Videos album in Facebook, the easier approach is to simply include the video in a normal status update. All videos you post are automatically added to the Videos album, and when you include the video in a post, your friends will all see it in their News Feeds.

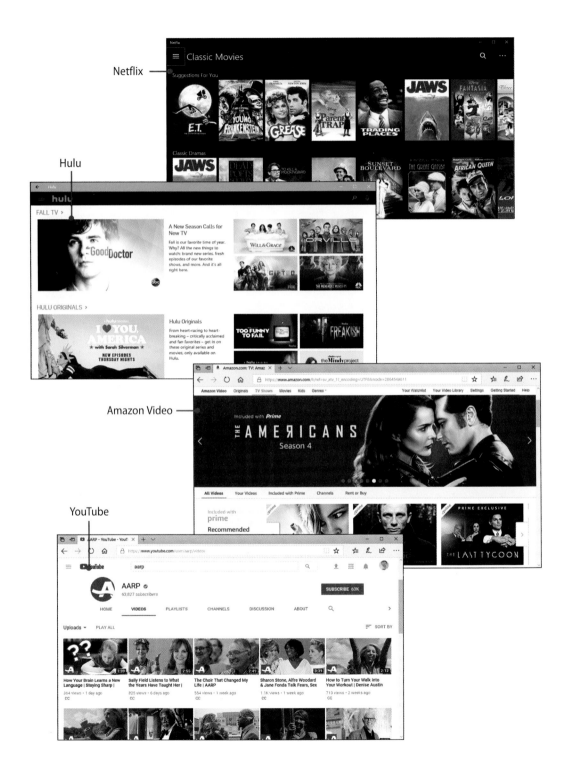

Netflix

Hulu

Amazon Video

YouTube

In this chapter, you discover how to watch your favorite TV shows, movies, and other videos on your Windows PC.

→ Watching Netflix
→ Watching Hulu
→ Watching Amazon Video
→ Viewing and Sharing Videos on YouTube

# Watching Movies and TV Shows on Your PC

Want to rewatch last night's episode of *Dancing with the Stars*? Or the entire season of *NCIS*? How about a classic episode of *Gunsmoke* or *Cheers*? Or that latest "viral video" you've been hearing about?

Here's the latest hot thing on the Web: watching your favorite television programs, films, and videos online, via your web browser. Assuming you have a broadband Internet connection, you can find tens of thousands of free and paid videos to watch at dozens of different websites, including Amazon, Hulu, Netflix, and YouTube.

## Watching Netflix

When it comes to watching movies and TV shows online, the most popular service today is Netflix (www.netflix.com). For a low $10.99/ month subscription (for the company's Basic plan), you can watch all the movies you want. Netflix offers a mix of both classic and newer movies,

a surprising number of classic and newer television programs, and a growing number of "made for Netflix" original programs. There's something there to
please just about everyone.

### DVD Rental

Netflix also offers a separate DVD-by-mail rental service, with a separate subscription fee. That's not what we're talking about here, however.

## Watch a Program on Netflix

Netflix offers a Windows app, downloadable from the Microsoft Store, that is the
best way to view its programming on your Windows 10 PC. (You can also watch
Netflix in your web browser, if you like, but the full-screen app experience is best.)

### Download the Netflix App

To download and install the Netflix app, open the Store app from either the Start
menu or the Windows taskbar. Once you're in the Store, search for **netflix** and
then click the Netflix tile in the search results. When you see the app's screen, click
the Free button. (The app is free.)

The first time you open the Netflix app,
you're prompted to either create a new
Netflix account or log in to an existing
one. Each subsequent time you open
the app, it automatically logs in to this
account and displays the appropriate
content tailored exclusively to your
viewing habits.

1. If you have multiple viewers on
your account, when you open the
app you'll be prompted to select
a viewer before proceeding. Click
the icon for the person who's
watching.

2. Programming on Netflix is organized into various sections—Top Picks, Popular on Netflix, New Releases, and so forth. Scroll down to view all sections.

3. Click the title of any section to view more options of that type.

4. Click the Options button to view the different genres available.

5. Click a genre to view movies of that type.

6. To search for a specific movie or show, click the Search (magnifying glass) icon to display the search box.

7. Enter the name of the movie or show into the Search box. Matching programs display as you type.

8. When you find a movie or show you want to watch, click it. The detail page for that movie or show displays.

## Watching TV Shows

If you choose to watch a TV show, you typically can choose from different episodes in different seasons. Select a season to see all episodes from that season and then click the episode you want to watch.

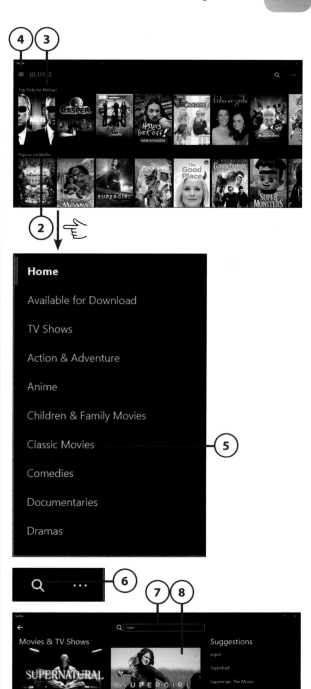

(9) Click the Play button on the image to watch the program.

(10) Netflix begins playing the movie or show you selected. Mouse over anywhere on the screen to display the transport controls at the bottom of the screen.

(11) Click the Fullscreen button to display the movie full screen.

(12) Click the Pause button to pause playback; the Pause button changes to a Play button. Click the Play button to resume playback.

(13) Click and drag the scrub (slider) control to move directly to another part of the movie.

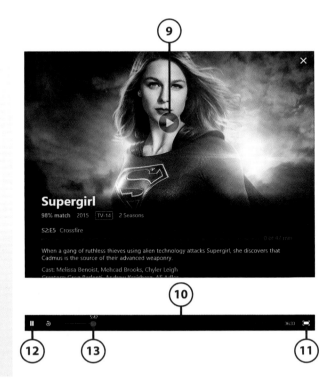

>>>*Go Further*

## NETWORK TV PROGRAMMING

Most major broadcast and cable TV networks offer their shows for viewing (for free) on their own websites. All you have to do is fire up your web browser and start watching. The most popular of these network TV sites include ABC (abc.go.com), CBS (www.cbs.com), Comedy Central (www.comedycentral.com), CW (www.cwtv.com), Fox (www.fox.com), NBC (www.nbc.com), Nick (www.nick.com), Showtime (www.sho.com), TNT (www.tntdrama.com), and USA Network (www.usanetwork.com).

In addition, some networks offer their own subscription services with additional exclusive programming. These include CBS All Access (www.cbs.com/all-access), HBO Go (www.hbogo.com), and Showtime (www.sho.com). You'll need to sign up for a (paid) subscription to view these services.

# Watching Hulu

If Netflix is the most popular streaming service for watching movies and classic TV shows, Hulu is a strong number two. Hulu offers a large selection of episodes from major TV networks, a variety of new and classic feature films, and a growing number of its own original programs. You can choose from two subscription plans.

Hulu offers two basic subscription plans. The standard $7.99/month plan lets you watch Hulu's streaming library but includes commercial interruptions; the No Commercials plan cost $11.99/month but, as the name implies, removes the commercials.

Hulu also offers a Live TV service that adds local TV stations, basic cable networks, and national sports networks to the company's base streaming library. This service, which starts at $39.99/month (with lots of add-ons available) is aimed primarily at those who want to cut the cable cord.

You can view any of Hulu's subscription service through the Hulu Windows app available (for free) from the Microsoft Store. (You can also watch the company's programming from the Hulu website, located at www.hulu.com.)

## Watch a Program on Hulu

You can use any web browser or the Hulu Windows app to watch programs on the Hulu website. We'll use the Hulu app for the following tasks.

1  After you launch the Hulu app and sign into the service, you see Hulu's home page, which displays a variety of featured programs. Scroll down to view recommended programming by type.

( 2 ) To view television programs by genre, click the menu button then go to the TV section and click Genres.

( 3 ) To view movies by genre, click the menu button then go to the Movies section and click Genres.

( 4 ) Click the tile of the genre you want to view. *Or…*

( 5 ) To search for a specific show, enter the name of the show into the top-of-page Search box and then press Enter.

( 6 ) Click the tile for the movie or show you want to watch.

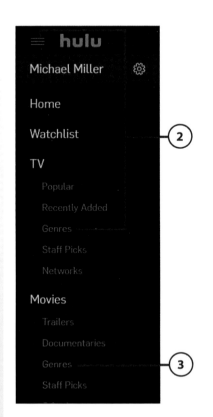

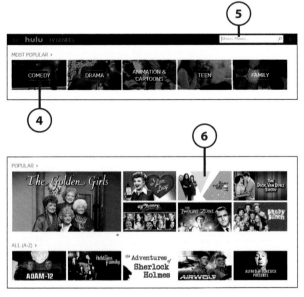

**7** When the detailed program page appears, scroll down to view available episodes, clips, and extras.

**8** To view TV shows by season, click the tile for the season you want.

**9** Click the tile for the episode you want to watch.

**10** Hulu begins playing the program you selected. Move your mouse over the screen to display the playback controls.

**11** Click the Pause button to pause playback; the Pause button changes to a Play button. Click the Play button to resume playback.

**12** Click and drag the scrub (slider) control to move directly to another part of the program.

**13** Click the Fullscreen button to view the program full screen on your computer display.

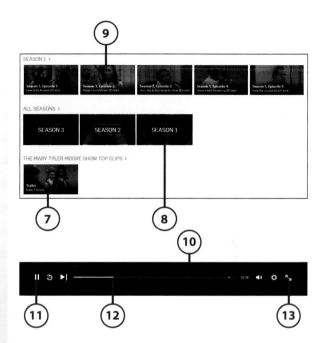

# >>>Go Further

## WATCHING STREAMING VIDEO ON YOUR LIVING ROOM TV

Watching movies and TV shows on your PC is fine if you're on the go, but it's not the same as watching programming on the big flat screen TV you have in your living room. Some newer TVs (sometimes called "smart" TVs) have built-in Internet, so you can watch Amazon, Hulu, Netflix, and other services directly from the TV itself. Not all TVs, however, have built-in streaming video, so you'll need to connect some sort of streaming media box or your computer to your TV to watch Internet-based programming.

If your computer has an HDMI connector, it's an easy task. HDMI is the cable technology used to connect high-definition Blu-ray players, cable boxes, and other equipment to flat screen TVs; the HDMI cable carries both audio and video signals. Just connect an HDMI cable from your PC to a similar HDMI input on your TV, and you're ready to go. Start your streaming video service of choice on your PC, as you would normally, and then switch your TV to the corresponding HDMI input. The programming you're playing on your PC is displayed on your TV. Sit back and start watching.

Learn more about connecting your PC to your TV in Chapter 5, "Connecting Printers and Other Peripherals."

# Watching Amazon Video

The newest streaming video service comes from the Internet's largest online retailer. Amazon Video, like Netflix and Hulu, offers a variety of movies, TV programs, and original programming.

You watch Amazon Video from Amazon's website. (There is not presently an Amazon Video app available in the Microsoft Store.) You can purchase or rent individual programs, episodes, and movies, or subscribe to Prime Video ($8.99/month—or free if you have an Amazon Prime membership) and get many—but not all—programs for free. (Not all shows and movies are available for free with Prime; you still have to purchase some of them separately.)

>>>*Go Further*

## AMAZON PRIME

Amazon Prime Video is both separate from and a part of Amazon Prime, the service that gives you free shipping on most Amazon orders. It's separate in that you can subscribe separately; there's an $8.99/month Prime Video subscription that just covers video streaming, not physical shipping. However, if you go with a full Amazon Prime subscription ($10.99/month or $99.99/year), you not only get free shipping on your Amazon purchases, you also get a full Prime Video membership. Depending on how much shopping you do at Amazon, that might be the best deal.

# View a Program on Amazon Video

Amazon doesn't have a dedicated app for viewing its online videos. Instead, you select a program from the Amazon website and watch it in your web browser.

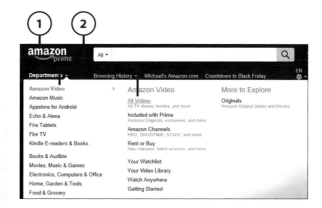

**1** Point your web browser to the Amazon website (www.amazon. com), sign into your account if necessary, and mouse over the Departments button.

**2** Click Amazon Video and then click All Videos.

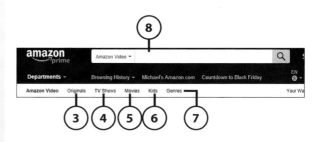

**3** Click the Originals tab to show only original Amazon programming.

**4** Click the TV Shows tab to view only TV shows.

**5** Click the Movies tab to view only movies.

**6** Click the Kids tab to view children's programming.

**7** Click Genres to browse different types of programming.

**8** Enter a query within the Search box to search for specific shows or movies.

**9** Scroll down the page to view suggestions by type.

**10** Click to select the item you want to watch.

**11** If you selected a TV show, click to select a season.

**12** Click the Play icon for the episode you want to watch.

**13** If you selected a movie, click Watch Now to watch now.

**14** Mouse over the screen to display the playback controls. Click Pause to pause playback; Click Play to resume playback.

**15** Click the Back icon to skip back 10 seconds.

**16** Click the Forward icon to skip forward 10 seconds.

**17** Drag the slider/scrubber to move to another point in the program.

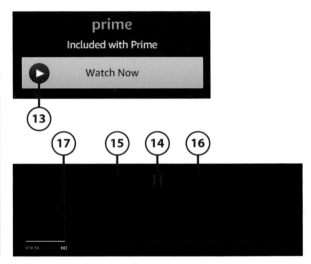

>>>Go Further

## PURCHASING AND RENTING MOVIES ONLINE

While streaming video is the big thing today, you can still purchase and rent movies and TV shows for downloading to your PC. When you purchase or rent a movie online, that video file is downloaded to your computer and you can watch it at any time.

The most popular sources for downloadable videos are Amazon (www.amazon.com) and Apple's iTunes Store (www.apple.com/itunes). Prices vary from $1 or so for individual TV episodes to $20 or so for a new-release movie. Rentals are typically around a third of the purchase price.

# Viewing and Sharing Videos on YouTube

Unlike Amazon, Hulu, and Netflix, YouTube doesn't specialize in commercial TV shows and movies. Instead, YouTube is a video-sharing community; users can upload their own videos and watch videos uploaded by other members.

YouTube is where you find all those homemade videos of cute cats and laughing babies that everybody's watching, as well as tons of "how-to" videos, video blogs, videogame tutorials, and more. And when you find a video you like, you can share it with your friends and family—which is what helps a video go "viral."

## View a Video

You access YouTube from any web browser. Unlike the commercial video services we've discussed, you use YouTube for free—no subscription necessary.

### Movies on YouTube

In addition to its user-uploaded videos, YouTube offers a variety of commercial movies. Some movies are free; others can be rented on a 48-hour pass for as low as $1.99.

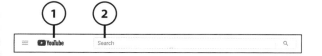

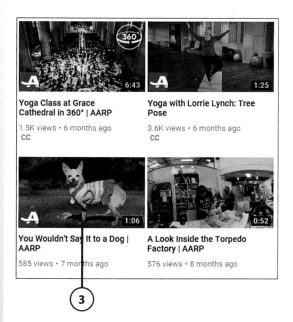

(1) From within your web browser, go to the YouTube site at www.youtube.com.

(2) To search for a particular video, enter what you're looking for into the Search box and then press Enter or click the Search (magnifying glass) button.

(3) Click the video you want to watch.

4) The video begins playing automatically when the video page displays.

5) Click the Pause button to pause playback; click the button again to resume playback.

6) Click the Fullscreen button to view the video on your entire computer screen.

7) Click the thumbs-up button to "like" the video, or the thumbs-down button to "dislike" it.

>>>Go Further

## SHARING VIDEOS

Find a video you think a friend would like? YouTube makes it easy to share any video with others.

Click the Share button under the video player to display the Share panel. You can then opt to email a link to the video, "like" the video on Facebook, or tweet a link to the video on Twitter.

## Upload Your Own Video

If you take movies with your camcorder or smartphone, you can transfer those movies to your computer and then upload them to YouTube. This is a great way to share your home videos with friends and family online. (You have to be signed into YouTube before you start uploading, of course.)

### Uploading from a Smartphone

If you shoot video with your smartphone or tablet, you might be able to upload to YouTube directly from your device or the YouTube mobile app. Check your device or app to see what's available.

1. Click the Upload button at the top of any YouTube page.

2. Click Select Files to Upload to display the Open dialog box.

3. Navigate to and select the video file you want to upload.

4. Click the Open button.

5. As the video is uploaded, YouTube displays the video information page. Enter a title for the video into the Title box.

6. Enter a description for the video into the Description box.

7. Enter one or more keywords to describe the video into the Tags box.

8. Click the Publish button to make your video live.

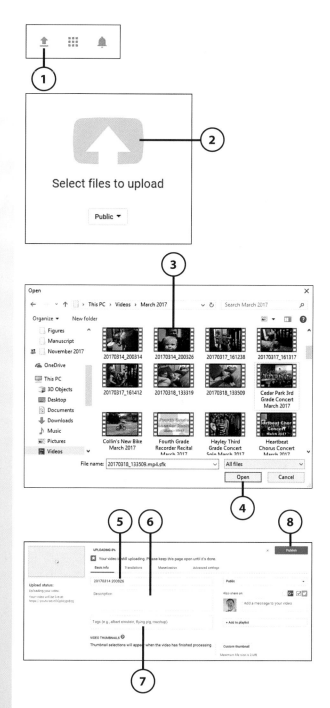

## >>>Go Further
## CUTTING THE CABLE CORD

For decades we've been slaves to the services available from our local cable or satellite TV companies. These services get more expensive every year, and if you're like me, you find that you're only watching a fraction of the hundreds of channels available.

This situation is driving millions of people to cut the cable cord and watch their programming over the Internet, using smart TVs and streaming media boxes and sticks. The problem, though, is that you can't watch your local TV channels on a Roku box or Amazon Fire stick. You can get most cable channels over the Internet, but you'll have to connect some sort of digital antenna to your TV to watch over-the-air (OTA) local channels.

One solution is to subscribe to a streaming service aimed at cord cutters, such as Hulu with Live TV (www.hulu.com/live-tv), PlayStation Vue (www.playstation.com/vue), or YouTube TV (tv.youtube.com). These services offer all the popular cable channels plus some or all of your local channels, all for much less than you pay for a typical cable TV package.

That said, you probably won't be doing this kind of cable cord cutting from your Windows computer. While you can view most of these cord-cutting services on your computer or smart phone, they're really designed for viewing on your living room TV. For this, you need some sort of streaming media device, such as an Amazon Fire box or stick or Roku —all of which are beyond the scope of this book. Suffice to say, though, you can save some big bucks by dumping your cable box and watching your TV over the Internet.

Pandora

Spotify

Groove Music app

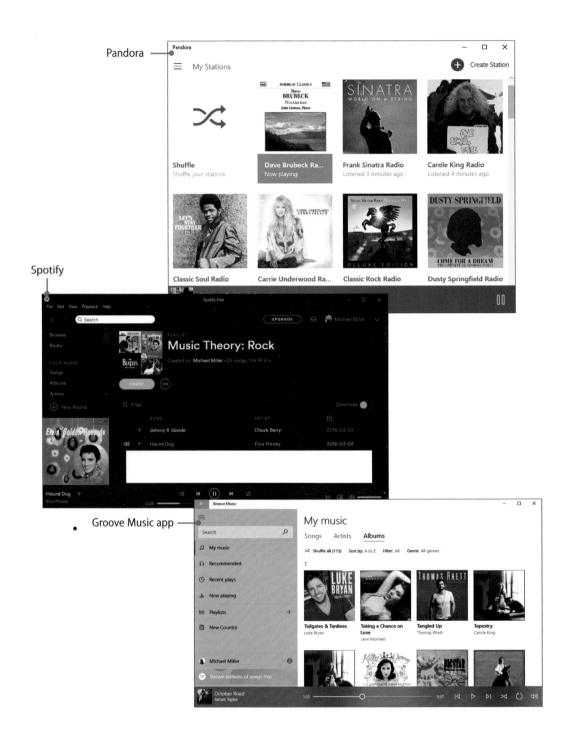

**21**

# Listening to Music on Your PC

Many folks like to listen to music on their computers. You can use the CD/DVD drive in your PC (if it has one) to play CDs, purchase and download tunes from online music stores, or stream music over the Internet to your computer. However you choose to listen, your computer—and Windows—will do the job.

## Listening to Streaming Music

People our age have been conditioned to purchase the music we like, whether on vinyl, cassette tape, compact disc, or via digital download. But there's an entire world of music on the Internet that you don't have to purchase. It's called *streaming music*, and it gives you pretty much all you can listen to for a low monthly subscription price—or even for free. There's nothing to download; the music is streamed to your computer in real time, over the Internet.

The two largest streaming music services are Pandora and Spotify. We'll look at each of these.

## >>>Go Further

## ON-DEMAND VERSUS PERSONALIZED SERVICES

There are two primary types of delivery services for streaming audio over the Internet. The first model, typified by Pandora, is like traditional radio in that you can't dial up specific tunes; you have to listen to whatever the service beams out, but in the form of personalized playlists or virtual radio stations. The second model, typified by Spotify, lets you specify which songs you want to listen to; these are *on-demand services*.

## Listen to Pandora

Pandora is much like traditional AM or FM radio, in that you listen to the songs Pandora selects for you, along with accompanying commercials. It's a little more personalized than traditional radio however, in that you create your own person-alized stations. All you have to do is choose a song or artist; Pandora then cre-ates a station with other songs like the one you picked. You access Pandora from the company's website (www.pandora.com) or, even better, from the Pandora Windows app, which is available for free download from the Microsoft Store.

### Free Versus Paid

Pandora's basic membership is free, but ad-supported. (You have to suffer through commercials.) To get rid of the commercials, pay for the $4.99/month Pandora One subscription.

Let's see how it works with the Pandora app. When you first launch the app, you're prompted to log into an existing account or sign up for a new one. Accounts are free, so do it.

1. The main screen of the Pandora app displays all the stations you've previously created. Click Recent to display your most recently listened-to stations, or click A–Z to view an alphabetical listing of your stations.

2. Click Shuffle to randomly play music from all your stations.

3. Click a station to play music from that station.

4. Information about the current track and artist is displayed.

5. Click Pause to pause playback. Click Play to resume playback.

6. "Like" the current song by clicking the thumbs-up icon. Pandora will now play more songs like this one.

7. If you don't like the current song, click the thumbs-down icon. Pandora skips to the next song, won't play the current one again, and will play fewer songs like it.

8. Skip to the next song without disliking it by clicking the Next Track button.

9. To create a new station, return to the main screen and click Create Station.

10. Enter the name of an artist, song, or genre and then press Enter.

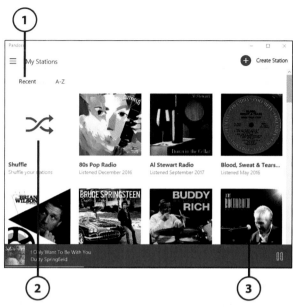

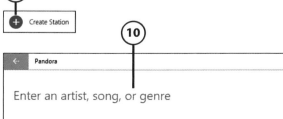

(11) Pandora lists stations that match your query. Click the one you want to add to your list.

(12) Pandora starts playing this station and adds it to your list of favorites.

## >>>Go Further
### LOCAL RADIO STATIONS ONLINE

If you'd rather just listen to your local AM or FM radio station—or to a radio station located in another city—you can do so over the Internet. Both iHeartRadio (www.iheart.com) and TuneIn (www.tunein.com) offer free access to local radio stations around the world.

# Listen to Spotify

The other big streaming music service today is Spotify. Unlike Pandora, Spotify lets you choose specific tracks to listen to.

Spotify offers a web-based version you can access via your web browser, or a standalone app that offers enhanced functionality. Access both at www.spotify.com; this section covers the Spotify app.

## Free Versus Paid

Spotify's basic membership is free, but you're subjected to commercials every few songs. If you want to get rid of the commercials (and get on-demand music on your mobile devices, too), you need to pay for a $9.99/month subscription.

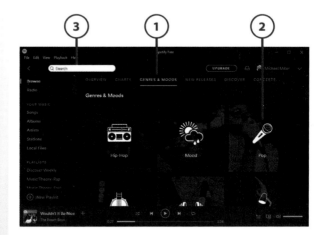

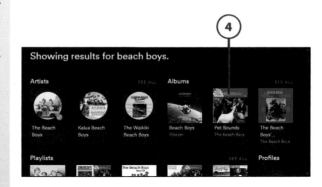

**1** Open the Spotify app and then click Genres & Moods to browse by musical genre.

**2** Click a genre tile to view music of that type.

**3** To search for a specific song, album, or artist, enter your query into the top-of-page Search box and then press Enter.

**4** Click a playlist, album, or artist to view all included songs.

**5** Click the green Play button to play all the songs in the playlist or album, or by that artist.

**6** Double-click a song title to play that particular track.

**(7)** Use the playback controls at the bottom to pause, rewind, or fast-forward playback, or to raise or lower the volume.

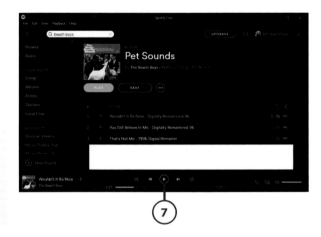

**(7)**

## >>>Go Further

### OTHER STREAMING MUSIC SERVICES

Pandora and Spotify aren't the only streaming music services on the Internet. You can check out and listen to any of these popular streaming music services using your web browser:

- Apple Music (www.apple.com/music)
- Google Play Music (play.google.com/ music)
- Napster (us.napster.com)
- Slacker (www.slacker.com)
- TIDAL (www.tidal.com)

# Purchasing Digital Music Online

Prior to streaming music services, the only way to get music online was to purchase and download individual tracks or complete albums from an online music store. The three biggest online music stores today are Amazon Digital Music, Apple's iTunes Store, and Google Play Music. Because Apple's store requires you to download and install the iTunes software to make a purchase, this section focuses on the Amazon and Google stores, both of which you can access from any web browser.

# Purchase Music from the Amazon Digital Music Store

The Amazon Digital Music Store is a major source of downloadable digital music, in MP3 format. The music you purchase from Amazon's online store can be played in any music playback app, including Microsoft's Groove Music app, which is covered later in this chapter.

Amazon offers tens of millions of tracks for purchase. Prices run from 69 cents to $1.29 per track, with complete albums also available.

**( 1 )** Point your web browser to www. amazon.com/mp3. The main page displays recommended releases.

**( 2 )** To search for a specific song, album, or artist, enter your query into the Search box at the top of the page and click the magnifying glass button or press Enter.

**( 3 )** Browse by genre by scrolling down to the Browse by Genre section in the left column; then click the genre you want.

**( 4 )** Click to select the artist or album you want.

**( 5 )** Purchase an entire album by clicking the Buy MP3 Album button. (Alternatively, click the Add to MP3 Cart button to purchase more than one item at this time.)

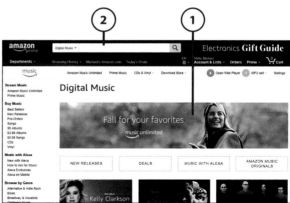

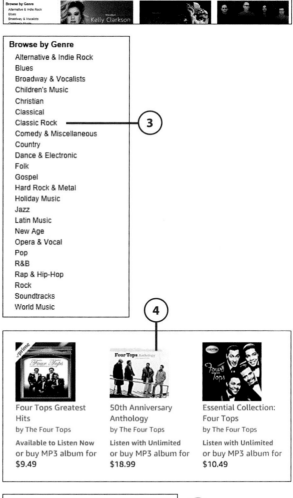

( 6 ) Purchase an individual track by clicking the price button for that track. (Alternatively, click the Add to MP3 Cart button to purchase more than one item at this time.)

( 7 ) You now see a Review Your Order page. If you want to make this purchase, click the Place Your Order button.

( 8 ) You now see Amazon's thank you page. To play this song now from the Amazon website, click the Play Now button.

( 9 ) To download your purchase to your PC, click the Download Purchases button.

( 10 ) You're now prompted to install the Amazon Music for PC app on your computer. You can do this if you want (it makes managing your Amazon downloads marginally easier), but you probably just want to download the track to your computer. To do so, click No Thanks, Just Download Music Files Directly and, when the Save As dialog box appears, select a location for the download and click Save. The track downloads to your computer.

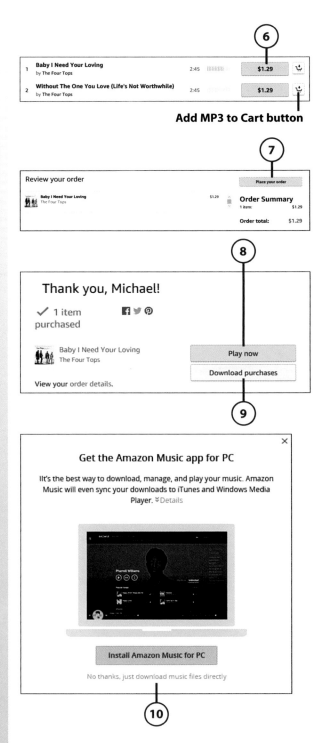

**Add MP3 to Cart button**

# Purchase Music from Google Play Music

Google offers its own online music store similar to the Amazon Digital Music Store. Google Play Music offers tens of millions of individual tracks and complete albums for purchase, at prices ranging from 69 cents to $1.29 per track.

( 1 ) Point your web browser to play. google.com/store/music. The main page displays recommended releases.

( 2 ) To search for a specific song, album, or artist, enter your query into the Search box at the top of the page and click the magnifying glass button or press Enter.

( 3 ) Browse by genre by clicking the Genres button and then selecting the genre you want.

( 4 ) Click to select the artist or album you want.

( 5 ) Purchase an entire album by clicking the price button at the top of the album page.

( 6 ) Purchase an individual track by clicking the price button for that track.

( 7 ) If you haven't yet purchased from Google, you're prompted to add a credit or debit card, or to pay via PayPal. Make a selection and follow the onscreen instructions to complete your purchase and download the track(s).

# Listening to Your Own Music in Windows 10

You can use your computer to listen to all sorts of music, including tracks you've downloaded from the Internet.

## Listen to Digital Music with the Groove Music App

How do you listen to the music you've downloaded from the Amazon or Google stores? There are several music player apps available, but the easiest one to use is the one that's included with Windows 10—the Groove Music app.

You launch the Groove Music app from the Windows Start menu.

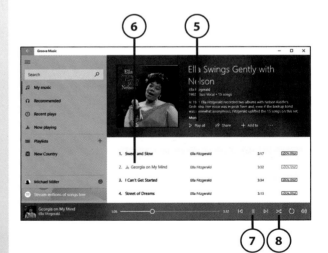

1. Click Albums to see all the albums in your collection.

2. Click Artists to see your music organized by artist.

3. Click Songs to display individual tracks.

4. Double-click an artist or album to view all tracks for that artist or album.

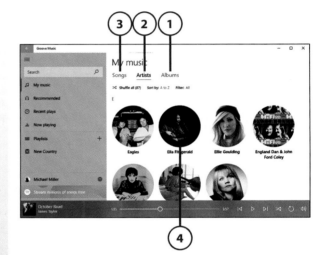

5. Click Play All to play all tracks within that artist or album.

6. Double-click a specific track to play only that track.

7. Click the Pause button to pause playback; click Play again to resume playback.

8. Click the Turn Shuffle On button to play tracks in a random order.

### Search for Music

To search for specific tunes or artists in your collection, click the Search button in the navigation pane and enter the name of the song or artist you're looking for.

## Listen to CDs

If you're like me, you probably have a fair number of compact discs in your collection. Unfortunately, there's no way to play these CDs on your Windows 10 computer—at least not right out of the box.

You see, the Groove Music app that we just discussed is for playing digital music only; it won't play CDs. And the Windows Media Player software included with older versions of Windows (which did play CDs) is no longer included with Windows 10, as of the Fall Creators Update.

So how can you play CDs on your Windows 10 PC? (Assuming your computer has a CD/DVD drive, of course; not all do.) What you have to do is download and install a music player app. Most of these third-party apps play both the digital music you've downloaded and physical music CDs. Many even let you copy ("rip") music from CDs to your computer, and burn physical CDs from the digital music on your PC.

Some of the more popular music player apps for Windows include the following:

- Media Monkey (www.mediamonkey.com)
- MusicBee (www.getmusicbee.com)
- VLC Media Player (www.videolan.org/vlc)

All of these programs are free.

Kindle app

NOOK app

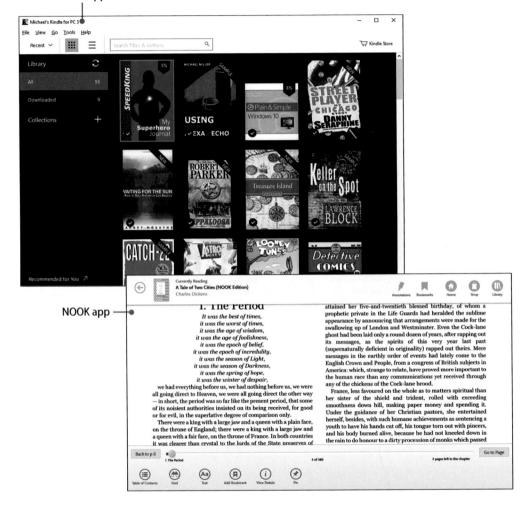

In this chapter, you discover where to find eBooks online and how to read them on your Windows PC.

→ Reading eBooks with Amazon's Kindle App
→ Reading eBooks with Barnes & Noble's NOOK App

# 22

# Reading Books on Your PC

Whether you love westerns, romance novels, or historical nonfiction, you can use your Windows PC to read many of your favorite books. Most books today are in digital format, what we call electronic books or eBooks. It's a great way to take your favorite books with you—especially if you have a notebook PC.

## Reading eBooks with Amazon's Kindle App

Two major eBook formats are in use today. Unfortunately, the two formats are incompatible, meaning you need separate eBook reader apps to read books in both formats.

Currently, the most popular seller of eBooks is Amazon, the online bookseller. Amazon sells both traditional printed books and electronic books in their own proprietary format. You can read Amazon's eBooks on Amazon's Kindle eBook reader devices, Kindle Fire tablets, and any PC using Amazon's Kindle app. This is a regular desktop computer program, not a Windows Store app; you can download it for free from

Amazon's website (www.amazon.com/Amazon-Digital-Services-LLC-Download/dp/B00UB76290).

After you have the Kindle desktop app installed on your PC, you can purchase new eBooks from Amazon's online bookstore. (You also can use the Kindle app to read free eBooks from many libraries.) Your eBooks are automatically downloaded to your PC, where you can read them using the Kindle app.

## Purchase eBooks from Amazon

Kindle-compatible eBooks are available from Amazon's online Kindle Store, which is accessible from the Kindle app. When you purchase a new eBook, it's immediately available for reading on your computer. (And if you're an Amazon Prime user, you also can "borrow" thousands of eBooks for free as part of your Prime membership.)

---

### First Time

The first time you open the Kindle app you're prompted to either sign in to your existing Amazon account, if you have one, or create a new account. Each subsequent time you open the app, it opens directly into your Amazon account.

---

(1) Launch the Kindle app and then click Kindle Store (in the top-right corner). This opens the Kindle Store in a new tab in your web browser. (You can also go directly to the Kindle Store by entering www.amazon.com/Kindle-eBooks into your web browser.)

(2) To search for a specific book, enter that book's title or author into the Search box and then click the magnifying glass icon or press Enter.

(3) Scroll down the page to see best-sellers, daily deals, and books recommended for you.

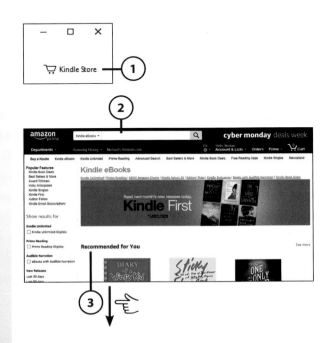

**4** Scroll down the Kindle eBooks section in the left column to view books in various categories.

**5** Click the title of the book you want to purchase; this displays the book's Amazon page.

**6** Click the Deliver To button and select *Your* Kindle for PC.

**7** Click the Buy or Buy Now with 1-Click button to purchase this book and make it available for reading on your PC.

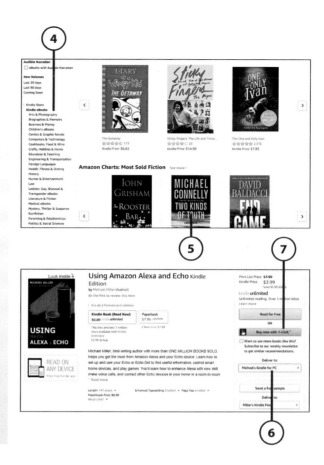

## Free Samples

Amazon offers free samples for many of the eBooks it sells. Look for and click the Send a Free Sample button to download a few pages.

## Kindle Unlimited

Amazon also offers the Kindle Unlimited program, which is kind of like a lending library for selected eBooks. Pay for a $9.99/month subscription and you get access to more than a million titles to read on your computer or other devices.

## Read an eBook

All the eBooks you purchase from Amazon are automatically *stored* online, in what Amazon calls the cloud. You can use the Kindle app to open any book you've purchased and read it on your computer screen.

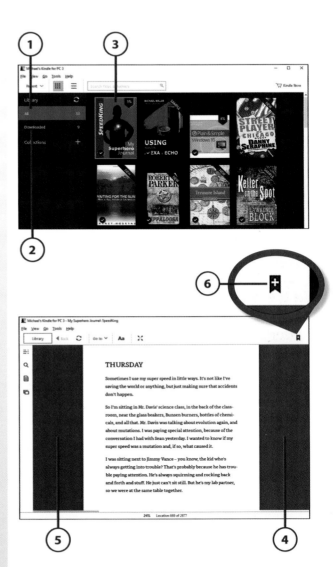

1. Open the Kindle app and, in the left column, click All. This displays all the books you've purchased that are currently stored online. (These might be books you're reading on other devices, such as your tablet or smartphone.)

2. Click Downloaded to view those books you've purchased that are stored on your PC.

3. Double-click a book cover to begin reading that book.

4. To turn the page, press the right-arrow key on your keyboard or click the right side of the screen with your mouse.

5. To return to the previous page, press the left-arrow key on your keyboard or click the left side of the screen with your mouse.

6. To bookmark the current page for future reference, click the Bookmark icon at the top-right corner of the screen.

**7** To jump to another location in the book, click Go To and then select Cover, Table of Contents, Beginning, or Page or Location (and then enter a page number).

**8** To return to your eBook library, click the Library button at the top-left corner of the screen.

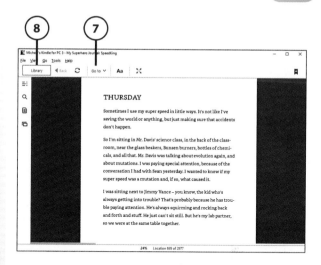

# Change How a Book Is Displayed Onscreen

One of the nice things about eBooks is that you can easily change how the text is displayed onscreen. You can make the text larger or smaller, change the page margins, and even change the color of the text and the page background.

**1** From within the book, click the Change (font) button to display the View Options pane.

**2** To change the display font, click the Font list and make a new selection.

**3** Drag the Font Size slider to a new position to make the text larger or smaller for easier reading.

**4** To force the book to display only a single column at a time, go to the Page Columns section and select Single.

**5** To change the justification, go to the Alignment section and select either Justified or Left-Aligned.

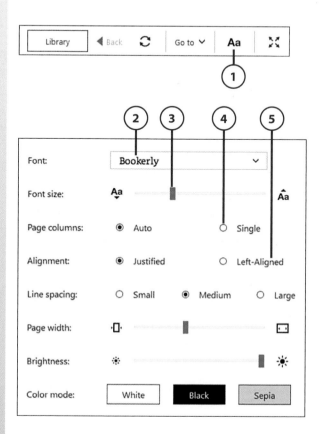

**6** To change the spacing between lines, go to the Line Spacing section and make a selection.

**7** To change the white space on the sides of the screen, go to the Page Width section and drag the slider left or right.

**8** To change the brightness of the displayed page, go to the Brightness section and drag the slider left or right.

**9** To change the way the text appears onscreen, go to the Color Mode section and select White (black text on a white background), Sepia (black text on a sepia background), or Black (white text on a black background).

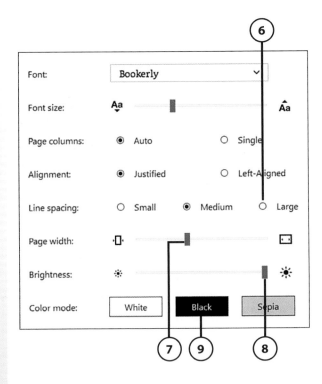

## >>>Go Further
### PDF FILES

Many eBooks you find online are also available in Adobe's PDF format. The advantage of PDF files is that they appear exactly as designed by the publisher; a PDF file is an exact representation of the original printed book. (Kindle- and ePub-format books, on the other hand, can be formatted by the reader for easier reading on any given device.)

As such, many readers prefer the PDF format for visually oriented books, such as children's books or four-color "coffee table" titles. For this reason, many publishers make their books available in PDF format, as well as Kindle and ePub formats.

You can use either the Kindle or NOOK app to read PDF-format eBooks. You can also use Adobe's Acrobat Reader app for PDF files.

# Reading eBooks with Barnes & Noble's NOOK App

Amazon's Kindle format is one of the two major eBook formats, and it's a proprietary one. That is, you can only read Kindle books on a Kindle eBook reader device or via the Kindle app, not with any other apps.

The other major eBook format is called ePub, and it's more universal. Although you can't read ePub books in the Kindle app, you can read them in other eBook apps, and on other eBook reader devices.

The most popular ePub-compatible eBook reader is the Barnes & Noble NOOK. Barnes & Noble makes a NOOK app available for Windows, which enables you to read all ePub-format eBooks on your computer, no matter where you purchase them. You can download the NOOK app from the Windows Store.

## Purchase eBooks from Barnes & Noble

You can purchase ePub-format eBooks from a number of different websites and retailers. Naturally, Barnes & Noble would prefer that you purchase your eBooks from their own online store.

### First Time

The first time you open the NOOK app, you're prompted to sign in with either your Microsoft account or a NOOK account. Your account information is remembered on subsequent logins.

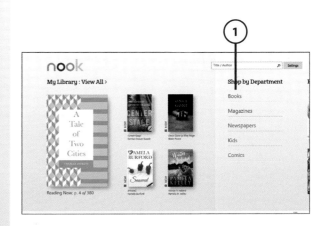

**1** From the Windows Start menu, open the NOOK app; then scroll to the Shop by Department list and click Books. (You can also purchase and read magazines, newspapers, comic books, and kids' books from within the app.)

**(2)** You see the NOOK store, with featured books displayed. To browse books by category, click the Browse Categories list and select a category.

**(3)** To search for a specific book, enter the title or author of the book you want into the Search box and then click the magnifying glass icon or press Enter.

**(4)** When the search results page displays, click the book you want to purchase.

**(5)** When the book page appears, click the Buy button to purchase and download the book.

## Free Samples

Barnes & Noble offers free samples for many of the eBooks it sells. Click the Free Sample button to download the sample chapter or section to your PC.

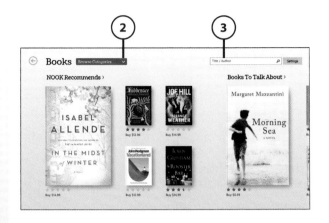

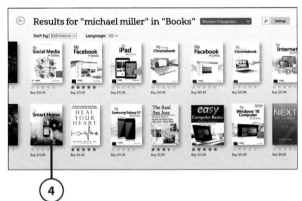

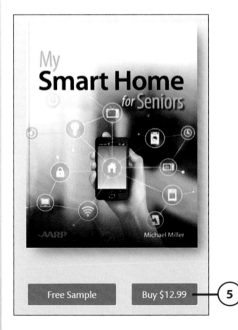

# Read an eBook

All the eBooks you purchase from Barnes & Noble are stored online until you're ready to read them. You can use the NOOK app to open and read any book you've purchased from Barnes & Noble, as well as ePub-format eBooks you've purchased elsewhere.

1. From the NOOK app, scroll to the My Library section and click View All to display all your books.

2. Click the cover of the book you want to read.

3. To turn the page, press the right-arrow key on your keyboard or click the right side of the screen with your mouse.

4. To return to the previous page, press the left-arrow key on your keyboard or click the left side of the screen with your mouse.

5. To view additional functions, right-click anywhere on the screen to display the top and bottom Options bars.

6. To return to your eBook library, click Library in the top Options bar.

7. To bookmark the current page for future reference, click Add Bookmark in the bottom Options bar.

8. To jump to another location in the book, click and drag the slider in the bottom Options bar.

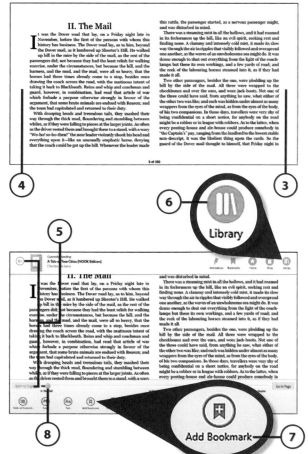

# Change How a Book Is Displayed Onscreen

The NOOK app, like the Kindle app, enables you to easily change how the text is displayed onscreen. You can make the text larger or smaller, change the page margins, and even change the color of the text and the page background.

( 1 ) From within the book, right-click to display the Options bars.

( 2 ) Click Text in the bottom Options bar to display the Text pane.

( 3 ) To make the text larger or smaller for easier reading, go to the Size section and click one of the seven available font sizes.

( 4 ) To change the spacing between lines, go to the Line Spacing section and click one of the three options.

( 5 ) To change the white space on the sides of the screen, go to the Margins section and click one of the three options.

( 6 ) To change the font used on the page, go to the Font section and make a new selection.

( 7 ) To change the way the text appears onscreen, go to the Theme section and make a selection from Normal, Night, Gray, Butter, Mocha, or Sepia.

( 8 ) To force a book to display as the publisher intended, click "on" the Publisher Defaults control.

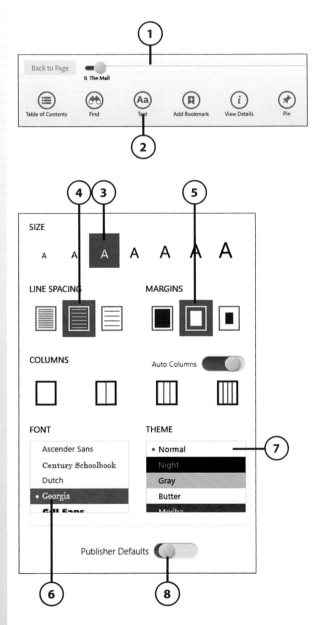

# >>>Go Further

## FREE EBOOKS

In addition to the eBooks you can purchase from Amazon, Barnes & Noble, and other online bookstores, there are also plenty of free eBooks available online. You can find a good selection of eBooks, typically in ePub format, at Free-eBooks.net (www.free-ebooks.net), ManyBooks (www.manybooks.net), and Project Gutenberg (www.gutenberg.org).

Additionally, your local public library likely has eBooks available for free download with a library card either online or within the library itself. These are typically limited-time downloads, so they are yours to read but not to keep—just like regular printed library books.

File Explorer

Ribbon

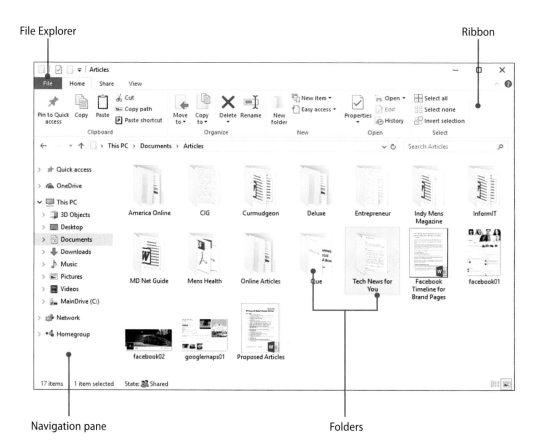

Navigation pane

Folders

In this chapter, you see how to use File Explorer to manage the files and folders on your PC's hard drive.

→ Using File Explorer
→ Working with Folders
→ Managing Files
→ Working with Microsoft OneDrive

23

# Using Files and Folders

All the data for documents and programs on your computer is stored in electronic files. A file can be a word processing document, a music track, a digital photograph—just about anything, really.

The files on your computer are organized into a series of folders and subfolders. It's just like the way you organize paper files in a series of file folders in a filing cabinet—only it's all done electronically.

## Using File Explorer

You might, from time to time, need to work with the files on your computer. You might want to copy files from an external USB memory drive, for example, or move a file from one folder to another. You might even want to delete unused files to free up space on your hard drive.

When you need to manage the files on your Windows 10 computer, you use an app called File Explorer. This app lets you view and manage all the files and folders on your PC—and on connected devices.

---

### A Different Name

Prior to Windows 8, File Explorer was called Windows Explorer—or just My Computer.

---

There are a few ways to open File Explorer:

- Click the File Menu icon on the taskbar.
- Click the Start button to open the Start menu, click the Windows System folder, and then click File Explorer.
- Right-click the Start button to open the Options menu; then click File Explorer.
- Press Windows+E.

## Navigate Folders and Libraries

All the files on your computer are organized into folders. Some folders have subfolders—that is, folders within folders. There are even sub-subfolders, and sub-sub-subfolders. It's a matter of nesting folders within folders, in a kind of hierarchy. Naturally, you use File Explorer to navigate the various folders and subfolders on your PC's hard disk.

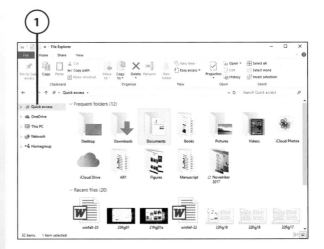

① In File Explorer's default view, Quick Access is selected and your most-used folders and documents are displayed. Double-click any item to view the contents.

(2) A given folder may contain multiple folders and subfolders. Double-click any item to view its contents.

(3) To move back to the disk or folder previously selected, click the Back button on the toolbar.

(4) To move up the hierarchy of folders and subfolders to the next highest item, click the up-arrow button on the toolbar.

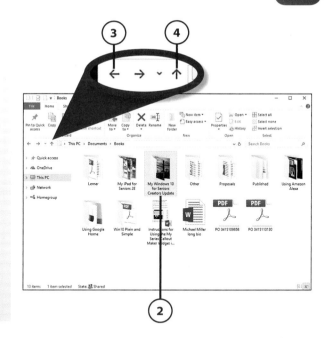

## >>>Go Further
### BREADCRUMBS

File Explorer includes an Address box at the top of the window, which displays your current location, in terms of folders and subfolders. This list of folders and subfolders presents a "breadcrumb" approach to navigation; it's like leaving a series of breadcrumbs behind as you delve deeper into the hierarchy of subfolders.

You can view additional folders within the hierarchy by clicking the separator arrow next to the folder icon in the Address box. This displays a pull-down menu of the recently visited and most popular items.

# Use the Navigation Pane

Another way to navigate your files and folders is to use the navigation pane on the left side of the File Explorer window. This pane displays both favorite links and hierarchical folder trees for your computer, libraries, and networks.

**1** Click the arrow icon next to any folder to display all the subfolders it contains.

**2** Click an icon in the navigation pane to open the contents of the selected item.

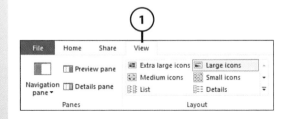

# Change the Folder View

You can choose to view the contents of a folder in a variety of ways. File Explorer lets you display files as Small Icons, Medium Icons, Large Icons, or Extra Large Icons. You also have the option of displaying files as Tiles, Details, or a List. There's even a Content view that displays information about the file beside it.

**1** From within File Explorer, click the View tab on the ribbon bar.

**2** Click Content to display files with content descriptions.

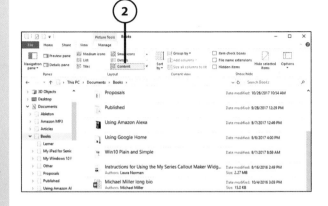

**3** Click Details to display columns of details about each file.

**4** Click List to display files in a simple list.

**5** Click Tiles to display files as small tiles.

**6** Click Small Icons, Medium Icons, Large Icons, or Extra Large Icons to display files as icons of various sizes.

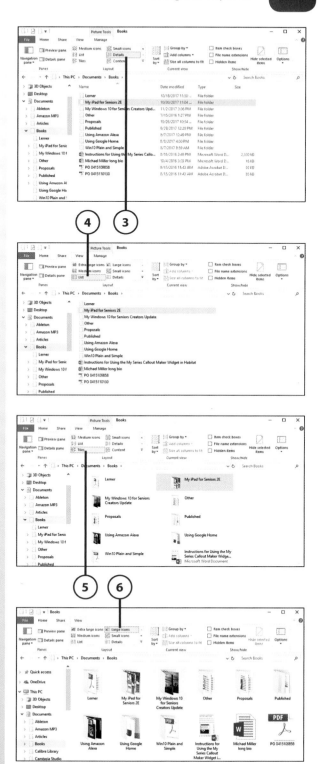

## Sort Files and Folders

When viewing files in File Explorer, you can sort your files and folders in a number of ways. To view your files in alphabetic order, choose to sort by Name. To see all similar files grouped together, choose to sort by Type. To sort your files by the date and time they were last edited, select Date Modified.

1. From within File Explorer, click the View tab on the ribbon bar.

2. Click the Sort By button.

3. Choose to sort by Name, Date Modified, Type, Size, Date Created, Authors, Categories, Tags, or Title.

4. By default, Windows sorts items in ascending order. To change the sort order, click Descending.

### Different Sorting Options

Different types of files have different sorting options. For example, if you're viewing music files, you can sort by Album, Artists, Bit Rate, Composers, Genre, and the like.

# Working with Folders

Windows organizes like files into folders. You can create new folders to hold new files, or rename existing folders if you like.

# Create a New Folder

The more files you create, the harder it is to organize and find things on your hard disk. When the number of files you have becomes unmanageable, you need to create more folders—and sub-folders—to better manage those files.

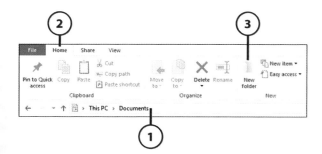

**(1)** From within File Explorer, navigate to the drive or folder where you want to place the new folder.

**(2)** Click the Home tab on the ribbon bar.

**(3)** Click the New Folder button.

**(4)** A new, empty folder now appears with the filename New Folder highlighted. Type a name for your folder and then press Enter.

## It's Not All Good

### Don't Click

When creating a new folder, do not click the folder until you've entered a new name for it. Clicking the folder locks in the current name as New Folder. You would then have to rename the folder (as described next) to change that name.

# Rename a Folder or File

When you create a new folder, it helps to give it a name that describes its contents. Sometimes, however, you might need to change a folder's name. Fortunately, Windows makes renaming an item relatively easy.

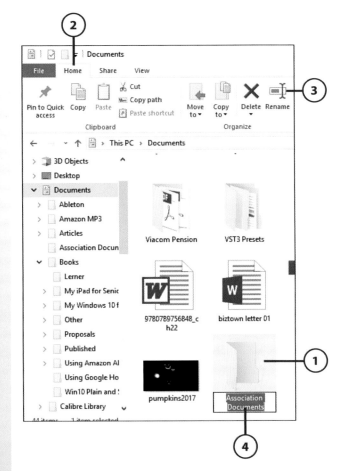

## Renaming Files

The steps in this lesson also apply to renaming files, not just folders.

(1) Click the file or folder you want to rename.

(2) Click the Home tab on the ribbon bar.

(3) Click the Rename button; this highlights the filename.

(4) Type a new name for your folder (which overwrites the current name) and then press Enter.

## Keyboard Shortcut

You can also rename a folder or file by selecting the item and pressing F2 on your computer keyboard. This highlights the name and readies it for editing.

# >>>*Go Further*

## WHY ORGANIZE YOUR FOLDERS?

You might never have occasion to open File Explorer and work with your files and folders. But there's some value in doing so, especially when it comes to organizing your own personal files.

Perhaps the best example of this is when you have a large number of digital photos—which, if you're a grandparent, you surely do. Instead of lumping hundreds or thousands of photos into a single Photos folder, you can instead create different subfolders for different types of photos. For example, you might want to create folders named Vacation Photos, Family Photos, Holiday Photos, and the like.

Personally, I like organizing my photos by year and month. Within my main Photos folder, I have subfolders for 2012, 2013, 2014, 2015, and the like. Then, within each year folder, I have subfolders for each month—January, February, March, and such. This way, I can quickly click through the folders to find photos taken in a particular month.

You can organize your photos and other files similarly, or use whatever type of organization suits you best. The point is to make all of your files easier to find, however you choose to do so.

# Managing Files

Tens of thousands of files are stored on a typical personal computer. From time to time, you might need to manage them in various ways. You can copy a file to create a duplicate in another location, or move a file from one location to another. You can even delete files from your hard drive, if you like. And you do all this with File Explorer.

# Copy a File

Copying a file places a duplicate of the original file into a new location. There are many ways to copy a file in Windows, the easiest is to use the Copy To button on File Explorer's Home ribbon.

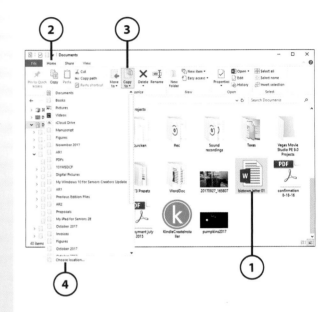

( **1** ) From within File Explorer, navigate to and click the item you want to copy.

( **2** ) Click the Home tab on the ribbon bar.

( **3** ) Click the Copy To button.

( **4** ) Select Choose Location (at the bottom of the pull-down menu). The Copy Items dialog box displays.

( **5** ) Navigate to the new location for the item.

( **6** ) Click the Copy button.

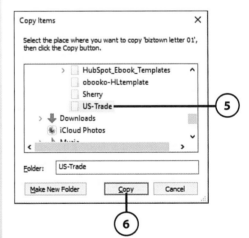

## Primary Folders

To copy an item directly to one of the primary Windows folders, click either Documents, Music, Pictures, or Videos from the Copy To menu.

# Move a File

Moving a file or folder is different from copying it. Moving cuts the item from its previous location and pastes it into a new location. Copying leaves the original item where it was and creates a copy of the item elsewhere.

1. From within File Explorer, navigate to and click the item you want to move.

2. Click the Home tab on the ribbon bar.

3. Click the Move To button.

4. Select Choose Location at the bottom of the pull-down menu. The Move Items dialog box displays.

5. Navigate to the new location for the item.

6. Click the Move button.

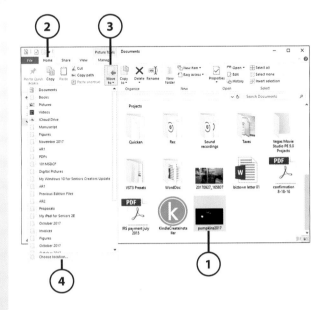

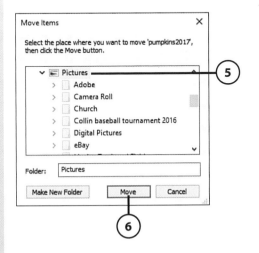

## Delete a File or Folder

Keeping too many files eats up a lot of hard disk space on your computer—which can be a bad thing. Because you don't want to waste disk space, you should periodically delete those files (and folders) you no longer need. When you delete a file, you send it to the Windows Recycle Bin, which is kind of a trash can for deleted files.

**1** From within File Explorer, navigate to and click the item you want to delete.

**2** Click the Home tab on the ribbon bar.

**3** Click the Delete button.

### Other Ways to Delete

You can also delete a file by dragging it from the File Explorer window onto the Recycle Bin icon on the desktop, or by selecting it and pressing the Delete key on your computer keyboard.

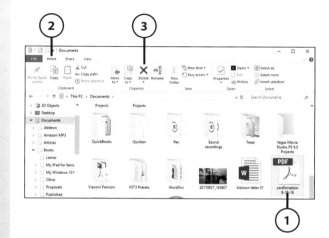

## Restore a Deleted File

Have you ever accidentally deleted the wrong file? If so, you're in luck. Windows stores the files you delete in the Recycle Bin, which is actually a special folder on your hard disk. For a short period of time, you can "undelete" files from the Recycle Bin back to their original locations—and save yourself from making a bad mistake.

**1** On the Windows desktop, double-click the Recycle Bin icon to open the Recycle Bin folder.

Recycle Bin

**2** Click the file you want to restore.

**3** Click the Manage tab on the ribbon bar.

**4** Click the Restore the Selected Items button.

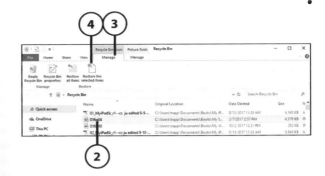

## Empty the Recycle Bin

By default, the deleted files in the Recycle Bin can occupy 4GB plus 5% of your hard disk space. When you've deleted enough files to exceed this limit, the oldest files in the Recycle Bin are automatically and permanently deleted from your hard disk. You can also manually empty the Recycle Bin and thus free up some hard disk space.

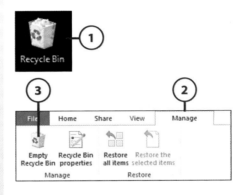

**1** From the Windows desktop, double-click the Recycle Bin icon to open the Recycle Bin folder.

**2** Click the Manage tab on the ribbon bar.

**3** Click the Empty Recycle Bin button.

**4** Click Yes in the Delete Multiple Items dialog box to completely erase the files.

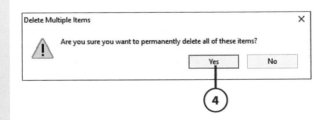

# Working with Microsoft OneDrive

Microsoft offers online storage for all your documents and data, via its OneDrive service. When you store your files on OneDrive, you can access them via any computer or mobile device connected to the Internet.

## Cloud Storage

Online file storage, such as that offered by OneDrive, Apple's iCloud, and Google Drive, is called *cloud storage*. The advantage of cloud storage is that you can access files from any computer (work, home, or other) at any location. You're not limited to using a given file on one particular computer.

# Manage OneDrive Files on the Web

Because OneDrive stores your files on the Web, you can manage all your OneDrive files with your web browser, from any Internet-connected computer. Just launch your browser and go to onedrive.live.com.

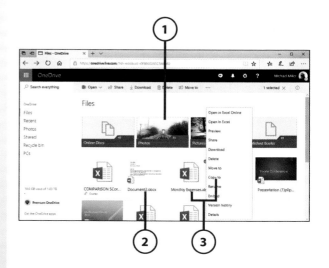

**1**   Your OneDrive files are stored in folders—Documents, Recent Docs, Photos, and so forth. Click a folder to view its contents.

**2**   Click a file to view it or, in the case of an Office document, open it in its host application.

**3**   To copy, cut, or rename a file, right-click the file to display the options menu, and then select the action you want to perform.

## Storage Plans

Microsoft gives you 5GB of storage in your free OneDrive account, which is more than enough to store most users' documents, digital photos, and the like. If you need more storage, you can purchase 50GB of storage for $1.99/month. (If you subscribe to Microsoft's Office 365 plan, you get 1TB of storage for free.)

# Manage OneDrive Files with File Explorer

You can also use File Explorer to view and manage the files stored online with OneDrive.

( 1 ) On your computer, open File Explorer and click OneDrive in the navigation pane. This displays all your OneDrive files and folders.

( 2 ) Double-click to open a folder.

( 3 ) Double-click to open a file.

( 4 ) To manage your files, click any file and then click the appropriate option on File Explorer's Home ribbon.

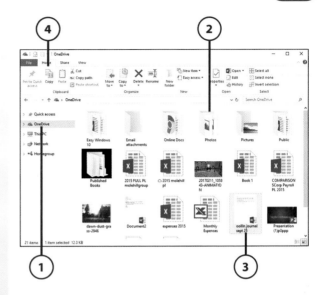

# Upload a File to OneDrive

Any file on your hard drive can be uploaded to OneDrive for storage online.

( 1 ) On the OneDrive website, navigate to and open the folder where you want to store the file. (If you don't select a folder, the file will be uploaded to the main OneDrive directory.)

( 2 ) Click Upload on the toolbar; then click Files to display the Open dialog box.

( 3 ) Navigate to and select the file(s) you want to upload.

( 4 ) Click the Open button.

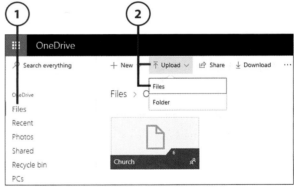

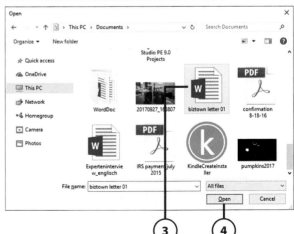

## >>>Go Further

### UPLOADING AND DOWNLOADING FROM FILE EXPLORER

You can also upload and download files to and from OneDrive from within File Explorer. To upload a file, copy that file from any other location to any folder within the OneDrive folder. To download a file, copy that file from the OneDrive folder to another location on your computer.

## Download a File to Your PC

Files stored on OneDrive can also be downloaded to your computer.

1. On the OneDrive website, select the file(s) you want to download.

2. Click Download. When prompted to save the file, do so. (Unless you specify otherwise, files downloaded from OneDrive are saved into the Download folder on your computer.)

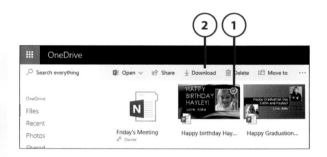

## Synchronizing Files On-Demand

The Windows 10 Fall Creators Update lets you work directly with files stored online with OneDrive, without first having to download those files to your computer. This lets you access the same files from multiple computers and devices, and have all your work show up on all your devices; make a change from one computer or device and all other versions of the file will automatically reflect that change. (You can also choose to download those files, if you want.)

## Enabling Files On-Demand

Files On-Demand should have been enabled by default when you installed the Fall Creators Update. You can check this by right-clicking the OneDrive icon in the notifications area of the Windows taskbar and then clicking Settings; when the Microsoft OneDrive dialog box opens, select the Settings tab, go to the File On-Demand section, and select Save Space and Download Files as You Use Them.

To use Files On-Demand, open File Explorer, select OneDrive, and double-click to open a given file. The file opens from within its native application, and any changes you make are automatically saved to the master file on OneDrive.

You can view the status of all your OneDrive files from within File Explorer.

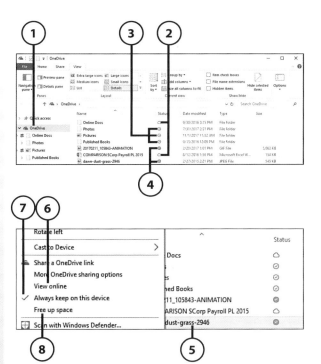

( 1 ) From within File Explorer, click OneDrive. You can view the On-Demand status of each file from the Status column in Details view, or next to the file name in any other view.

( 2 ) Online Only files are only available online in OneDrive.

( 3 ) Locally Available files are stored on your computer.

( 4 ) Always Available files are stored online but can be edited on your computer or other devices.

( 5 ) To change the On-Demand status of any file, right-click that file to view the context menu.

( 6 ) Select View Online to make a file Always Available.

( 7 ) Select Always Keep on This Device to make a file Locally Available.

( 8 ) Click Free Up Space to make a file Online Only.

Windows Task Manager

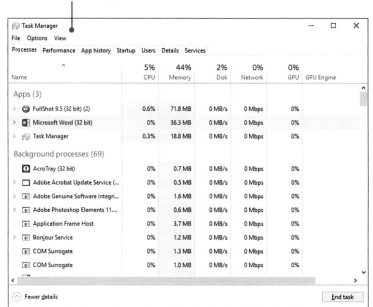

In this chapter, you find out how to deal with common computer problems—and prevent those problems from happening.

→ Performing Necessary Maintenance
→ Backing Up Important Files
→ Fixing Simple Problems
→ Recovering from Serious Problems

# Dealing with Common Problems

Have you ever had your computer freeze on you? Or refuse to start? Or just start acting weird? Maybe you've had problems trying to print a document, or open a given program, or find a particular file. Or maybe you just can't figure out how to do a specific something.

Computer problems happen. When issues do occur, you want to get things fixed and running again as fast and as painlessly as possible. That's what this chapter is all about—dealing with those relatively common computer problems you might encounter.

## Performing Necessary Maintenance

Before we deal with fixing computer problems, let's deal with how to prevent those problems. That's right—a little preventive maintenance can stave off a lot of future problems. Take care of your PC on a regular basis, and it will take care of you.

To ease the task of protecting and maintaining your system, Windows 10 includes several utilities to help you keep your computer running smoothly. You should use these tools as part of your regular maintenance routine—or if you experience specific problems with your computer system.

## How Often to Run?

It's a good idea to run all these system utilities at least once a month, just to ensure that your system stays in tip-top condition.

# Delete Unnecessary Files

Even with today's very large hard disks, you can still end up with too many useless files taking up too much hard disk space—especially if you're obsessed with taking vacation pictures or photos of your very cute grandkids. Fortunately, Windows includes a utility that identifies and deletes unused files. The Disk Cleanup tool is what you should use when you need to free up extra hard disk space for more frequently used files.

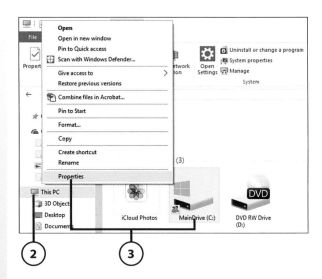

1. Click the File Explorer icon on the taskbar or Start menu to open File Explorer.

2. Click This PC section in the navigation pane.

3. Right-click the drive you want to clean up (usually the C: drive), and click Properties to open the Properties dialog box.

4. Select the General tab (displayed by default) and click the Disk Cleanup button.

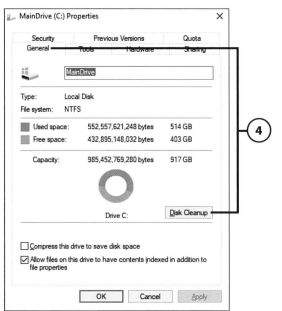

**5** Disk Cleanup automatically analyzes the contents of your hard disk drive. When it's finished analyzing, it presents its results in the Disk Cleanup dialog box. Select which types of files you want to delete.

**6** Click OK to begin deleting.

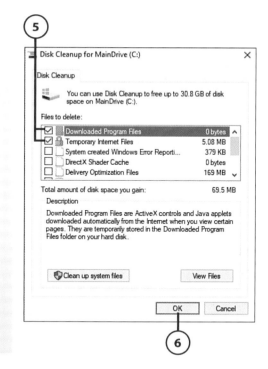

**Which Files to Delete?**

You can safely choose to delete all files suggested by Disk Cleanup *except* the setup log files and hibernation files. These files are needed by the Windows operating system, and you should not delete them.

## Delete Unused Programs

Another way to free up valuable hard disk space is to delete those programs you never use. This is accomplished using the Uninstall or Change a Program utility.

**1** Click the Start button and then click Settings (or open the Action Center and select All Settings) to open the Settings window.

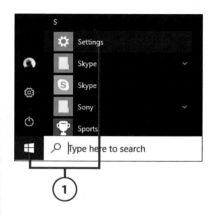

**2** Click Apps to open the Apps page.

**3** Click to select the Apps & Features tab.

**4** Click the program you want to delete; this expands the app's listing.

**5** Click Uninstall.

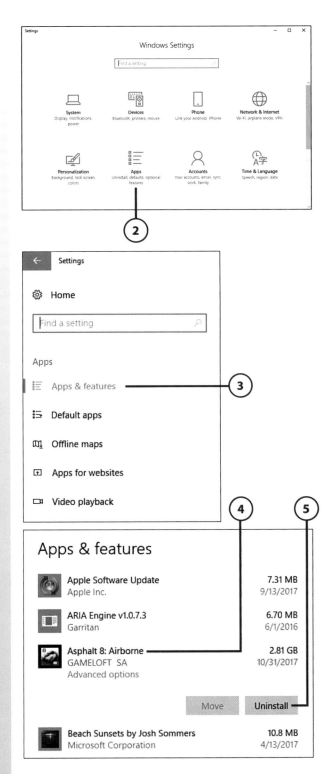

# Backing Up Important Files

The data stored on your computer's hard disk is valuable, and perhaps irreplaceable. We're talking about your personal photos, home movies, favorite music, spreadsheets, and word processing documents, and maybe even a tax return or two.

That's why you want to keep a backup copy of all these valuable files. The easiest way to store backup copies is on an external hard disk drive. These drives provide lots of storage space for a relatively low cost, and they connect to your PC via USB. There's no excuse not to do it!

>>>*Go Further*

## OTHER BACKUP OPTIONS

Many people find that the easiest way to back up their files is with an external hard drive. Get a big enough external drive (about the same size as your main hard disk), and you can copy your entire hard disk to the external drive. Then, if your system ever crashes, you can restore your backed-up files from the external drive to your computer's hard drive.

Most external hard drives come with some sort of backup software installed, or you can use a third-party backup program. The backup process can be automated so that it occurs once a day or once a week and only backs up those new or changed files since your last backup.

Other users prefer to back up their data over the Internet, using an online backup service. This type of service copies your important files from your computer to the service's own servers, over the Internet. This way, if your local data is lost or damaged, you can then restore the files from the online backup service's servers.

Several popular online backup services are designed for home users, including the following:

- Carbonite (www.carbonite.com)
- IDrive (www.idrive.com)
- Mozy (www.mozy.com)
- Norton Online Backup (us.norton.com/online-backup)
- SOS Online Backup (www.sosonlinebackup.com)

The benefit of using an online backup service is that the backup copy of your library is stored off-site, so you're protected in case of any local physical catastrophe, such as fire or flood. Most online backup services also work in the background, so they're constantly backing up new and changed files in real time. Expect to pay $50 or more per year, per computer, for one of these services.

# Activate File History

In Windows 10, you can back up important data files using the File History feature. When enabled, File History automatically creates copies of all the different versions of your files and enables you to restore them in case they get lost or destroyed. To protect your valuable files, then, there's little you need to do except turn on File History.

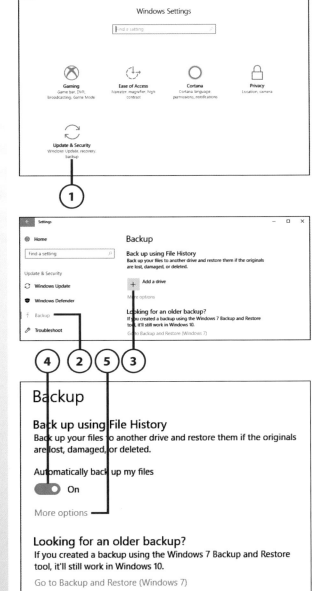

1. Open the Settings window and click Update & Security to open the Update & Security page.

2. Click to select the Backup tab.

3. If you have not yet selected a backup drive, click + Add a Drive and select a drive—typically an external hard disk or another computer on your home network. Or...

4. If you've previously selected a backup drive, make sure the Automatically Back Up My Files switch is clicked "on."

5. Click More Options.

6. Click the Back Up My Files control and select how often you want to perform a backup—from every 10 minutes to daily.

7. Click the Keep My Backups control and select how long you want to keep your backed up files. (The default is "forever," although you can select other options.)

8. By default, File History backs up all the folders in your User folder. To add another folder to the backup, go to the Back Up These Folders section, click the +, and select a folder.

9. To *not* back up a specific folder, go to the Exclude These Folders section, click the +, and select a folder.

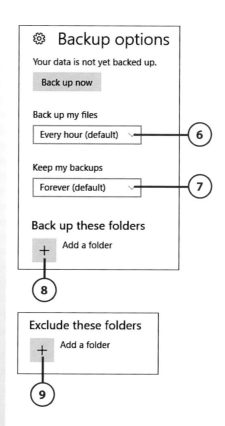

⚙ **Backup options**

Your data is not yet backed up.

Back up now

Back up my files

Every hour (default)    — 6

Keep my backups

Forever (default)    — 7

**Back up these folders**

+    Add a folder

8

**Exclude these folders**

+    Add a folder

9

# >>>Go Further

## RESTORING BACKUP FILES

What do you do if you have a serious enough computer problem that you lose access to your important files? Well, if you've employed File History, it's easy enough to restore any or all files you've backed up from your backup medium. It's a matter of selecting which files to restore, and to where.

From the Settings app, select the Backup tab, and click More Options. Scroll down the left column and click Restore Files from a Current Backup. Navigate to and select those files or folders you want to restore then click the Restore button to restore these files to their original locations.

By the way, you can also use File History to restore a given file to an earlier state. This is useful if you're editing a document, for example, and want to use an earlier version of the document before more recent editing. Just select the version of the file you want to restore and click the Restore button.

# Fixing Simple Problems

Computers aren't perfect—even new ones. It's always possible that at some point in time, something will go wrong with your PC. It might refuse to start; it might freeze up; it might crash and go dead. Then what do you do?

When something goes wrong with your computer, there's no need to panic (even though that's what you'll probably feel like doing). Most PC problems have easy-to-find causes and simple solutions. The key thing is to keep your wits about you and attack the situation calmly and logically.

## You Can't Connect to the Internet

This problem is likely caused by a bad connection to your Wi-Fi network or hotspot. Fix the Wi-Fi problem and you can get back online lickity-split.

1. Try turning off and then turning back on your PC's wireless functionality. You might be able to do this from a button or switch on your computer, or you can do it within Windows. Click the Connections icon on the taskbar to display the Connections pane. Click "off" the Wi-Fi control, wait a few moments, and then turn the Wi-Fi option back "on" and reconnect to your network.

2. It's possible that your computer is too far away from the wireless signal. Move your computer nearer to the closest Wi-Fi router or hotspot.

3. If you're using a public Wi-Fi hotspot, you might need to log on to the hotspot to access the Internet. Open your web browser and try to access any web page; if you're greeted with a log-in page for the hotspot, enter the appropriate information to get connected.

4. If nothing else works, it's possible that the hotspot to which you're trying to connect has Internet issues. Report your problem to whomever is in charge at the moment.

5. If you're on your home network, it's possible that your Wi-Fi router or cable modem (or combination gateway device) is the problem. Try turning off the router and modem or gateway device for five minutes or so, and then turning them back on.

6. It's also possible that your home Internet service provider (ISP) is having issues. If the problem persists, call your ISP and report the problem.

# You Can't Go to a Specific Web Page

If you have a good connection to the Internet and can open some web pages, trouble opening a specific web page is probably isolated to that particular website.

1. The site might be having temporary connection issues. Refresh the web page to try loading it again.

2. You might have typed the wrong address for this particular site. Try entering the address again.

3. You might have the wrong address for a specific page on the website. Try shortening the address to include only the main URL—that is, go directly to the site's home page, not to an individual page on the site. For example, instead of going to www.quepublishing.com/articles/article.aspx?p=2832580, just go to the main page at www.quepublishing.com and navigate from there.

4. If you continue to have issues with this website, it's probably a problem with the site itself. That is, it's nothing you're doing wrong. Wait a few moments and try again to see if the problem is fixed.

# You Can't Print

What do you do when you try to print a document on your printer and nothing happens? This problem could have several causes.

1. Click the Print button or command to open the Printer page or dialog box and then make sure the correct printer is selected.

2. Make sure the printer is turned on. (You'd be surprised….)

3. Check the printer to make sure it has plenty of paper and isn't jammed. (And if it is jammed, follow the manufacturer's instructions to unjam it.)

4. Check the cable between your computer and the printer. Make sure both ends are firmly connected. Lots of printer problems are the result of loose cables.

## Your Computer Is Slow

Many computers will start to slow down over time. There are many reasons for this, from an overly full hard disk to an unwanted malware infection.

1. Close any open programs that don't need to be open at the moment.

2. Run the Disk Cleanup utility to remove unnecessary files and free up hard disk space. (See the "Delete Unnecessary Files" task earlier in this chapter for more information on the Disk Cleanup Utility.)

3. Install and run a reputable anti-malware utility to find and remove any computer viruses or malware unknowingly installed on your system. (Learn more about anti-malware utilities in Chapter 15, "Protecting Yourself Online.")

4. Ask a knowledgeable friend or professional computer technician to check your computer's startup programs; these are programs that load automatically when Windows starts up and run in the background, using valuable computer memory. Have your friend or technician remove those unnecessary startup programs.

### Task Manager

You can view and manage your startup programs from the Task Manager utility. To open the Task Manager, press Ctrl+Alt+Del and then select Task Manager. Select the Startup tab to view those programs that launch during startup, and disable those you don't want to launch.

## A Specific Program Freezes

Sometimes Windows works fine but an individual software program stops working. Fortunately, Windows presents an exceptionally safe environment; when an individual application crashes or freezes or otherwise quits working, it seldom messes up your entire system. You can then use the Task Manager utility to close any frozen program without affecting other Windows programs.

1. When an application freezes, press Ctrl+Alt+Del.

2. Click the Task Manager option to launch the Task Manager utility.

3. Click the Processes tab.

4. Go to the Apps section and click the program that's frozen.

5. Click the End Task button.

## Your Entire Computer Freezes

If you're like many users, the worst thing that can happen is that your computer totally freezes, and you can't do anything—including shut it off. Well, there is a way to shut down a frozen computer and then restart your system.

1. Hold down the Windows key on your keyboard and simultaneously press your PC's power button. If that doesn't work, press and hold the PC's power button for several seconds, until the PC shuts down.

2. Wait a few moments and then turn your computer back on. It should restart normally. If not, you might need to consult a computer technician or repair service.

## >>>Go Further

### TROUBLESHOOTING PC PROBLEMS

No matter what kind of computer-related problem you're experiencing, you can take the following six basic steps to track down the cause of the problem. Work through these steps calmly and deliberately, and you're likely to find what's causing the current problem—and then be in a good position to fix it yourself:

1. Don't panic! Just because there's something wrong with your PC is no reason to get frustrated or angry or just plain crazy. That's because it's likely that there's nothing seriously wrong. Besides, getting all panicky won't solve anything. Keep your wits about you and proceed logically, and you can probably find what's causing your problem and get it fixed.

2. Check for operator errors. That is, look for something that you did wrong. Maybe you clicked the wrong button, pressed the wrong key, or plugged something into the wrong port. Retrace your steps and try to duplicate your problem. Chances are the problem won't recur if you don't make the same mistake twice.

3. Check that everything is plugged in to the proper place and that the system unit itself is getting power. Take special care to ensure that all your cables are securely connected—loose connections can cause all sorts of strange results.

4. Make sure you have the latest versions of all the software and apps installed on your system. That's because old versions of most programs probably haven't been updated with the latest bug fixes and compatibility patches. (These are small updates that typically fix known issues within a program.)

5. Try to isolate the problem by when and how it occurs. Walk through each step of the process to see if you can identify a particular program or process that might be causing the problem.

6. When all else fails, call in professional help. If you have a brand-new PC and you think it's a Windows-related issue, contact Microsoft's technical support department. If you think it's a problem with a particular program or app, contact the tech support department of the program's manufacturer. If you think it's a hardware-related problem, contact the manufacturer of your PC or the dealer you bought it from. The pros are there for a reason—when you need technical support, go and get it.

Above all, don't be afraid of your PC. It's really difficult to break a computer these days; even if you did something wrong, most mistakes can be easily fixed.

## Recovering from Serious Problems

If you have a frozen computer that won't unfreeze or a computer that refuses to start properly, and this issue continues over time (that is, restarting your computer doesn't fix it), you might have a serious problem on your hands. At this point, you bring in a professional computer technician or attempt a few simple fixes on your own.

# Restore Your Computer to a Previous State

If your computer system crashes or freezes on a regular basis, your best course of action is to reboot your system and then run the System Restore utility. This utility can automatically restore your system to the state it was in before the crash occurred—and save you the trouble of reinstalling any damaged software programs. It's a great safety net for when things go wrong!

## Before You Restore

Be sure to close all programs before you use System Restore because Windows will need to be restarted when the utility has done its work. The full process might take a half-hour or more.

1. From the Cortana search box on the taskbar, enter **recovery**.

2. Select Recovery from the search results. This opens the Recovery panel.

3. Click Open System Restore to display the System Restore window.

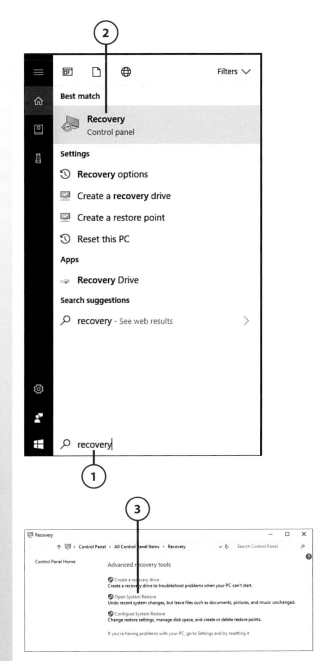

(4) Click the Next button.

(5) Select a restore point from the list.

(6) Click the Next button.

(7) Click the Finish button to begin the restore process.

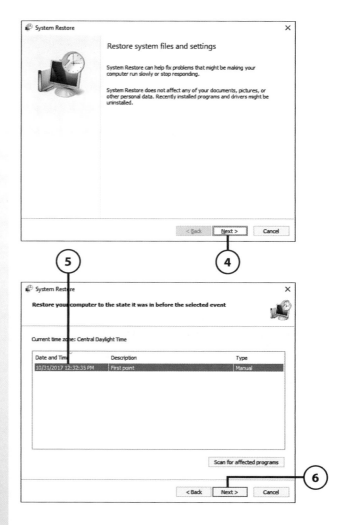

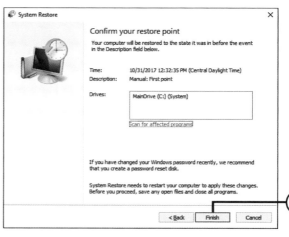

## *It's Not All Good*

**System Files Only—No Documents**

System Restore helps you recover any damaged programs and system files, but it doesn't help you recover any documents or data files. This is why you need to use the File History utility to back up all your data on a regular basis—and restore that backed-up data in the case of an emergency. Read the "Activate File History" task earlier in this chapter for more information about the File History utility.

# Refresh System Files

Your computer can get seriously out of whack if key system files somehow become damaged or deleted. Fortunately, Windows 10 includes the ability to "refresh" your system with the current versions of important system files. This refresh function works by checking whether key system files are working properly or not; if it finds any issues, it attempts to repair those files—and only those files.

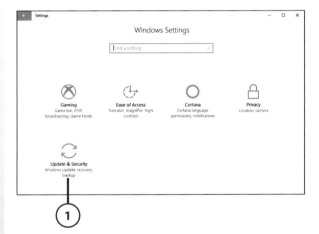

## System Files Only

Refreshing your PC doesn't remove any of your personal files or documents. It only refreshes Windows system files.

( 1 ) From the Settings window, click Update & Security.

( 2 ) Click to select the Recovery tab.

( 3 ) Go to the Reset This PC section and click Get Started.

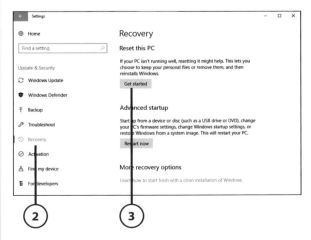

(4) When prompted, click the Keep My Files option and follow the onscreen instructions to complete the refresh.

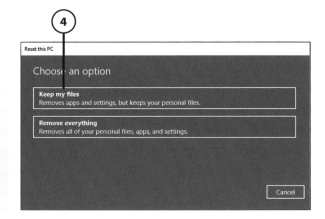

## Reset Your System

In the event of a catastrophic system failure, you can reset your computer to its factory-fresh condition by wiping clean the hard disk and reinstalling Windows from scratch.

Resetting your system is more drastic than simply refreshing it. The Reset PC utility wipes your hard disk clean and reinstalls Windows from scratch. That leaves you with a completely reset system—but without any of the apps you've installed or the files you created.

*It's Not All Good*

**Everything Is Deleted**

The Reset PC utility completely deletes all the files, documents, and programs you have on your system. You'll want to back up your files before taking this extreme step, and then restore your files from the backup and reinstall all the apps you use.

**1** From the Settings window, click Update & Security.

**2** Click to select the Recovery tab.

**3** Go to the Reset This PC section and click Get Started.

**4** When prompted, click the Remove Everything option; then follow the onscreen instructions to complete the reset process.

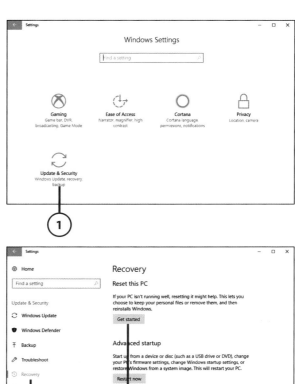

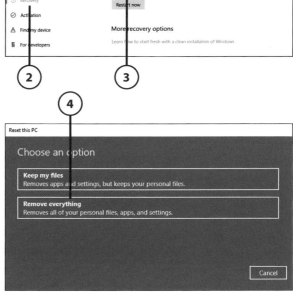

## >>>Go Further
### GETTING HELP

Many computer users easily become befuddled when it comes to dealing with even relatively simple computer problems. I understand completely; there's little that's readily apparent or intuitive about figuring out how to fix many PC-related issues.

If you feel over your head or out of your element when it comes to dealing with a particular computer problem, that's okay; you don't have to try to fix everything yourself. You have many options available to you, from Best Buy's ubiquitous Geek Squad to any number of local computer repair shops. Google **computer repair** for your location, check your local Yellow Pages, or just ask around to see who your friends use for computer support. It might prove faster and less aggravating in the long run to pay a professional to get your computer working properly again.

# Glossary

## 1–10

**2-in-1 computer**   A portable computer that combines the functionality of a touchscreen tablet and traditional notebook PC.

## A

**Action Center**   The pop-up pane that appears when you click the Notifications button in the Windows taskbar; it displays system messages and quick links to key Windows functions.

**address**   The location of an Internet host. An email address might take the form johndoe@xyz.com; a web address might look like www.xyztech.com. See also *URL*.

**all-in-one computer**   A desktop computer where the system unit, monitor, and speakers are housed in a single unit. Often the monitor of such a system has a touchscreen display.

**app**   *See application.*

**application**　A computer program designed for a specific task or use, such as word processing, accounting, or missile guidance.

**attachment**　A file, such as a Word document or graphics image, attached to an email message.

# B

**backup**　A copy of important data files.

**boot**　The process of turning on your computer system.

**broadband**　A high-speed Internet connection; it's faster than the older dial-up connection.

**browser**　A program, such as Microsoft Edge or Google Chrome, used to view pages on the Web.

**bug**　An error in a software program or the hardware.

# C

**CD-ROM (compact disc read-only memory)**　A CD that can be used to store computer data. A CD-ROM, similar to an audio CD, stores data in a form readable by a laser, resulting in a storage device of great capacity and quick accessibility.

**computer**　A programmable device that can store, retrieve, and process data.

**Cortana**　The virtual assistant built into Windows 10; it's designed to provide personalized information and search capabilities.

**CPU (central processing unit)**　The group of circuits that direct the entire computer system by (1) interpreting and executing program instruction and (2) coordinating the interaction of input, output, and storage devices.

**cursor**　The highlighted area or pointer that tracks with the movement of your mouse or arrow keys onscreen.

# D

**data**　Information—on a computer, in digital format.

**desktop**　The background in Windows upon which all other apps and utilities sit.

**desktop computer**    A personal computer designed for use on a typical office desktop. A traditional desktop computer system consists of a system unit, monitor, keyboard, mouse, and speakers.

**device**    A computer file that represents some object—physical or nonphysical—installed on your system.

**disk**    A device that stores data in magnetic or optical format.

**disk drive**    A mechanism for retrieving information stored on a magnetic disk. The drive rotates the disk at high speed and reads the data with a magnetic head similar to those used in tape recorders.

**domain**    The identifying portion of an Internet address. In email addresses, the domain name follows the @ sign; in website addresses, the domain name follows the www.

**download**    A way to transfer files, graphics, or other information from the Internet to your computer.

**driver**    A support file that tells a program how to interact with a specific hardware device, such as a hard disk controller or video display card.

**DVD**    An optical disc, similar to a CD, that can hold a minimum of 4.7GB, enough for a full-length movie.

# E

**email**    Electronic mail; a means of corresponding with other computer users over the Internet through digital messages.

**encryption**    A method of encoding files so only the recipient can read the information.

**Ethernet**    A popular computer networking technology; Ethernet is used to network, or hook together, computers so that they can share information.

**executable file**    A program you run on your computer system.

# F

**Fall Creators Update**   The latest version of Windows 10, released in October, 2017.

**favorite**   A bookmarked site in a web browser.

**file**   Any group of data treated as a single entity by the computer, such as a word processor document, a program, or a database.

**File Explorer**   The utility used to navigate and display files and folders on your computer system. Previously known as Windows Explorer.

**firewall**   Computer hardware or software with special security features to safeguard a computer connected to a network or to the Internet.

**folder**   A way to group files on a disk; each folder can contain multiple files or other folders (called *subfolders*). Folders are sometimes called *directories*.

**freeware**   Free software available over the Internet. This is in contrast with *shareware*, which is available freely but usually asks the user to send payment for using the software.

# G

**gigabyte (GB)**   One billion bytes.

**graphics**   Pictures, photographs, and clip art.

# H

**hard disk**   A sealed cartridge containing a magnetic storage disk(s) designed for long-term mass storage of computer data.

**hardware**   The physical equipment, as opposed to the programs and procedures, used in computing.

**home page**   The first or main page of a website.

**hover**   *See mouse over.*

**hyperlink**   A connection between two tagged elements in a web page, or separate sites, that makes it possible to click from one to the other.

# I–J

**icon**   A graphic symbol on the display screen that represents a file, peripheral, or some other object or function.

**Internet**   The global network of networks that connects millions of computers and other devices around the world.

**Internet service provider (ISP)**   A company that provides end-user access to the Internet via its central computers and local access lines.

# K–L

**keyboard**   The typewriter-like device used to type instructions to a personal computer.

**kilobyte (KB)**   A unit of measure for data storage or transmission equivalent to 1024 bytes; often rounded to 1000.

**LAN (local-area network)**   A system that enables users to connect PCs to one another or to minicomputers or mainframes.

**laptop**   A portable computer small enough to operate on one's lap. Also known as a *notebook* computer.

# M–N

**malware**   Short for *malicious software*, any software program designed to do damage to or take over your computer system.

**megabyte (MB)**   One million bytes.

**megahertz (MHz)**   A measure of microprocessing speed; 1MHz equals one million electrical cycles per second. (One thousand MHz equals 1 gigahertz, or GHz.)

**memory**   Temporary electronic storage for data and instructions, via electronic impulses on a chip.

**microprocessor**   A complete central processing unit assembled on a single silicon chip.

**Microsoft Edge**   The web browser included with Windows 10.

**Microsoft Store**    Microsoft's online store that offers Windows apps for sale and download.

**modem (modulator demodulator)**    A device capable of converting a digital signal into an analog signal, typically used to connect to the Internet.

**monitor**    The display device on a computer, similar to a television screen.

**motherboard**    Typically the largest printed circuit board in a computer, housing the CPU chip and controlling circuitry.

**mouse**    A small handheld input device connected to a computer and featuring one or more button-style switches. When moved around on a flat surface, the mouse causes a symbol on the computer screen to make corresponding movements.

**mouse over**    The act of selecting an item by placing your cursor over an icon without clicking. Also known as *hovering*.

**network**    An interconnected group of computers.

**notebook computer**    A portable computer with all components (including keyboard, screen, and touchpad) contained in a single unit. Notebook PCs can typically be operated via either battery or wall power.

# O–P

**operating system**    A sequence of programming codes that instructs a computer about its various parts and peripherals and how to operate them. Operating systems, such as Windows, deal only with the workings of the hardware and are separate from software programs.

**path**    The collection of folders and subfolders (listed in order of hierarchy) that hold a particular file.

**peripheral**    A device connected to the computer that provides communication or auxiliary functions.

**phishing**    The act of trying to "fish" for personal information via means of a deliberately deceptive email or website.

**pixel**    The individual picture elements that combine to create a video image.

**port**   An interface on a computer to which you can connect a device, either internally or externally.

**printer**   The piece of computer hardware that creates hard copy printouts of documents.

# Q–R

**RAM (random-access memory)**   A temporary storage space in which data can be held on a chip rather than being stored on disk or tape. The contents of RAM can be accessed or altered at any time during a session but will be lost when the computer is turned off.

**resolution**   The degree of clarity an image displays, typically expressed by the number of horizontal and vertical pixels or the number of dots per inch (dpi).

**ribbon**   A toolbar-like collection of action buttons, used in many newer Windows programs.

**ROM (read-only memory)**   A type of chip memory, the contents of which have been permanently recorded in a computer by the manufacturer and cannot be altered by the user.

**root**   The main directory or folder on a disk.

**router**   A piece of hardware or software that handles the connection between your home network and the Internet.

# S

**scanner**   A device that converts paper documents or photos into a format that can be viewed on a computer and manipulated by the user.

**server**   The central computer in a network, providing a service or data access to client computers on the network.

**shareware**   A software program distributed on the honor system; providers make their programs freely accessible over the Internet, with the understanding that those who use them will send payment to the provider after using them. See also *freeware*.

**software** The programs and procedures, as opposed to the physical equipment, used in computing.

**spam** Junk email. As a verb, it means to send thousands of copies of a junk email message.

**spreadsheet** A program that performs mathematical operations on numbers arranged in large arrays; used mainly for accounting and other record keeping.

**spyware** Software used to surreptitiously monitor computer use (that is, spy on other users).

**Start menu** The pop-up menu, activated by clicking the Start button, that displays all installed programs on a computer.

**system unit** The part of a desktop computer system that looks like a big gray or black box. The system unit typically contains the microprocessor, system memory, hard disk drive, floppy disk drives, and various cards.

# T–U–V

**tablet computer** A small, handheld computer with no keyboard or mouse, operated solely via its touchscreen display.

**Task View** The Windows function that enables the creation of multiple virtual desktops, each with its own collection of open apps.

**terabyte (TB)** One trillion bytes.

**touchscreen display** A computer display that is touch sensitive and can be operated with a touch of the finger.

**trackpad** The pointing device used on most notebook PCs, in lieu of an external mouse.

**upgrade** To add a new or improved peripheral or part to your system hardware. Also to install a newer version of an existing piece of software.

**upload**   The act of copying a file from a personal computer to a website or Internet server. The opposite of *download*.

**URL (uniform resource locator)**   The address that identifies a web page to a browser. Also known as a *web address*.

**USB (universal serial bus)**   The most common type of port for connecting peripherals to personal computers.

**virus**   A computer program segment or string of code that can attach itself to another program or file, reproduce itself, and spread from one computer to another. Viruses can destroy or change data and in other ways sabotage computer systems.

# W–X–Y–Z

**web page**   An HTML file, containing text, graphics, and/or mini-applications, viewed with a web browser.

**website**   An organized, linked collection of web pages stored on an Internet server and read using a web browser. The opening page of a site is called a *home page*.

**Wi-Fi**   The radio frequency (RF)–based technology used for home and small business wireless networks and for most public wireless Internet connections. Short for wireless fidelity.

**window**   A portion of the screen display used to view simultaneously a different part of the file in use or a part of a different file than the one in use.

**Windows**   The generic name for all versions of Microsoft's graphical operating system.

**Windows app**   A type of application, sold in the Microsoft Store, designed to take best advantage of Windows 10's graphical user interface.

**World Wide Web (WWW)**   A vast network of information, particularly business, commercial, and government resources, that uses a hypertext system for quickly transmitting graphics, sound, and video over the Internet.

**Zip file**   A file that has been compressed for easier transmission.

# Index

## F